MW01234499

The Epistles of John, Jude and the Book of Revelation

EXPOSITIONS OF HOLY SCRIPTURE

Expositions of Holy Scripture

A COMMENTARY ON THE BIBLE
COMPLETE IN 32 VOLUMES

By the Rev. Alexander Maclaren
D.D., D.Lit.

Contents of the First Series, Six Volumes, $7.50

1. The Book of Genesis.
2. The Book of Isaiah (Chapters I—XLVIII).
3. The Gospel of St. Matthew, Vol. I (Chapters I—VIII).
4. The Gospel of St. Matthew, Vol. II (Chapters IX—XVII).
5. The Gospel of St. Matthew, Vol. III (XVIII—XXVIII).
6. The Book of Isaiah (Chapters XLIX—LXVI) and the Book of Jeremiah.

Contents of the Second Series, Six Volumes, $7.50

1. The Gospel of St. Mark, Vol. I (Chapters I—VIII).
2. The Gospel of St. Mark, Vol. II (Chapters VIII—XVI).
3. The Books of Exodus, Leviticus and Numbers.
4. The Books of Deuteronomy, Joshua, Judges, Ruth and I. Samuel.
5. Second Book of Samuel, First Book of Kings, Second Book of Kings (to Chapter VII).
6. The Acts of the Apostles, Vol. I (Chapters I—XIII).

Contents of the Third Series, Six Volumes, $7.50

1. The Acts of the Apostles, Vol. II (Chapters XIII to end).
2. The Gospel of St. John, Vol. I (Chapters I—VIII).
3. The Gospel of St. John, Vol. II (Chapters IX—XIV).
4. The Gospel of St. John, Vol. III (Chapters XV—XXI).
5. The Second Book of Kings (from Chapter VIII), The Books of Chronicles, Ezra, Nehemiah.
6. The Books of Esther, Job, Proverbs and Ecclesiastes.

Contents of the Fourth Series, Six Volumes, $7.50

1. The Book of Psalms, Vol. I.
2. The Book of Psalms, Vol. II.
3. Ezekiel, Daniel and the Minor Prophets.
4. The Book of St. Luke, Vol. I.
5. The Book of St. Luke, Vol. II.
6. The Epistle to the Romans.

Contents of the Fifth Series, Eight Volumes, $10.00

1. First and Second Corinthians.
2. Ephesians.
3. Galatians and Philippians.
4. Colossians to Timothy.
5. Timothy, Titus, Philemon.
6. Hebrews, James.
7. First and Second Peter, First John.
8. Second and Third John, Jude, Revelation.

Dr. Alexander Maclaren's incomparable position as the prince of expositors has for more than a generation been recognized throughout the English-speaking world. He holds an unchallenged position, and it is believed that this series, embodying as it does the treasure store of Dr. Maclaren's lifework, will be found of priceless value by preachers, teachers, and readers of the Bible generally.

SOLD ONLY IN SERIES

THE EPISTLES OF
JOHN, JUDE
AND THE BOOK OF
REVELATION

BY

ALEXANDER MACLAREN

D.D., LITT.D.

NEW YORK
A. C. ARMSTRONG AND SON
3 & 5 WEST EIGHTEENTH STREET
LONDON: HODDER AND STOUGHTON
MCMX

CONTENTS

CONTENTS

CONTENTS

I. JOHN

FAITH CONQUERING THE WORLD

'This is the victory that overcometh the world, even our faith.'—1 JOHN v. 4.

No New Testament writer makes such frequent use of the metaphors of combat and victory as this gentle Apostle John. None of them seem to have conceived so habitually of the Christian life as being a conflict, and in none of their writings does the clear note of victory in the use of that word 'overcometh' ring out so constantly as it does in those of the very Apostle of Love. Equally characteristic of John's writings is the prominence which he gives to the still contemplation of, and abiding in, Christ. These two conceptions of the Christian life appear to be discordant, but are really harmonious.

There is no doubt where John learned the phrase. Once he had heard it at a time and in a place which stamped it on his memory for ever. 'Be of good cheer, I have overcome the world,' said Christ, an hour before Gethsemane. Long years since then had taught John something of its meaning, and had made him to understand how the Master's victory might belong to the servants. Hence in this letter he has much to say about 'overcoming the wicked one,' and the like; and in the Apocalypse we never get far away from hearing the shout of victory, whether we consider the sevenfold promises of the letters that stand at the beginning of the visions, or whether we listen to such sayings as

A

this :—'They overcame by the blood of the Lamb,' or
the last promise of all :—'He that overcometh shall
inherit all things.'

Thus bound together by that link, as well as by a
great many more, are all the writings which the tradition of the Church has attributed to this great Apostle.

But to come to the words of my text. They appear
in a very remarkable context here. If you read a verse
or two before, you will get the full singularity of their
introduction. 'This is the love of God,' says he, 'that
we keep His commandments : and His commandments
are not grievous.' They *are* very heavy and hard in
themselves ; it is very difficult to do right, and to walk
in the ways of God, and to please Him. His commandments *are* grievous, *per se* ; a heavy burden, a difficult
thing to do—but let us read on :—'They are not grievous,
for whatsoever is born of God'—keepeth the commandments ? No! 'Whatsoever is born of God *overcometh the world.*' That, thinks John, is the same thing
as keeping God's commandments. 'This is the victory
that overcometh the world, even our faith.' Notice,
then, first, What is the true notion of conquering the
world ? secondly, How that victory may be ours.

I. What is the true notion of conquering the world ?
Let us go back to what I have already said. Where
did John learn the expression ? Who was it that first
used it ? It comes from that never-to-be-forgotten
night in that upper room ; where, with His life's
purpose apparently crushed into nothing, and the
world just ready to exercise its last power over Him
by killing Him, Jesus Christ breaks out into such a
strange strain of triumph, and in the midst of apparent
defeat lifts up that clarion note of victory :—'I have
overcome the world !'

He had not made much of it, according to usual standards, had He? His life had been the life of a poor man. Neither fame nor influence, nor what people call success, had He won, judged from the ordinary points of view, and at three-and-thirty is about to be murdered; and yet He says, ' I have beaten it all, and here I stand a conqueror!' That threw a flood of light for John, and for all that had listened to Christ, on the whole conditions of human life, and on what victory and defeat, success and failure in this world mean. Not so do men usually estimate what conquering the world is. Not so do you and I estimate it when we are left to our own folly and our own weakness. Our notion of being victorious in life is when each man, according to his own ideal of what is best, manages to wring that ideal out of a reluctant world. Or, to put it into plainer words, a man desires, say, conspicuous notoriety and fame. He accounts that he has conquered when he scrambles over all his fellows, and writes his name, as boys do, upon a wall, higher than anybody else's name, with a bit of chalk, in writing that the next winter's storm will obliterate! That is victory! The ultra-commercial ideal says, 'Found a big business and make it pay.' That is to conquer! Other notions, higher and nobler than that, all partake of the same fallacy that if a man can get the world, the sum of external things, into his grip, and squeeze it as one does a grape, and get the last drop of sweetness out of it into his thirsty lips, he is a conqueror.

Well! and you may get all that, whatever it is, that seems to you best, sweetest, most needful, most toothsome and delightsome—you may get it all; and in a sense you may have conquered the world, and yet you may be utterly beaten and enslaved by it. Do you remember the old story—I make no apology for the plainness of it—of the man that said to his commanding officer, 'I have taken a prisoner.' 'Bring him along with you.' 'He won't let me.' 'Come yourself, then.' 'I can't'? So you think you have conquered the world when it yields you the things you want, and all the while it has conquered and captivated *you*.

You say 'Mine'! It would be a great deal nearer the truth if the possessions, or the love, or the wealth, or the culture, or whatever else it may be, that you have set your desire upon, were to rise up and say you are theirs! Utterly beaten and enslaved many a man is by the things that he vainly fancies *he* has mastered and conquered. If you think of how in the process of getting, you narrow yourselves; of how much you throw away; of how eyes become blind to beauty or goodness or graciousness; of how you become the slaves of the thing that you have won; of how the gold gets into a man's blood and makes his complexion as yellow as jaundice—if you think of all that, and how desperate and wretched you would be if in a minute it was all swept away, and how it absorbs your thoughts in keeping it and looking after it, say, is it you that are its master, or it that is yours?

Now let us turn for a moment to the teaching of this Epistle. Following in the footsteps of Jesus Christ Himself, the poor man, the beaten man, the unsuccessful man, may yet say, 'I have overcome the world.' What does that mean? Well, it is built upon this—the world, meaning thereby the sum total of outward things, considered as apart from God—the world and God we make to be antagonists to one another. And the world woos me to trust to it, to love it; crowds in upon my eye and shuts out the greater things beyond; absorbs my attention, so that if I let it have its own way I have no leisure to think about anything but itself. And the world conquers me when it succeeds in hindering me from seeing, loving, holding communion with and serving my Father, God.

On the other hand, I conquer it when I lay my hand upon it and force it to help me to get nearer Him, to get liker Him, to think more often of Him, to do His will more gladly and more constantly. The one victory over the world is to bend it to serve me in the highest things—the attainment of a clearer vision of the Divine nature, the attainment of a deeper love to God Himself, and of a more glad consecration and service to Him. That is the victory—when you can make the world a ladder to lift you to God. That is its right use, that is victory, when all its tempting voices do not draw you away from listening to the Supreme Voice that bids you keep His commandments. When the world comes between you and God as an obscuring screen, it has conquered you. When the world comes between you and God as a transparent medium, you have conquered it. To win victory is to get it beneath your feet and stand upon it, and reach up thereby to God.

Now, dear brethren, that is the plain teaching of all this context, and I would lay it upon your hearts and upon my own. Do not let us be deceived by the false estimates of the men around us. Do not let us forget that the one thing we have to live for is to know God, and to love and to please Him, and that every life is a disastrous failure, whatsoever outward artificial apparent success it may be enriched and beautified with, that has not accomplished that.

You rule Nature, you coerce winds and lightnings and flames to your purposes. Rule the world! Rule the world by making it help you to be wiser, gentler, nobler, more gracious, more Christ-like, more Christ-conscious, more full of God, and more like to Him, and then you will get the deepest delight out of it. If a man wanted to find a wine-press that should squeeze out of the vintage of this world its last drop of sweetest sweetness, he would find it in constant recognition of the love of God, and in the coercing of all the outward and the visible to be his help thereto.

There are the two theories; the one that we are all apt to fall into, of what success and victory is; the other the Christian theory. Ah! many a poor, battered Lazarus, full of sores, a pauper and a mendicant at Dives' gate; many a poor old cottager; many a lonely woman in her garret; many a man that has gone away from Manchester, for instance, unable to get on in business, and obliged to creep into some corner and hide himself, not having succeeded in making a fortune, is the victor! And many a Dives, fettered by his own possessions, and the bond-slave of his own successes, is beaten by the world shamefully and disastrously! Pray and strive for the purged eyesight which shall teach you what it is to conquer the world, and what it is to be conquered by it.

II. And now let me turn for a moment to the second of the points that I have desired to put before you, viz., the method by which this victory over the world, of making it help us to keep the commandments of God, is to be accomplished. We find, according to John's fashion, a threefold statement in this context upon this matter, each member of which corresponds to and heightens the preceding. We read thus:—'Whatsoever is born of God overcometh the world.' 'This is the victory that overcometh the world,' or more accurately,

'*hath overcome* the world, even our faith.' Who is
he that overcometh the world? He that believeth
that Jesus Christ is 'the Son of God.' Wherein there
are, speaking roughly, these three statements, that
the true victory over the world is won by a new life, born
of and kindred with God; that that life is kindled in
men's souls through their faith; that the faith which
kindles that supernatural life, the victorious antagonist
of the world, is the definite, specific faith in Jesus as
the Son of God. These are the three points which the
Apostle puts as the means of conquest of the world.

The first consideration, then, suggested by these
statements is that the one victorious antagonist of all
the powers of the world which seek to draw us away
from God, is a life in our hearts kindred with God, and
derived from God.

Now I know that a great many people turn away
from this central representation of Christianity as if
it were mystical and intangible. I desire to lay it upon
your hearts, dear brethren, that every Christian man
has received and possesses through the open door of his
faith, a life supernatural, born of God, kindred with
God, therefore having nothing kindred with evil, and
therefore capable of meeting and mastering all the
temptations of the world.

It is a plain piece of common-sense, that God is
stronger than this material universe, and that what is
born of God partakes of the Divine strength. But there
would be no comfort in that, nor would it be anything
germane and relevant to the Apostle's purpose, unless
there was implied in the statement what in fact is distinctly asserted more than once in this Epistle, that
every Christian man and woman may claim to be thus
born of God. Hearken to the words that almost im-

mediately precede our text, ' Whosoever believeth that
Jesus is the Christ is born of God.' Hearken to other
words which proclaim the same truth, 'To as many as
received Him, to them gave He power to become the
sons of God, which were born, not of the will of the
flesh, nor of the will of man, but of God.' He does come
with all the might of His regenerating power into our
poor natures, if and when we turn ourselves with
humble faith to that dear Lord ; and breathes into our
deadness a new life, with new tastes, new desires, new
motives, new powers, making us able to wrestle with and
to overcome the temptations that were too strong for us.

Mystical and deep as this thought may be, God's
nature is breathed into the spirits of men that will
trust Him! and if you will put your confidence in that
dear Lord, and live near Him, into your weakness will
come an energy born of the Divine, and you will be
able to do all things in the might of the Christ that
strengthens you from within, and is the life of your
life, and the soul of your soul. To the little beleaguered
garrison surrounded by strong enemies through whom
they cannot cut their way, the king sends reliefs, who
force their passage into the fortress, and hold it against
all the power of the foe. You are not left to fight by
yourselves, you can conquer the world if you will trust
to that Christ, trusting in whom God's own power will
come to your aid, and God's own Spirit will be the
strength of your spirit.

And then there is the other way of looking at this
same thing, viz., you can conquer the world if you will
trust in Jesus Christ, because such trust will bring you
into constant, living, loving contact with the Great
Conqueror. There is a beautiful accuracy and refine-
ment in the language of these three clauses which is

not represented in our Authorised Version. The central one which I have read as my text this morning might be translated as it is translated in the Revised Version—'This is the victory that hath overcome the world, even our faith.' By which I suppose the Apostle means very much what I am saying now, viz., that my faith brings me into contact with that one great victory over the world which for all time was won by Jesus Christ. I can appropriate Christ's conquest to myself if I trust Him. The might of it and some portion of the reality of it passes into my nature in the measure in which I rely upon Him. He conquered once for all, and the very remembrance of His conquest by faith will make me strong—will 'teach my hands to war and my fingers to fight.' He conquered once for all, and His victory will pass, with electric power, into my life if I trust Him. I am brought into living fellowship with Him. All the stimulation of example, and all that lives lofty and pure can do for us, is done for us in transcendent fashion by the life of Jesus Christ. And all that lives lofty and pure can never do for us is done in unique fashion by the life and death of Him whose life and death are alike the victory over the world and the pattern for us.

So if we join ourselves to Him by faith, and bring into our daily life, in all its ignoble effort, in all its little duties, in all its wearisome monotonies, in all its triviality, the thought, the illuminating thought, the ennobling thought, of the victorious Christ our companion and our Friend—*in hoc signo vinces*—in this sign thou shalt conquer! They that keep hold of His hand see over the world and all its falsenesses and fleetingnesses. They that trust in Jesus are more than conquerors by the might of His victory.

And then there is the last thought, which, though it be not directly expressed in the words before us, is yet closely connected with them. You can conquer the world if you will trust Jesus Christ, because your faith will bring into the midst of your lives the grandest and most solemn and blessed realities. Faith is the true anæsthesia of the soul;—the thing that deadens it to the pains and the pleasures that come from this fleeting life. As for the pleasures, I remember reading lately of some thinker of our own land who was gazing through a telescope at the stars, and turned away from the solemn vision with one remark,—'I don't think much of our county families!' And if you will look up at Christ through the telescope of your faith, it is wonderful what Lilliputians the Brobdingnagians round about you will dwindle into, and how small the world will look, and how coarse the pleasures.

If a man goes to Italy, and lives in the presence of the pictures there, it is marvellous what daubs the works of art, that he used to admire, look when he comes back to England again. And if he has been in communion with Jesus Christ, and has found out what real sweetness is, he will not be over-tempted by the coarse dainties that people eat here. Children spoil their appetites for wholesome food by sweetmeats; we very often do the same in regard to the bread of God, but if we have once really tasted it, we shall not care very much for the vulgar dainties on the world's stall.

Dear brethren, set your faith upon that great Lord, and the world's pleasures will have less power over you, and as for its pains—

'There's nothing either good or bad,
But thinking makes it so.'

If a man does not think that the world's pains are of

much account, they are not of much account. He who
sees athwart the smoke of the fire of Smithfield, the
face of the Captain of his warfare, who has conquered,
will dare to burn and will not dare to deny his Master
or his Master's truth. The world may threaten in hope
of winning you to its service, but if its threats, turned
into realities, fail to move you, it is the world which
inflicts, and not you who suffer, that is beaten. In the
extremest case they 'kill the body and after that have
no more that they can do,' and if they have done all
they can, and have not succeeded in wringing the in-
cantation from the locked lips, they are beaten, and
the poor dead martyr that they could only kill has
conquered them and their torments. So fear not all
that the world can do against you. If you have got a
little spark of the light of Christ's presence in your
heart, the darkness will not be very terrible, and you
will not be alone.

So, brethren, two questions :—Does your faith do
anything like that for you? If it does not, what do
you think is the worth of it? Does it deaden the
world's delights? Does it lift you above them? Does
it make you conqueror? If it does not, do you think
it is worth calling faith?

And the other question is: Do you want to beat, or
to be beaten? When you consult your true self, does
your conscience not tell you that it were better for you
to keep God's commandments than to obey the world?
Surely there are many young men and women in this
place to-day who have some desires high, and true,
and pure, though often stifled, and overcome, and
crushed down; and many older folk who have
glimpses, in the midst of predominant regard for the
things that are seen and temporal, of a great calm,

pure region away up there that they know very little about.

Dear friends, my one word to you all is: Get near Jesus Christ by thought, and love, and trust. Trust to Him and to the great love that gave itself for you. And then bring Him into your life, by daily reference to Him of it all: and by cultivating the habit of thinking about Him as being present with you in the midst of it all, and so holding His hand, you will share in His victory; and at the last, according to the climax of His sevenfold promises, 'To Him that overcometh will I give to sit down with Me on My throne, even as I also overcame, and am sat down with My Father on His Throne.'

I.—TRIUMPHANT CERTAINTIES

'We know that whosoever is born of God sinneth not; but he that is begotten of God keepeth himself, and that wicked one toucheth him not.'—1 JOHN v. 18.

JOHN closes his letter with a series of triumphant certainties, which he considers as certified to every Christian by his own experience. 'We know that whosoever is born of God sinneth not . . . we know that we are of God . . . and we know that the Son of God is come.' Now, that knowledge which he thus follows out on these three lines is not merely an intellectual conviction, but it is the outcome of life, and the broad seal of experimental possession is stamped upon it. Yet the average Christian reads this text, and shrugs his shoulders and says, 'Well! perhaps I do not understand it, but, so far as I do, it seems to me to say a thing which is contradicted by the whole experience of life.' 'We know that whosoever is born of God sinneth not'; and some of us are driven by such words, and

parallel ones which occur in other places, to a presumptuous over-confidence, and some of us to an
equally unscriptural despondency; and a great many
of us to laying John's triumphant certainty up upon
the shelf where the unintelligible things are getting
covered over with dust.

So I wish, in this sermon, to try, if I can, to come to
the understanding, that in some measure I may help
you to come to the joyful possession, of the truth which
lies here, and which the Apostle conceives to belong to
the very elements of the Christian character.

I. First, then, I ask the question—of whom is the
Apostle speaking here?

'We know that whosoever is born of God'—or, as the
Revised Version reads it, '*begotten* of God'—'sinneth
not.' Now we must go back a little—and sometimes to
go a long way from a subject is the best way to get at
it. Let me recall to you the Master's words with which
He all but began His public ministry, when He said to
Nicodemus, 'Except a man be born again he cannot see
the kingdom of God.' There is the root of all that this
epistle is so full of, the conception of a regeneration, a
being born again, which makes men, by a new birth,
sons of God, in a fashion and in a sphere of their nature
in which they were not the sons of the Heavenly
Father before that experience. Jesus Christ laid
down, as the very first principle which He would insist
upon, to a man who was groping in the midst of mere
legal conceptions of righteousness as the work of his
own hands, this principle,—there must be a radical
change, and there must be the entrance into every
human nature of a new life-principle before there is
any vision, any possession of, or any entrance into,
that region in which the will of God is supreme, and

where He reigns and rules as King. John is only
echoing his Master when he here, and in other places
of this letter, lays all the stress, in regard to practical
righteousness and to noble character, upon being born
again, subjected to that change which is fairly paralleled with the physical fact of birth, and has, as its
result, the possession by the man who passes through
it of a new nature, sphered in and destined to dominate
and cleanse his old self.

Then there is a further step to be taken, and that is
that this sonship of God, which is the result of being
born again, is mediated and received by us through our
faith. Remember the prologue of John's Gospel, where,
as a great musician will hint all his subsequent themes
in his overture, he gathers up in one all the main
threads and points of his teaching. There he says, 'To
as many as received Him, to them gave He power to
become the sons of God.' Long years afterwards, when
an old man in Ephesus, he writes down in this last
chapter of his first epistle the same truth which he
there set blazing in the forefront of his Gospel when he
says, in the first verse of this chapter, 'Whosoever
believeth that Jesus is the Christ is born of God.' On
condition, then, of a man's faith in Jesus Christ, there
is communicated to him a new life direct from God,
kindred with the Divine, and which dwells in him, and
works in him precisely in the measure of his personal
faith.   That is the first point that I desire to
establish.

You will remember, I suppose, that this same conception of the deepest result of the Christian faith being
no mere external forgiveness of sins, nor alteration of
a man's position in reference to the Divine judgments,
but the communication of a new life-power and prin-

ciple to him, is not the property of the mystic John only, but it is the property likewise of the legal James, who says, ' Of His own will begat He us by the word of truth, that we should be a kind of first-fruits of His creatures'; and it is set forth with great emphasis and abundance in all the writings of the Apostle Paul, who insists that we are sons through the Son, who insists that the gift of God is a new nature, formed in righteousness 'after the image of Him that created Him,' and who is ever dwelling upon the necessity that this new nature should be cultivated and increased by the faith and effort of its recipient.

Keeping these things in mind, I take the second step, and that is that this new birth, and the new Divine life which is its result, co-exist along with the old nature in which it is planted, and which it has to coerce and subdue, sometimes to crucify, and always to govern. For I need not remind you that if the analogy of birth is to be followed, we have to recognise that that Divine life, too, like the physical life, which is also God's gift, has to pass through stages; and that just as the perfect man, God manifest in the flesh, 'increased in wisdom and stature, and in favour with God and man,' so the Divine life in a soul comes to it in germ, and has its period of infancy and growth up into youth and manhood. This Apostle puts great emphasis upon that idea of advancement in the Divine life. For you remember the long passage in which he twice reiterates the notion of the stages of children and young men and fathers. So the new life has to grow, grow in its own strength, grow in its sphere of influence, grow in the power with which it purges and hallows the old nature in the midst of which it is implanted. But growth is not the only word for its development. That new nature has to fight for its life. There must be effort, in order that it may rule; there must be strenuous and continuous diligence, directed not only to strengthen it, but to weaken its antagonist, in order that it may spread and permeate the whole nature. Thus we have the necessary foundation laid for that which characterises the Christian life, from the beginning to the end, that it is a working out of that which is implanted, a working out, with ever widening area of influence, and a working in with ever deeper and more thorough power of transforming the character. There may be indefinite approximation to the entire suppression and sanctification of the old man; and whatsoever is born of God manifests its Divine kindred in this, that sooner or later it overcomes the world.

Now, if all that which I have been saying is true—and to me it is undeniably so—I come to a very plain answer to the first question that I raised: Who is it that John is speaking about? 'Whosoever is born of God' is the Christian man, in so far as the Divine life which he has from God by fellowship with His Son, through His own personal faith, has attained the supremacy in Him. The Divine nature that is in a man is that which is born of God. And that the Apostle does not mean the man in whom that nature is implanted, whether he is true to the nature or no, is obvious from the fact that, in another part of this same chapter, he substitutes '*what*soever' for '*whoso*-ever,' as if he would have us mark that the thing which he declares to be victorious and sinless is not so much the person as the power that is lodged in the person. That is my answer to the first question.

II. What is asserted about this Divine life?

'Whosoever is born of God sinneth not.' That is by

no means a unique expression in this letter. For, to say nothing about the general drift of it, we have a precisely similar statement in a previous chapter, twice uttered. 'Whosoever abideth in Him sinneth not'; 'whosoever is born of God doth not commit sin, for His seed remaineth in him, and he cannot sin, because he is born of God.' Nothing can be stronger than that. Yes, and nothing can be more obvious. I think, then, that the Apostle does not thereby mean to declare that, unless a man is absolutely sinless in regard of his individual acts, he has not that Divine life in him. For look at what precedes our text. Just before he has said, and it is the saying which leads him to my text, 'If any man seeth his brother sin a sin which is not unto death, he shall ask, and he shall give him life.' So, then, he contemplated that within the circle of sons of God, who were each other's brethren because they were all possessors of that Divine birth, there would exist 'sin not unto death,' which demanded a brother's brotherly intercession and help. And do you suppose that any man, in the very same breath in which he thus declared that brotherhood was to be manifested by the way in which we help a brother to get rid of his sins, would have stultified himself by a blank, staring contradiction such as has been extracted from the words of my text? I say nothing about inspiration; I only say common-sense forbids it. The fact of the matter is that John, in his simple, childlike way, does not wait to concatenate his ideas, or to show how the one limits and explains the other, but he lays them down before us, and the fact of their juxtaposition limits, and he does not expect that his readers are quite fools. So he says in the one breath, 'If any man see his brother sin a sin,' and in the next breath, 'Who-

soever is born of God sinneth not.' Surely there is **a**
way to bring these two sayings into harmony. And it
seems to me to be the way that I have been suggesting
to you—viz., to take the text to mean—not that a Christian is, or must be, in order to vindicate his right to be
called a Christian, sinless, but that there is a power in
him, a life-principle in him which is sinless, and whatsoever in him is born of God overcometh the world
and 'sinneth not.'

Now, then, that seems to me to be the extent of the
Apostle's affirmation here; and I desire to draw two
plain, practical conclusions. One is, that this notion of
a Divine life-power, lodged in, and growing through,
and fighting with the old nature, makes the hideousness and the criminality of a Christian man's transgressions more hideous and more criminal. The
teaching of my text has sometimes been used in the
very opposite direction. I do not need to say anything
about that. There have been people that have said
'It is no more *I*, but *sin*, that dwelleth in me; *I* am
not responsible.' There have been types of so-called
Christianity which have used this loftiest and purest
thought of my text as a minister of sin. I do not suppose that there are any representatives of that caricature and travesty here, so I need not say a word about
it. The opposite inference is what I urge now. In
addition to all the other foulnesses which attach to
any man's lust, or lechery, or drunkenness, or ambition,
or covetousness, this super-eminent brand and stigma
is burned in upon yours and mine, Christian men and
women, that it is dead against, absolutely inconsistent
with, the principle of life that is bedded within us.
And whilst all men, by every transgression, flout God
and degrade themselves, the Christian man who comes

down to the level of living for flesh and sense and time and self, has laid the additional and heaviest of all weights of guilt upon his back in that he has done despite to the Spirit of grace, and grieved and contradicted and thwarted the life of God that is within him. The deepest guilt and the darkest condemnation attach to the sins of the man who, with a Divine life in his spirit, obeys the flesh. 'To whomsoever much is given, of him shall much be required.'

Another consideration may fairly be urged as drawn from this text, and that is that the one task of Christians ought to be to deepen and to strengthen the life of God, which is in their souls, by faith. There is no limit, except one of my own making, to the extent to which my whole being may be penetrated through and through and ruled absolutely by that new life which God has given.

> ''Tis life, whereof our nerves are scant,
> Oh life, not death, for which we pant;
> More life, and better, that I want.'

It is all very well to cultivate specific and sporadic virtues and graces. Get a firmer hold and a fuller possession of the life of Christ in your own souls, and all graces and virtues will come.

III. Now, I have one last question—what is the ground of John's assertion about him 'that is born of God'?

My text runs on, 'but he that is begotten of God keepeth himself.' If any of you are using the Revised Version, you will see a change there, small in extent, but large in significance. It reads, 'He that is begotten of God keepeth him.' And although at this stage of my sermon it would be absurd in me to enter upon exegetical considerations, let me just say in a sentence

that the original has considerable variation in expression in these two clauses, which variation makes it
impossible, I think, to adopt the idea contained in the
Authorised Version, that the same person is referred
to in both clauses. The difference is this. In the first
clause, 'He that is begotten of God' is the Christian
man; in the second, 'He that is begotten of God' is
Christ the Saviour.

There is the guarantee that 'Whosoever is begotten
of God sinneth not,' because round his weakness is
cast the strong defence of the Elder Brother's hand;
and the Son of God keeps all the sons who, through
Him, have derived into their natures the life of God.
If, then, they are kept by the only begotten Son of the
Father, who, that 'He might bring many sons unto
glory,' has Himself worn the likeness of our flesh apart
from sin, then the one thing for us to do, in order
to nourish and deepen and strengthen, and bring to
sovereign power in our poor natures that previous and
enduring principle of life, is to take care that we do not
run away from the keeping hand nor wander far from
the only safety. When a little child is sent out for a
walk by the parent with an elder brother, if it goes
staring into shop windows, and gaping at anything
that it sees upon the road, and loses hold of the
brother's hand, it is lost, and breaks into tears, and can
only be consoled and secured by being brought back.
Then the little fingers clasp round the larger hand, and
there is a sense of relief and of safety.

Dear brethren, if we stray away from Christ we lose
ourselves in muddy ways. If we keep near Him, as
merchantmen in time of war keep near the men-of-war
convoy, or as pilgrims across a dangerous desert keep
close to the heels of the horses of their escort, 'that

wicked one toucheth us not.' And so we may be sure that 'that which is born of God' will come to the sovereign power within us, and He that was born of the Spirit will cast out him that was born of the flesh.

II.—TRIUMPHANT CERTAINTIES

'We know that we are of God, and the whole world lieth in wickedness.'—
1 JOHN v. 19.

THIS is the second of the triumphant certainties which John supposes to be the property of every Christian. I spoke about the first of them in my last sermon. It reads, 'We know that whosoever is born of God sinneth not.' Now, there is a distinct connection and advance, as between these two statements. The former of them is entirely general. It is particularised in my text; the 'whosoever' there is pointed into 'we' here. The individuals who have the right to claim these prerogatives are none other than the body of Christian people.

Then there is another connection and advance. 'Born of God' refers to an act; 'of God' to a state. The point is produced into a line. There is still another connection and advance. 'Whosoever is born of God sinneth not,' 'and that wicked one toucheth him not.' That glance at a dark surrounding, from which he that is born of God is protected, is deepened in my text into a vision of the whole world as 'lying in the wicked one.'

Now, I know that sayings like this of my text, which put into the forefront the Christian prerogative, and which regard mankind, apart from the members of Christ's body, as in a dark condition of subjection under an alien power, have often been spoken of as if they were presumptuous, on the one hand, and narrow, un-charitable, and gloomy on the other. I am not concerned to deny that, on the lips of some professing Christian, they have had a very ugly sound, and have ministered to distinctly un-Christlike sentiments. But, on the other hand, I do believe that there are few things which the average Christianity of to-day wants more than a participation in that joyous confidence and buoyant energy which throb in the Apostle's words; and that for lack of this triumphant certitude many a soul has been lamed, its joy clouded, its power trammelled, and its work in the world thwarted. So I wish to try to catch some of that solemn and joyous confidence which the Apostle peals forth in these triumphant words.

I. I ask you, then, to look first at the Christian certainty of belonging to God.

'We know that we are of God.' Where did John get that form of expression, which crops up over and over again in his letter? He got it where he got most of his terminology, from the lips of the Master. For, if you remember, our Lord Himself speaks more than once of men being 'of God.' As, for instance, when He says, 'He that is of God heareth God's words. Ye therefore hear them not because ye are not of God.' And then He goes on to give the primary idea that is conveyed in the phrase when He says, in strong contrast to that expression, 'Ye are of your father, and the lusts of your father ye will do.' So, then, plainly, as I said, what was a point in the previous certitude, is here prolonged into a line, and expresses a permanent state.

The first conception in the phrase is that of life derived, communicated from God Himself. Fathers of the flesh communicate life, and it is thenceforth independent. But the life of the Spirit, which we draw from God, is only sustained by the continual repetition of the same gift by which it was originated. So the second idea that lies in the expression is that of a life dependent upon Him from whom it originally comes. The better life in the Christian soul is as certain to fade and die if the supply from Heaven is cut off or dammed back, as is the bed of a stream to become parched and glistering in the fierce sunshine, if the head-waters flow into it no more. You can no more have the life of the Spirit in the spirit of a man without continual communication from Him than a sunbeam can subsist if it be cut off from the central source. Therefore, the second of the ideas in this expression is, the continual dependence of that derived life upon God. Christian people are 'of God,' in so far as they partake of that new life, in an altogether special sense, which has a feeble analogy in the dependence of all creation upon the continual effluence of the Divine power. Preservation is a continual creation, and unless God operated in all physical phenomena and change there would neither be phenomena, nor change, nor substance, which could show them forth. But high above all that is the dependence of the renewed soul upon Him for the continual communication of His gifts and life.

If that life is thus derived and dependent, there follows the last idea in our pregnant phrase, viz., that it is correspondent with its source. 'Ye are of God,' kindred with Him and developing a life which, in its measure, being derived and dependent, is cognate with, and assimilated to, His own. This is the prerogative of every Christian soul.

Then there is another step to be taken. The man that has that life *knows* it. 'We know,' says the Apostle, 'that we are of God.' That word 'know' has been usurped, or at all events illegitimately monopolised by certain forms of knowledge. But surely the inward facts of my own consciousness are as much facts, and are certified to me as validly and reliably as are facts in other regions which are attested by the senses, or arrived at by reasoning. Christian people have the same right to lay hold of that great word, 'we know,' and to apply it to the facts of their spiritual experience, as any scientist in the world has to apply it to the facts of his science. I do not for a moment forget the differences between the two kinds of knowledge, but I do feel that in regard of certitude the advantage is at least shared, and some of us would say that we are surer of ourselves than we are of anything besides. How do you know that you *are* at all? The only answer is, 'I feel that I am.' And precisely the same evidence applies in regard to these lofty thoughts of a Divine kindred and a spiritual life. I know that I am of God. I have passed through experiences, and I am aware of consciousness which certify that to me.

But that is not all For, as I tried to show in my last sermon, the condition of being 'born of God' is laid plainly down in this very chapter by the Apostle, as being the simple act of faith in Jesus Christ. So, then, if any man is sure that he believes, he knows that he is born of God, and is of God.

But you say, 'Do you not know that men deceive themselves by a profession of being Christians, and that many of us estimate their professions at a very different rate of genuineness from what they estimate them at?' Yes, I know that. And this whole letter

of John goes to guard us against the presumption of
entertaining inflated thoughts about ourselves as being
kindred with God, unless we verify the consciousness
by certain plain facts. You remember how continually
in this epistle there crops up by the side of the most
thorough-going mysticism, as people call it, the
plainest, home-spun practical morality, and how all
these lofty, towering thoughts are brought down to
this sharp test, 'Let no man deceive you; he that
doeth not righteousness is not of God; neither he that
loveth not his brother.' That is a test which, applied
to many a fanatical dream, shrivels it up.

There is another test which the Master laid down in
the words that I have quoted already for another
purpose, when He said, 'He that is of God heareth
God's words. Ye, therefore, hear them not because ye
are not of God.' Christian people, take these two
plain tests—first, righteousness of life, common practical morality, the doing and the loving to do, the
things that all the world recognises to be right and
true; and, second, an ear attuned and attent to catch
God's voice—and control your consciousness of being
God's son by these, and you will not go far wrong.

And now, before I go further, one word. It is a
shame, and a laming and a weakening of any Christian
life, that this triumphant confidence should not be
clear in it. 'We *know* that we are of God.' Can you
and I echo that with calm confidence? 'I sometimes
half hope that I am.' 'I am almost afraid to say it.'
'I do not know whether I am or not.' 'I trust I may
be.' That is the kind of creeping attitude in which
hosts of Christian people are contented to live; and
they stare at a man as if he was presumptuous, and
soaring up into a region that they do not know any-

thing about, when he humbly echoes the Apostle, and
says, ' We know that we are God's.'   Why should our
skies be as grey and sunless as those of a northern
winter's day when all the while, away down on the
sunny seas, to which we may voyage if we will, there
are unbroken sunshine, ethereal blue, and a perpetual
blaze of light?   Christian men and women! it concerns
the power of your lives, their progress in holiness, and
their possession of peace, that you should be far more
able than, alas! many of us are, to say, and that
without presumption, ' We know that we are of God.'

II. We have here the Christian view of the surrounding world.

I need not, I suppose, remind you that John learned
from Jesus to use that phrase 'the world,' not as
meaning the aggregate of material things, but as
meaning the aggregate of godless men.   If you want a
modern translation of the word, it comes very near a
familiar one with us nowadays, and that is 'Society';
the mass of people that are not of God.

Now, the more a man is conscious that he himself, by
faith in Jesus Christ, has passed into the family of God,
and possesses the life that comes from Him, the more
keen will be his sense of the evil that lies round him,
and of the contrast between the maxims and prevalent
practices and institutions and ways of the world, and
those which belong to Christ and Christ's people.   Just
as a native of Central Africa, brought to England for
a while, when he gets back to his kraal, will see its
foulnesses and its sordidnesses as he did not before, or
as, according to old stories, those that were carried
away into fairyland for a little while came back to the
work-a-day life of the world, and felt themselves alien
from it, and had visions of what they had seen ever

floating before them; so the measure of our conscious belonging to God is the measure of our perception of the contrast between us and the ways of the men about us.

I am not concerned for a moment to deny, rather, I most thankfully recognise the truth, that a great deal of 'the world' has been ransomed by the Cross, by which its prince has been cast out, and that much of Christian morality, and of the Christian way of looking at things, has passed into the general atmosphere in which we live, so as that, between the true Christian community and the surrounding world in which it is plunged, there is less antagonism than there was when John in Ephesus wrote these words beneath the shadow of Diana's temple. But the world is a world still, and the antagonism is there; and if a man will live true to the life of God that is in him, he will find out soon enough that the gulf is not bridged over. It never will be bridged. The only way by which the antagonism can be ended is for the kingdoms of this world to become the kingdoms of our God and of His Christ. Society is not of God, and the institutions of every nation upon earth have still in them much of the evil one. Christian people are set down in the midst of these, and the antagonism is perennial.

III. Lastly, consider the consequent Christian duty.

Let me put two or three plain exhortations. I beseech you, Christian people, cultivate the sense of belonging to a higher order than that in which you dwell. A man in a heathen land loses his sense of home, and of its ways; and it needs a perpetual effort in order that we should not forget our true affinities. 'We are of God' may be so said as to be the parent of all manner of un-Christlike sentiments, as I have

already remarked. It may be the mother of contempt
and self-righteousness, and a hundred other vices; but,
rightly said, it has no such tendency. But unless we
are ever and anon seeking to renew that consciousness,
it will fade and become dim, and we shall forget the
imperial palace whence we came, and be content to live
in the barren fields of the citizens of that country, and
even to feed upon the husks that are in the swine's
trough. So I say, cultivate the sense of belonging
to God.

Again, I say, be careful to avoid infection. Go as
men do in a plague-stricken city. Go as our soldiers in
that Ashanti expedition had to go, on your guard
against malaria, the 'pestilence that walketh in darkness,' and smites ere we are aware, bringing down our
notions, our views of life, our thoughts of duty, to the
low level of the people around us. Go as these same
soldiers did, on the watch for ambuscades and lurking
enemies behind the trees. And remember that the
only safety is keeping hold of Christ's hand.

Look on the world as Christ looked on it. There
must be no contempt; there must be no self-righteousness; there must be no pluming ourselves on our own
prerogatives. There must be sorrow caught from Him,
and tenderness of pity, like that which forced itself
to His eyes as He gazed across the valley at the city
sparkling in the sunshine, or such as wrung His heart
when He looked upon the multitude as sheep without
a shepherd.

Work for the deliverance of your brethren from the
alien tyrant. Notice the difference between the two
clauses in the text. 'We are *of* God'; that is a permanent relation. 'The world lieth *in* the wicked one';
that is not necessarily a permanent relation. The world

is not *of* the wicked one; it is '*in*' him, and that may be altered. It is in the sphere of that dark influence. As in the old stories, knights hung their dishonoured arms upon trees, and laid their heads in the lap of an enchantress, so men have departed from God, and surrendered themselves to the fascinations and the control of an alien power. But the world may be taken out of the sphere of influence in which it lies. And that is what you are here for. 'For this purpose the Son of God was manifested, that He might destroy the works of the devil'; and for that purpose He has called us to be His servants. So the more we feel the sharp contrast between the blessedness of the Divine life which we believe ourselves to possess, and the darkness and evils of the world that lies around us, the more should sorrow, and the more should sympathy, and the more should succour be ours. Brethren, for ourselves let us remember that we cannot better help the world to get away from the alien tyrant that rules it than by walking in the midst of men, with the aureola of this joyful confidence and certitude around us. The solemn alternative opens before every one of us—Either I am 'of God,' or I am 'in the wicked one.' Dear friends, let us lay our hearts and hands in Christ's care, and then that will be true of us which this Apostle declares for the whole body of believers : ' Ye are of God, little children, and have overcome, because greater is He that is in you than he that is in the world.'

III.—TRIUMPHANT CERTAINTIES

'And we know that the Son of God is come, and hath given us an understanding, that we may know Him that is true, and we are in Him that is true, even in His Son Jesus Christ.'—1 JOHN v. 20.

ONCE more John triumphantly proclaims ' We know.' Whole-souled conviction rings in his voice. He is sure

of his footing. He does not say 'We incline to think,'
or even 'We believe and firmly hold,' but he says 'We
know.' A very different tone that from that of many
of us, who, influenced by currents of present opinions,
feel as if what was rock to our fathers had become
quagmire to us! But John in his simplicity thinks
that it is a tone which is characteristic of every
Christian. I wonder what he would say about some
Christians now.

This third of his triumphant certainties is connected
closely with the two preceding ones, which have been
occupying us in former sermons. It is so, as being in
one aspect the ground of these, for it is because 'the
Son of God is come' that men are born of God, and
are of Him. It is so in another way also, for properly
the words of our text ought to read not '*And* we know,'
rather '*But* we know.' They are suggested, that is to
say, by the preceding words, and they present the only
thought which makes them tolerable. 'The whole world
lieth in the wicked one. But we know that the Son of
God is come.' Falling back on the certainty of the
Incarnation and its present issues, we can look in the
face the grave condition of humanity, and still have hope
for the world and for ourselves. The certainty of the
Incarnation *and its issues*, I say. For in my text John
not only points to the past fact that Christ has come in
the flesh, but to a present fact, the operation of that
Christ upon Christian souls—'He hath given us an
understanding.' And not only so, but he points, further,
to a dwelling in God and God in us as being the abiding
issue of that past manifestation. So these three things
—the coming of Christ, the knowledge of God which
flows into a believing heart through that Incarnate Son,
and the dwelling in God which is the climax of all His

gifts to us—these three things are in John's estimation
certified to a Christian heart, and are not merely
matters of opinion and faith, but matters of knowledge.

Ah! brethren, if our Christianity had that firm strain,
and was conscious of that verification, it would be less
at the mercy of every wind of doctrine; it would be less
afraid of every new thought; it would be more powerful
to rule and to calm our own spirits, and it would be
more mighty to utter persuasive words to others. We
must *know* for ourselves, if we would lead others to
believe. So I desire to look now at these three points
which emerge from my text, and

I. I would deal with the Christian's knowledge that
the Son of God is come.

Now, our Apostle is writing to Asiatic Christians of
the second generation at the earliest, most of whom had
not been born when Jesus Christ was upon earth, and
none of whom had any means of acquaintance with Him
except that which we possess—the testimony of the
witnesses who had companied with Him. And yet, to
these men—whose whole contact with Christ and the
Gospel was, like yours and mine, the result of hearsay
—he says, 'We know.' Was he misusing words in his
eagerness to find a firm foundation for a soul to rest on?
Many would say that he was, and would answer this
certainty of his 'We *know*,' with, How *can* he know?
You may go on the principle that probability is the
guide of life, and you may be morally certain, but the
only way by which you know a fact is by having seen
it; and even if you have seen Jesus Christ, all that you
saw would be the life of a man upon earth whom you
believed to be the Son of God. It is trifling with
language to talk about knowledge when you have only
testimony to build on.

Well! there is a great deal to be said on that side, but there are two or three considerations which, I think, amply warrant the Apostle's declaration here, and our understanding of his words, 'We know,' in their fullest and deepest sense. Let me just mention these briefly. Remember that when John says 'The Son of God is come' he is not speaking—as his language, if any of you can consult the original, distinctly shows —about a past fact only, but about a fact which, beginning in a historical past, is permanent and continuous. In one aspect, no doubt, Jesus Christ had come and gone, before any of the people to whom this letter was addressed heard it for the first time, but in another aspect, if I may use a colloquial expression, when Jesus Christ came, He 'came to stay.' And that thought, of the permanent abiding with men, of the Christ who once was manifest in the flesh for thirty years, and

> ' Walked the acres of those blessed fields
> For our advantage,'

runs through the whole of Scripture. Nor shall we understand the meaning of Christ's Incarnation unless we see in it the point of beginning of a permanent reality. He has come, and He has *not* gone—'Lo! I am with you alway'—and that thought of the fulness and permanence of our Lord's presence with Christian souls is lodged deep and all-pervading, not only in John's gospel, but in the whole teaching of the New Testament. So it is a present fact, and not only a past piece of history, which is asserted when the Apostle says ' The Son of God is come.' And a man who has a companion knows that he has him, and by many a token not only of flesh but of spirit, is conscious that he is not alone, but that the dear and strong one is by his side. Such consciousness belongs to all the maturer and deeper forms of the Christian life.

Further, we must read on in my text if we are to find all which John declares to be a matter of knowledge. 'The Son of God is come, and hath given us an understanding.' I shall have a word or two more to say about that presently, but in the meantime I simply point out that what is here declared to be known by the Christian soul is a present operation of the present Christ upon his nature. If a man is aware that, through his faith in Jesus Christ, new perceptions and powers of discerning solid reality where he only saw mist before have been granted to him, the Apostle's triumphant assertion is vindicated.

And, still further, the words of my text, in their assurance of possessing something far more solid than an opinion or a creed, in Christ Jesus and our relation to Him, are warranted, on the consideration that the growth of the Christian life largely consists in changing belief that rests on testimony into knowledge grounded in vital experience. At first a man accepts Jesus Christ because, for one reason or another, he is led to give credence to the evangelical testimony and to the apostolic teaching: but as he goes on learning more and more of the realities of the Christian life, creed changes into consciousness; and we can turn round to apostles and prophets, and say to them, with thankfulness for all that we have received from them, 'Now we believe, not because of your saying, but because we have seen Him ourselves, and know that this is indeed the Christ, the Saviour of the world.' That is the advance which Christian men should all make, from the infantile, rudimentary days, when they accepted

Christ on the witness of others, to the time when they
accepted Him because, in the depth of their own experience, they have found Him to be all that they took
Him to be. The true test of creed is life. The true way
of knowing that a shelter is adequate is to house in it,
and be defended from the pelting of every pitiless
storm. The medicine we know to be powerful when
it has cured us. And every man that truly grasps
Jesus Christ, and is faithful and persevering in his
hold, can set his seal to that which to others is
but a thing believed on hearsay, and accepted on
testimony.

'We know that the Son of God is come.' Christian
people, have you such a first-hand acquaintance with
the articles which constitute your Christian creed as
that? Over and above all the intellectual reasons
which may lead to the acceptance, as a theory, of the
truths of Christianity, have you that living experience of them which warrants you in saying 'We
know'? Alas! Alas! I am afraid that this supreme
ground of certitude is rarely trodden by multitudes of
professing Christians. And so in days of criticism and
upheaval they are frightened out of their wits, and all
but out of their faith, and are nervous and anxious lest
from this corner or that corner or the other corner of
the field of honest study and research, there may come
some sudden shock that will blow the whole fabric of
their belief to pieces. 'He that believeth shall not
make haste,' and a man who *knows* what Christ has
done for him may calmly welcome the advent of any
new light, sure that nothing that can be established can
touch that serene centre in which his certitude sits
enshrined and calm. Brother, do you seek to be able
to say, 'I know in whom I have believed'?

II. Note the new power of knowing God given by the Son who is come.

John says that one issue of that Incarnation and permanent presence of the Lord Christ with us is that 'He hath given us an understanding that we may know Him that is true.' Now, I do not suppose that he means thereby that any absolutely new faculty is conferred upon men, but that new direction is given to old ones, and dormant powers are awakened. Just as in the miracles of our Lord the blind men had eyes, but it needed the touch of His finger before the sight came to them, so man, that was made in the image of God, which he has not altogether lost by any wandering, has therein lying dormant and oppressed the capacity of knowing Him from whom he comes, but he needs the couching hand of the Christ Himself, in order that the blind eyes may be capable of seeing and the slumbering power of perception be awakened. That gift of a clarified nature, a pure heart, which is the condition, as the Master Himself said, of seeing God— that gift is bestowed upon all who, trusting in the Incarnate Son, submit themselves to His cleansing hand.

In the Incarnation Jesus Christ gave us God to see; by His present work in our souls He gives us the power to see God. The knowledge of which my text speaks is the knowledge of 'Him that is true,' by which pregnant word the Apostle means to contrast the Father whom Jesus Christ sets before us with all men's conceptions of a Divine nature; and to declare that whilst these conceptions, in one way or another, fall beneath or diverge from reality and fact, our God manifested to us by Jesus Christ is the only One whose nature corresponds to the name, and who is essentially that which is included in it.

But what I would dwell on especially for a moment
is that this gift, thus given by the Incarnate and present
Christ, is not an intellectual gift only, but something
far deeper. Inasmuch as the Apostle declares that the
object of this knowledge is not a truth about God but
God Himself, it necessarily follows that the knowledge
is such as we have of a person, and not of a doctrine.
Or, to put it into simpler words: to know *about* God is
one thing, and to know God is quite another. We may
know all about the God that Christ has revealed and
yet not know Him in the very slightest degree. To
know about God is theology, to know Him is religion.
You are not a bit better, though you comprehend the
whole sweep of Christ's revelation of God, if the God
whom you in so far comprehend remain a stranger to
you. That we may know Him as a man knows his
friend, and that we may enter into relations of familiar
acquaintance with Him, Jesus Christ has come in the
flesh, and this is the blessing that He gives us—not an
accurate theology, but a loving friendship. Has Christ
done that for you, my brother?

That knowledge, if it is real and living, will be
progressive. More and more we shall come to know.
As we grow like Him we shall draw closer to Him; as
we draw closer to Him we shall grow like Him. So
the Christian life is destined to an endless progress,
like one of those mathematical spirals which ever climb,
ever approximate to, but never reach, the summit and
the centre of the coil. So, if we have Christ for our
medium both of light and of sight, if He both gives us
God to see and the power to see Him, we shall begin a
course which eternity itself will not witness completed.
We have landed on the shores of a mighty continent,
and for ever and for ever and ever we shall be pressing

deeper and deeper into the bosom of the land, and learning more and more of its wealth and loveliness. 'We know that we know Him that is true.' If the Son of God has come to us, we know God, and we know that we know Him. Do you?

III. Lastly, note here the Christian indwelling of God, which is possible through the Son who is come.

Friendship, familiar intercourse, intimate knowledge as of one with whom we have long dwelt, instinctive sympathy of heart and mind, are not all which, in John's estimation, Jesus Christ brings to them that love Him, and live in Him. For he adds, 'We are *in* Him that is true.' Of old Abraham was called the Friend of God, but an auguster title belongs to us. 'Know ye not that ye are the temples of the living God, and that the Spirit of God dwelleth in you?' Oh! brethren, do not be tempted, by any dread of mysticism, to deprive yourselves of that crown and summit of all the gifts and blessings of the Gospel, but open your hearts and your minds to expect and to believe in the actual abiding of the Divine nature in us. Mysticism? Yes! And I do not know what religion is worth if there is not mysticism in it, for the very heart of it seems to me to be the possible interpenetration and union of man and God—not in the sense of obliterating the personalities, but in the deep, wholesome sense in which Christ Himself and all His apostles taught it, and in which every man who has had any profound experience of the Christian life feels it to be true.

But notice the words of my text for a moment, where the Apostle goes on to explain and define how 'we are in Him that is true,' because we are 'in His Son Jesus Christ.' That carries us away back to 'Abide in Me, and I in you.' John caught the whole strain of such

thoughts from those sacred words in the upper room.
Christ in us is the deepest truth of Christianity. And
that God is in us, if Christ is in us, is the teaching not
only of my text but of the Lord Himself, when He said,
'We will come unto him and make our abode with
him.'

And will not a man '*know*' that? Will it not be something deeper and better than intellectual perception
by which he is aware of the presence of the Christ in
his heart? Cannot we all have it if we will? There is
only one way to it, and that is by simple trust in Jesus
Christ. Then, as I said, the trust with which we began
will not leave us, but will be glorified into experience
with which the trust will be enriched.

Brethren, the sum and substance of all that I have
been trying to say is just this: lay your poor personalities in Christ's hands, and lean yourselves upon
Him; and there will come into your hearts a Divine
power, and, if you are faithful to your faith, you will
know that it is not in vain. There is a tremendous
alternative, as I have already pointed out, suggested
by the sequence of thoughts in my text, 'the whole
world lieth in the wicked one' but 'we are in Him that
is true.' We have to choose our dwelling-place, whether
we shall dwell in that dark region of evil, or whether
we shall dwell in God, and know that God is in us.

If we are true to the conditions, we shall receive the
promises. And then our Christian faith will not be
dashed with hesitations, nor shall we be afraid lest any
new light shall eclipse the Sun of Righteousness, but,
in the midst of the babble of controversy, we may be
content to be ignorant of much, to hold much in
suspense, to part with not a little, but yet with quiet
hearts to be sure of the one thing needful, and with

unfaltering tongues to proclaim 'We know that the Son of God is come, and we are in Him that is true.'

THE LAST WORDS OF THE LAST APOSTLE

'This is the true God, and eternal life. 21. Little children, keep yourselves from idols. Amen.'—1 JOHN v. 20, 21.

So the Apostle ends his letter. These words are probably not only the close of this epistle, but the last words, chronologically, of Scripture. The old man gathers together his ebbing force to sum up his life's work in a sentence, which might be remembered though much else was forgotten. Last words stick. Perhaps, too, some thought of future generations, to whom his witness might come, passed across his mind. At all events, some thought that we are here listening to the last words of the last Apostle may well be in ours. You will observe that, in this final utterance, the Apostle drops the triumphant 'we know,' which we have found in previous sermons reiterated with such emphasis. He does so, not because he doubted that all his brethren would gladly attest and confirm what he was about to say, but because it was fitting that his last words should be his very own; the utterance of personal experience, and weighty with it, and with apostolic authority. So he smelts all that he had learned from Christ, and had been teaching for fifty years, into that one sentence. The feeble voice rings out clear and strong; and then softens into tremulous tones of earnest exhortation, and almost of entreaty. The dying light leaps up in one bright flash: the lamp is broken, but the flash remains. And if we will let it shine into our lives, we shall not walk in darkness, but have the light of life.

I. Here we have the sum of all that we need to know about God.

'This is the true God.' The first question is, What or whom does John mean by 'this'?

Grammatically, we may refer the word to the immediately preceding name, Jesus Christ. But it is extremely improbable that the Apostle should so suddenly shift his point of view, as he would do if, having just drawn a clear distinction between 'Him that is true,' and the Christ who reveals Him, he immediately proceeded to apply the former designation to Jesus Christ Himself. It is far more in accordance with his teaching, and with the whole scope of the passage, if by 'this' we understand the Father of whom he has just been speaking. It is no tautology that he reiterates in this connection that He is 'true.' For he has separated now his own final attestation from the common consciousness of the Christian community with which he has previously been dealing. And when he says, 'This is the true God' he means to say, 'This God of whom I have been affirming that Jesus Christ is His sole Revealer, and of whom I have been declaring that through Jesus Christ we may know Him and dwell abidingly in Him,' 'this'—and none else—'is the true God.'

Then the second question that I have to answer briefly is, What does John mean by 'true'? I had occasion, in a previous sermon on the foregoing words, to point out that by that expression he means, whenever he uses it, some person or thing whose nature and character correspond to his or its name, and who is essentially and perfectly that which the name expresses. If we take that as the signification of the word, we just come to this, that the final assertion into which the old Apostle flings all his force, and which he wishes to stand

out prominent as his last word to his brethren and to
the world, is that the God revealed in Jesus Christ,
and with whom a man through Jesus Christ may have
fellowship of knowledge and friendship—that He and
none but He answers to all that men mean when they
speak of a God; that He, if I might use such an expression, fully fills the part.

Brethren, if we but think that, however it comes
(no matter about that), every man has in him a capacity
of conceiving of a perfect Being, of righteousness,
power, purity, and love, and that all through the ages
of the world's yearnings there has never been presented
to it the realisation of that dim conception, but that
all idolatry, all worship, has failed in bodying out
a Person who would answer to the requirements of a
man's spirit, then we come to the position in which
these final words of the old fisherman go down to a
deeper depth than all the world's wisdom, and carry a
message of consolation and a true gospel to be found
nowhere besides.

Whatsoever embodiments men may have tried to give
to their dim conception of a God, these have been
always limitations, and often corruptions, of it. And
to limit or to separate is, in this case, to destroy. No
pantheon can ever satisfy the soul of man who yearns
for One Person in whom all that he can dream of
beauty, truth, goodness shall be ensphered. A galaxy of
stars, white as the whitest spot in the Milky Way, can
never be a substitute for the sun. '*This* is the true
God'; and all others are corruptions, or limitations, or
divisions, of the indissoluble unity.

Then, are men to go for ever and ever with 'the
blank misgivings of a creature, moving about in worlds
not realised'? Is it true that I can fancy some one far

greater than is? Is it true that my imagination can paint a nobler form than reality acknowledges? It is so, alas! unless we take John's swan-song and last testimony as true, and say:—This God, manifest in Jesus Christ, on whose heart I can lay my head, and into whose undying and unstained light I can gaze, and in whose righteousness I can participate, this God is the *real* God; no dream, no projection from my own nature, magnified and cleansed, and thrown up first from the earth that it may come down from heaven, but the reality, of whom all human imaginations are but the faint transcripts, though they be the faithful prophets.

For, consider what it is that the world owes to Jesus Christ, in its knowledge of God. Remember that to us orphaned men He has come and said, as none ever said, and showed as none ever showed: ' Ye are not fatherless, there is a Father in the heavens.' Consider that to the world, sunk in sense and flesh, and blotting its most radiant imaginations of the Divine by some veil and hindrance, of corporeity and materialism, He comes, and has said, 'God is a Spirit.' Consider that, taught of Him, this Apostle, to whom was committed the great distinction of in monosyllables preaching central truths, and in words that a child can apprehend, setting forth the depths that eternity and angels cannot comprehend, has said, ' God is Light, and in Him is no darkness at all.' And consider that he has set the apex on the shining pyramid, and spoken the last word when he has told us, 'God is Love.' And put these four revelations together, the Father; Spirit; unsullied Light; absolutely Love; and then let us bow down and say, ' Thou hast said the truth, O aged Seer. This is our God; we have waited for Him, and He will save us. This—and none beside—is the true God.'

I know not what the modern world is to do for a God if it drifts away from Jesus Christ and His revelations. I know that it is always a dangerous way of arguing to try to force people upon alternatives, one of which is so repellent as to compel them to cling to the other. But it does seem to me that the whole progress of modern thought, with the advancement of modern physical science, and other branches of knowledge which perhaps are not yet to be called science, are all steadily converging on forcing us to this choice —will you have God in Christ, or, will you wander about in a Godless world, and for your highest certitude have to say, 'Perhaps'? 'This is the true God,' and if we go away from Him I do not know where we are to go.

II. Here we have the sum of His gifts to us.

'This is the true God, and eternal life.' Now, let us distinctly and emphatically put first that what is here declared is primarily something about God, and not about His gift to men; and that the two clauses, 'the true God,' and 'eternal life,' stand in precisely the same relation to the preceding words, 'This is.' That is to say, the revelation which John would lay upon our hearts, that from it there may spring up in them a wondrous hope, is that, in His own essential self, the God revealed in Jesus Christ, and brought into living fellowship with us by Him, is 'eternal life.' By 'eternal life' he means something a great deal more august than endless existence. He means a life which not only is not ended by time, but which is above time, and not subject to its conditions at all. Eternity is not time spun out for ever. And so we are not lifted up into a region where there is little light, but where the very darkness is light, just as the curtain was the picture, in the old story of the painter,

That seems to part us utterly from God. He is
'eternal life'; then, we poor creatures down here,
whose being is all 'cribbed, cabined, and confined' by
succession, and duration, and the partitions of time,
what can we have in common with Him? John answers
for us. For, remember that in the earlier part of this
epistle he writes that 'the life was manifested, and we
shew unto you that eternal life which was with the
Father, and was manifested unto us,' and 'we declare
it unto you; that ye also may have fellowship with us;
and our fellowship is with the Father and with His
Son.' So, then, strange as it is, and beyond our thoughts
as it is, there may pass into creatures that very eternal
life which is in God, and was manifested in Jesus. We
have to think of Him because we know Him to be love,
as in essence self-communicating, and whatsoever a
creature can receive, a loving Father, the true God,
will surely give.

But we are not left to wander about in regions of
mysticism and darkness. For we know this, that however strange and difficult the thought of eternal life as
possessed by a creature may be, to give it was the very
purpose for which Jesus Christ came on earth. 'I am
that Bread of Life.' 'I am come that they might have
life, and have it more abundantly.' And we are not
left to grope in doubt as to what that eternal life consists in; for He has said: 'This is life eternal, that they
might know Thee, the only true God, and Jesus Christ
whom Thou hast sent.' Nor are we left in any more
doubt as to that bond by which the whole fulness of
this Divine gift may flow into a man's spirit. For over
and over again the Master Himself has declared, 'He
that believeth hath everlasting life.'

Thus, then, there is a life which belongs to God on

His throne, a life lifted above the limitations of time,
a life communicated by Jesus Christ, as the waters of
some land-locked lake may flow down through a sparkling river, a life which consists in fellowship with God,
a life which may be, and is, ours, on the simple condition of trusting Him who gives it, and a life which,
eternal as it is, and destined to a glory all undreamed
of, in that future beyond the grave, is now the possession of every man that puts forth the faith which is its
condition. 'He that believeth hath'—not *shall have*, in
some distant future, but has to-day—'everlasting life,'
verily here and now. And so John lays this upon our
hearts, as the ripe fruit of all his experience, and the
meaning of all his message to the world, that God revealed in Christ 'is the true God,' and as Himself the
possessor, is the source for us all, of life eternal.

III. Lastly, we have here the consequent sum of
Christian effort.

'Little children, keep yourselves from idols,' seeing
that 'this is the true God,' the only One that answers
to your requirements, and will satisfy your desires.
Do not go rushing to these shrines of false deities that
crowd every corner of Ephesus—ay! and every corner
of Manchester. For what does John mean by an idol?
Does he mean that barbarous figure of Diana that
stood in the great temple, hideous and monstrous?
No! he means anything, or any person, that comes
into the heart and takes the place which ought to be
filled by God, and by Him only. What I prize most,
what I trust most utterly, what I should be most for-
lorn if I lost ; what is the working aim of my life, and
the hunger of my heart—that is my idol. We all know
that.

Is the exhortation not needed, my brother? In

Ephesus it was hard to have nothing to do with
heathenism. In that ancient world their religion,
though it was a superficial thing, was intertwined with
daily life in a fashion that puts us to shame. Every
meal had its libation, and almost every act was knit by
some ceremony or other to a god. So that Christian
men and women had almost to go out of the world, in
order to be free from complicity in the all-pervading
idol-worship. Now, although the form has changed,
and the fascinations of old idolatry belong only to a
certain stage in the world's culture and history, the
temptation to idolatry remains just as subtle, just as
all-pervasive, and the yielding to it just as absurd.
You and I call ourselves Christians. We say we believe
that there is nothing else, and nobody else, in the whole
sweep of the universe that can satisfy our hearts, or be
what our imagination can conceive, but God only.
Having said that on the Sunday, what about Monday?
  They have forsaken Me, the fountain of living water,
and hewed to themselves broken cisterns that can hold
no water.' 'Little children'—for we are scarcely more
mature than that—'little children, keep yourselves
from idols.'

  And how is it to be done? 'Keep yourselves.'
Then you can do it, and you have to make a dead lift
of effort, or be sure of this—that the subtle seduction
will slide into your heart, and before you know it, you
will be out of God's sanctuary, and grovelling in
Diana's temple. But it is not only our own effort that
is needed, for just a sentence or two before, the Apostle
had said: 'He that is born of God'—that is, Christ—
'keepeth us.' So our keeping of ourselves is essentially
our letting Him keep us. Stay inside the walls of the
citadel, and you need not be afraid of the besiegers; go

outside by letting your faith flag, and you will be
captured or killed. Keep yourselves by clinging 'to
Him that is able to keep you from falling, and to present you faultless.' Make experience by fellowship
with Him who is the only true God, and able to
satisfy your whole nature, mind, heart, will, and these
false deities, the whole rabble of them, will have no
power to tempt you to bow the knee.

Brethren! here is the sum of the whole matter.
There is one truth on which we can stay our hearts,
one God in whom we can utterly trust, the God revealed in Jesus Christ. If we do not see Him in Christ,
we shall not see Him at all, but wander about all our
days in a world empty of solid reality. There is one
gift which will satisfy all our needs, the gift of eternal
life in Jesus Christ. There is one practical injunction
which will save us from many a heartache, and which
our weakness can never afford to neglect, and that is
to keep ourselves from all false worship. These golden
words of my text, in their simplicity, in their depth, in
their certainty, in their comprehensiveness, are worthy
to be the last words of Revelation; and to stand to all
the world, through all ages, as the shining apex, or the
solid foundation, or the central core of Christianity.
'This'—*this*, and none else—'is the true God and
eternal life. Little children, keep yourselves from
idols.'

GRACE, MERCY, AND PEACE

'Grace be with you, mercy, and peace, from God the Father, and from the Lord
Jesus Christ, the Son of the Father, in truth and love.'—2 JOHN 3.

WE have here a very unusual form of the Apostolic
salutation. 'Grace, mercy, and peace' are put together
in this fashion only in Paul's two Epistles to Timothy,

and in this the present instance; and all reference to
the Holy Spirit as an agent in the benediction is, as
there, omitted.

The three main words, 'Grace, mercy, and peace,'
stand related to each other in a very interesting
manner. If you will think for a moment you will see,
I presume, that the Apostle starts, as it were, from the
fountain-head, and slowly traces the course of the
blessing down to its lodgment in the heart of man.
There is the fountain, and the stream, and, if I may
so say, the great still lake in the soul, into which its
waters flow, and which the flowing waters make.
There is the sun, and the beam, and the brightness
grows deep in the heart of man. Grace, referring
solely to the Divine attitude and thought : mercy, the
manifestation of grace in act, referring to the workings
of that great Godhead in its relation to humanity : and
peace, which is the issue in the soul of the fluttering
down upon it of the mercy which is the activity of the
grace. So these three come down, as it were, a great,
solemn, marble staircase from the heights of the Divine
mind, one step at a time, down to the level of earth ;
and the blessings which are shed along the earth. Such
is the order. All begins with grace ; and the end and
purpose of grace, when it flashes into deed, and becomes
mercy, is to fill my soul with quiet repose, and shed
across all the turbulent sea of human love a great
calm, a beam of sunshine that gilds, and miraculously
stills while it gilds, the waves.

If that be, then, the account of the relation of these
three to one another, let me just dwell for a moment
upon their respective characteristics, that we may get
more fully the large significance and wide scope of this
blessing. Let us begin at what may be regarded either

as the highest point from which all the stream descends, or as the foundation upon which all the structure rests. 'Grace from God the Father and from the Lord Jesus Christ, the Son of the Father.' These two, blended and yet separate, to either of whom a Christian man has a distinct relation, these two are the sources, equally, of the whole of the grace.

The Scriptural idea of grace is love that stoops, and that pardons, and that communicates. I say nothing about that last characteristic, but I would like to dwell for a moment or two upon the other phases of this great word, a key-word to the understanding of so much of Scripture.

The first thing then that strikes me in it is how it exults in that great thought that there is no reason whatsoever for God's love except God's will. The very foundation and notion of the word 'grace' is a free, undeserved, unsolicited, self-prompted, and altogether gratuitous bestowment, a love that is its own reason, as indeed the whole of the Divine acts are, just as we say of Him that He draws His being from Himself, so the whole motive for His action and the whole reason for His heart of tenderness to us lies in Himself. We have no power. We love one another because we apprehend something deserving of love, or fancy that we do. We love one another because there is something in the object on which our love falls; which, either by kindred or by character, or by visible form, draws it out. We are influenced so, and love a thing because the thing or the person is perceived by us as being worthy, for some reason or other, of the love. God loves because He cannot help it; God loves because He is God. Our love is drawn out—I was going to say pumped out—by an application of external causes.

D

God's love is like an artesian well, whensoever you
strike, up comes, self-impelled, gushing into light
because there is such a central store of it beneath
everything, the bright and flashing waters. Grace is
love that is not drawn out, but that bursts out, self-
originated, undeserved. 'Not for your sakes, be it
known unto you, O house of Israel, but for Mine own
name's sake, do I this.' The grace of God is above that,
comes spontaneously, driven by its own fulness, and
welling up unasked, unprompted, undeserved, and
therefore never to be turned away by our evil, never to
be wearied by our indifference, never to be brushed
aside by our negligence, never to be provoked by our
transgression, the fixed, eternal, unalterable centre
of the Divine nature. His love is grace.

And then, in like manner, let me remind you that
there lies in this great word, which in itself is a gospel,
the preaching that God's love, though it be not turned
away by, is made tender by our sin. Grace is love
extended to a person that might reasonably expect,
because he deserves, something very different; and
when there is laid, as the foundation of everything,
'the grace of our Father and of the Son of the Father,'
it is but packing into one word that great truth which
we all of us, saints and sinners, need—a sign that God's
love is love that deals with our transgressions and
shortcomings, flows forth perfectly conscious of them,
and manifests itself in taking them away, both in their
guilt, punishment, and peril. 'The grace of our Father'
is a love to which sin-convinced consciences may certainly appeal; a love to which all sin-tyrannised souls
may turn for emancipation and deliverance. Then, if
we turn for a moment from that deep fountain, 'Love's
ever-springing well,' as one of our old hymns has it, to

the stream, we get other blessed thoughts. The love, the grace, breaks into mercy. The fountain gathers itself into a river, the infinite, Divine love concentrates itself in act, and that act is described by this one word, mercy. As grace is love which forgives, so mercy is love which pities and helps. Mercy regards men, its object, as full of sorrows and miseries, and so robes itself in garb of compassion, and takes wine and oil into its hands to pour into the wound, and lays often a healing hand, very carefully and very gently, upon the creature, lest, like a clumsy surgeon, it should pain instead of heal, and hurt where it desires to console. God's grace softens itself into mercy, and all His dealings with us men must be on the footing that we are not only sinful, but that we are weak and wretched, and so fit subjects for a compassion which is the strangest paradox of a perfect and divine heart. The mercy of God is the outcome of His grace.

And as is the fountain and the stream, so is the great lake into which it spreads itself when it is received into a human heart. Peace comes, the all-sufficient summing up of everything that God can give, and that men can need, from His loving-kindness, and from their needs. The world is too wide to be narrowed to any single aspect of the various discords and disharmonies which trouble men. Peace with God; peace in this anarchic kingdom within me, where conscience and will, hopes and fears, duty and passion, sorrows and joys, cares and confidence, are ever fighting one another; where we are torn asunder by conflicting aims and rival claims, and wherever any part of our nature asserting itself against another leads to intestine warfare, and troubles the poor soul. All that is harmonised and quieted down, and made concordant and co-operative to one great end, when the grace and the mercy have flowed silently into our spirits and harmonised aims and desires.

There is peace that comes from submission ; tranquillity of spirit, which is the crown and reward of obedience ; repose, which is the very smile upon the face of faith, and all these things are given unto us along with the grace and mercy of our God. And as the man that possesses this is at peace with God, and at peace with himself, so he may bear in his heart that singular blessing of a perfect tranquillity and quiet amidst the distractions of duty, of sorrows, of losses, and of cares. 'In everything by prayer and supplication with thanksgiving let your requests be known unto God; and the peace of God which passeth all understanding shall keep your hearts and minds in Christ Jesus.' And he who is thus at friendship with God, and in harmony with himself, and at rest from sorrows and cares, will surely find no enemies amongst men with whom he must needs be at war, but will be a son of peace, and walk the world, meeting in them all a friend and a brother. So all discords may be quieted ; even though still we have to fight the good fight of faith, we may do, like Gideon of old, build an altar to ' Jehovah-shalom,' the God of peace.

And now one word, as to what this great text tells us are the conditions for a Christian man, of preserving, vivid and full, these great gifts, ' Grace, mercy, and peace be unto you,' or, as the Revised Version more accurately reads, ' shall be with us in truth and love.' Truth and love are, as it were, the space within which the river flows, if I may so say, the banks of the stream. Or, to get away from the metaphor, these are set forth as being the conditions abiding in which, for our parts, we shall receive this benediction—'In truth and in love.'

I have no time to enlarge upon the great thoughts that these two words, thus looked at, suggest; let me put it into a sentence. To 'abide in the truth' is to keep ourselves conscientiously and habitually under the influence of the Gospel of Jesus Christ, and of the Christ who is Himself the Truth. They who, keeping in Him, realising His presence, believing His word, founding their thinking about the unseen, about their relations to God, about sin and forgiveness, about righteousness and duty, and about a thousand other things, upon Christ and the revelation that He makes, these are those who shall receive ' Grace, mercy, and peace.' Keep yourselves in Christ, and Christ coming to you, brings in His hands, and *is*, the 'grace and the mercy and the peace' of which my text speaks. And in love, if we want these blessings, we must keep ourselves consciously in the possession of, and in the grateful response of our hearts to, the great love, the incarnate Love, which is given in Jesus Christ.

Here is, so to speak, the line of direction which these great mercies take. The man who stands in their path, they will come to him and fill his heart; the man that steps aside, they will run past him and not touch him. You keep yourselves in the love of God, by communion, by the exercise of mind and heart and faith upon Him; and then be sure—for my text is not only a wish, but a confident affirmation—be sure that the fountain of all blessing itself, and the stream of petty benedictions which flow from it, will open themselves out in your hearts into a quiet, deep sea, on whose calm surface no tempests shall ever rave, and on whose unruffled bosom God Himself will manifest and mirror His face.

A PROSPEROUS SOUL

'Beloved, I wish above all things that thou mayest prosper and be in health,
even as thy soul prospereth.'—3 JOHN 2.

THIS little letter contains no important doctrinal
teaching nor special revelation of any kind. It is the
outpouring of the Christian love of the old Apostle to
a brother about whom we know nothing else except
that John, the beloved, loved him in the truth. And
this prayer—for it is a prayer rather than a mere
wish, since a good man like John turned all his wishes
into prayers—this prayer in the original is even more
emphatic and beautiful than in our version. 'Beloved,
I pray that in all things thou mayest prosper and be in
health, even as thy soul prospereth,' says the Revised
Version, and that slight change in the position of one
clause is at once felt to be an improvement. We can
scarcely suppose an Apostle praying for anybody 'above
all things' that he might get on in the world. But the
wish that Gaius may prosper outwardly in all things,
as his soul prospers, is eminently worthy of John. He
sets these two types of prosperity over against one
another, and says, 'My wish for you is that you may
be as prosperous and robust in spiritual matters as you
are in bodily and material things.'

I. Now note in the first place, What makes a prosperous soul? That question might be answered in a
great variety of ways, but I purpose for the present to
answer it by confining myself to this letter, and seeing
what we can find out about the man to whom it was
addressed. 'I rejoiced greatly when the brethren came
and testified of the truth that is in thee.' There is the
starting-point of true health of soul. That soul, and

only that soul, is prosperous, in which what the Apostle calls here ' the truth' is lodged and rooted; and by ' the truth' he means, of course, the whole great revelation of God in Jesus Christ; and eminently Jesus Christ Himself who is the embodied Truth. Whether we take the phrase as meaning the abiding of Jesus Christ in the heart, or whether we take it as meaning more simply the incorporation into the very substance of the being, of the motives and principles that lie in the Gospel, comes to pretty much the same thing. The one thing which makes a man's soul healthy is to get Jesus Christ into it. That acts like an amulet that banishes all diseases and corruptions. That is like the preserving salt which, rubbed into a perishable substance, arrests corruption and makes food sweet and savoury. It is the engrafted word that is able to save the soul, and howsoever many other things may contribute to the inner well-being and prosperity of a man, such as intellectual acquirements, refined tastes, the gratification of pure affections, the fulfilment of innocent and legitimate hopes, and the like, the one thing that makes the soul prosperous is to have Christ in His word deeply planted and inseparably enshrined in its personality and being.

And how is that enshrining to be brought about? Alas, we all know the way a great deal better than we practise it. The prosperous soul is the soul that has opened itself in docile obedience for the entrance of the quickening and cleansing word. And just as a flower will open its calyx in the sunshine, and being opened by the sunshine playing upon its elastic filaments, will, because it is opened, receive into itself the sun that opened it and so grow; in like manner, that heart that disparts itself at the touch of Christ's hand, and welcomes Him into the inner chambers and shrine of its being, will find that where He comes He brings warmth and fragrance and growth and all blessing. The prosperous soul is the Christ-inhabited soul. By willing reception, by patient waiting, by the study of God's word, by the endeavour to bring ourselves more and more under the influence of the truth as it is in Jesus, does that truth that makes prosperity take up its abode within us.

But the letter gives another of the characteristics of the truly prosperous and healthy soul. 'Thy brethren came and testified of the truth that is in thee, even as thou walkest in the truth.' The Apostle is not afraid of a confusion of metaphors which shocks sticklers for rhetorical propriety. The truth is, first of all, regarded as being in the man; and then it is regarded as being a road on which, and within the limits of which he walks, or an atmosphere in which he moves. The incongruity is no real incongruity, but it strikingly brings out the great and blessed fact of the Gospel that the man who has the grace of God, the truth as it is in Jesus, within him, thereby finds that there is prepared for him a path within the limits of that truth in which he can safely walk. There will be progress if there be prosperity. The prosperous spirit is the active and advancing spirit, not content merely with sitting and saying, 'I have the truth in my soul. Thy word have I hid in my heart that I sin not against Thee'; but recognising that that truth is the law of his life, and prescribes for him a course of conduct. The prosperous soul is the soul that confines its activity within the fence which 'the truth as it is in Jesus,' who is the pattern, and the motive, and the law, and the power, has laid down for us; and within those limits makes

daily and hourly advance to a more entire conformity
with the example of the Lord. The prosperous soul is
the soul that *walks*—not that sits idle—for action is the
end of thought, and the purpose of the truth is to make
men good, and not merely wise—a soul that acts and
advances, yet never passing out of the atmosphere of
the Gospel, nor going beyond the principles and motives
that are laid down there.

There is a third characteristic in this letter, which
we may also take for an illustration of the Apostle's
idea. For he says: 'Thou doest faithfully whatsoever
thou doest.'

Now 'faithfully' is not here used in the sense of
righteously discharging all obligations and fulfilling
one's stewardship, but it means something deeper than
that. The root idea is 'whatever thou doest thou
doest as a work of Christian faith'; or, to put it into
other words, the prosperous soul is the soul all whose
activity is based upon that one great truth made its
own by faith, that Jesus Christ loves it, and so is all
the result of trust in Him. Faith in Christ is the
mother-tincture, out of which every virtue can be com-
pounded, according to the liquid to which you add it.
The basis of all, the 'stock' from which all the rest is
really made, is the act of faith in Jesus Christ. And
so the prosperous soul is the soul that has the truth in
it, and walks in the truth which it has, and does everything because it trusts in the living God and in Jesus
Christ His Son.

Is that your notion of the ideal of human nature, of
the true and noble prosperity of an immortal spirit?
Unless it be you have yet to learn the loftiest elevation
and the fairest beauty that are possible for men. The
prosperous soul filled with Christ within, and walking

with Christ by its side, and drawing laws and motives,
pattern and power from Him, is the soul that truly
has fulfilled its ideal, and is journeying on the right
road.   For that is the literal meaning of the word that
is rendered here 'prosper'; journeying on the right
road to the true goal of human nature.

II. Look at the wished-for correspondence between
this soul-prosperity and outward prosperity. 'Beloved,'
says John, 'I wish above all things,' or rather, 'I wish
that in regard to all things, thou mayest prosper and
be in health as thy soul prospereth.'

How would you like that standard applied to your
worldly prosperity?   Would you like not to get on any
better in business than you do in religion?   Would you
be content that your limbs should be no more healthy
than your soul, or that you should be making no more
advances in worldly happiness and material prosperity
than you are in the Divine life?   Would you be content
to have your worldly prosperity doled out to you out
of the same spoon, of the same dimensions, with which
you are content to receive your spiritual prosperity?
'As thy soul prospereth'—that would mean a very
Lenten diet for a good many of us, and a very near
approach to insolvency for some commercial men.
Brethren, there is a sharp test in these words. I
suppose this good Gaius to whom the letter was written
was very likely in humble circumstances, and not im-
probably in enfeebled health.   And John was probably
wishing for him more than he had, when he wished
him to get on as well in the world as he did in his
spiritual life, and desired that his soul might prosper as
much as his body.   It would be a bad thing for some of
us if the same standard of proportion were applied to us.

Another consideration is suggested by this correspondence, and that is that it is always a disastrous thing for Christian people when outward prosperity gets ahead of inward. It is the ruin of a good many so-called Christian people. When a man gets on in the world he begins, too often, to decline in the truth. It is difficult for us to carry a full cup without spilling it. And the worst thing that could happen to many Christian people would be what they fret, and fume, and work themselves into a fever, and live careful days and sleepless nights in order to secure—and that is, outward prosperity. The best thing is that the soul should be more prosperous than the body, and the worst adversity is the outward prosperity that ruins or harms the inward life.

III. So, lastly, note the superiority of the inward prosperity. There is no overstrained spiritualism here. John has set us an example that we need not be afraid to follow. If he that leaned upon Christ's bosom, and had drunk in more of the spirit of his Master than any of the Twelve, was not afraid to pray for this good brother that he might have worldly good and health, we need not doubt that for ourselves, and for those that are dear to us, it is perfectly legitimate and right that we should desire and pray for both things. There is no unnatural, artificial, hypocritical pretence of despising the present and the outward in the words here. Although the Apostle does put the two things side by side, he does not fall into the error of casting contempt upon either. He is a true disciple of the Master who said, 'Your Father knoweth that ye have need of these things.' And if your Father knows that you have need, then you may be quite sure that you will get them, and it is a lie to pretend that you do not want them when you do.

But then, that being admitted, look how the higher towers above the legitimate lower. It will always be the case that if a man seeks first the Kingdom of God and His righteousness, there will be—in his simple devotion to the truth, and walking within the limits that it prescribes, and making all his life an act of faith—a direct tendency in a great many directions to secure the best possible use, and the largest possible enjoyment, from the things that are seen and temporal. 'Godliness hath promise of the life which now is'; and the first Psalm, which perhaps may have been in the Apostle's mind here, contains a truth that was not exhausted in the Old Testament days, because the man whose heart is set on the law of God, and who meditates upon that law day and night, all that he doeth shall prosper. There is in godliness a distinct and constant tendency to make the best of both worlds; but the best is not made of the present world unless we subordinate it and feel distinctly its insignificance in comparison with the future, which is also the present, unseen world.

And even when, as is often the case, the devout and inwardly prosperous soul is compassed about with sorrows that never can be stanched, with griefs through which anything but an immortal life would bleed itself away; or with poverty and want and anxiety arising from causes which no personal devotion can ever touch or affect—even then if the soul prospers it has the power, the magic power, of converting poison into food, and sorrow into a means of growth; and they whose spirits are joined to Jesus Christ, and whose souls ever move in harmony with Him—and therefore are prosperous souls—will find that there is nothing in this world that is really adverse to them. For 'all

things work together for good to them that love God,'
since he who loves God thinks nothing bad that helps
him to love Him better; and since he who loves God
finds occasion for loving and trusting Him more in
every variety and vicissitude of earthly fortune.

Therefore, brethren, if we will follow the directions
that this Apostle gives us as to how to secure the
prosperity of our souls, God is faithful and He will
measure to us prosperity in regard of outward things
by the proportion which our faith in Him bears to His
faithfulness. The more we love Him, the more certainly will all things be our servants. If we can say
'We are Christ's,' then all things are ours.

FOR THE SAKE OF THE NAME

'For His name's sake.'—3 JOHN 7.

THE Revised Version gives the true force of these words
by omitting the 'His,' and reading merely 'for the sake
of the Name.' There is no need to say whose name.
There is only One which could evoke the heroism and
self-sacrifice of which the Apostle is speaking. The expression, however, is a remarkable one. The name
seems almost, as it were, to be personified. There are
one or two other instances in the New Testament
where the same usage is found, according to the true
reading, though it is obscured in our Authorised
Version, because it struck some early transcribers as
being strange, and so they tried to mend and thereby
spoiled it.

We read, for instance, in the true reading, in the
Acts of the Apostles, as to the disciples, on the first
burst of persecution, that 'they rejoiced that they

were counted worthy to suffer shame for *the* Name.'
And again, in Philippians, that in recompense and
reward for ' His obedience unto death '—the Father
hath given unto the Son—' *the* Name which is above
every name.' Once more, though less obviously, we
find James speaking about ' the worthy name by which
we are called.'

Then the other part of this phrase is quite as significant as this principal one. The word rendered 'for
the sake of,' does not merely mean—though it does
mean that—' on account of,' or ' by reason of,' but ' on
behalf of,' as if, in some wonderful sense, that mighty
and exalted Name was furthered, advantaged, or
benefited by even men's poor services. So, you see,
a minute study of the mere words of the Scripture,
though it may seem like grammatical trifling and
pedantry, yields large results. Men do sometimes
' gather grapes of thorns'; and the hard, dry work of
trying to get at the precise shade of meaning in Scriptural words always repays us with large lessons and
impulses. So let us consider the thoughts which
naturally arise from the accurate observation of the
very language here.

I. And, first, let us consider the pre-eminence
implied in ' *the* Name.'

Now I need not do more than remind you in a sentence that eminently in the Old Testament, and also in
the New, a name is a great deal more than the syllables
which designate a person or a thing. · It describes, not
only who a man is, but what he is ; and implies qualities,
characteristics, either bodily or spiritual, which were
either discerned in or desired for a person. So when
the creatures are brought to Adam that he might give
them names, that expresses the thought of the primitive

man's insight into their nature and characteristics.
So we find our Lord changing the names of His disciples, in some cases in order to express either the deep
qualities which His eye discerned lying beneath the
more superficial ones, and to be evolved in due time, or
declaring some great purpose which He had for them,
official or otherwise.

So here the name substantially means the same
thing as the Person Jesus. It is not the syllables by
which He is called, but the whole character and nature
of Him who is called by these syllables, that is meant
by ' the Name.' The distinction between it, as so used,
and Person, is simply that the former puts more stress
on the qualities and characteristics as known to us.

Thus ' the Name ' means the whole Christ as we
know Him, or as we may know Him, from the Book,
in the dignity of His Messiahship, in the mystery of
His Divinity, in the sweetness of His life, in the depth
of His words, in the gentleness of His heart, in the
patience and propitiation of His sacrifice, in the might
of His resurrection, in the glory of His ascension, in
the energy of His present life and reigning work for
us at the right hand of God. All these, the central
facts of the Gospel, are gathered together into that
expression *the Name*, which is the summing up in one
mighty word, so to speak, which it is not possible for
a man to utter except in fragments, of all that Jesus
Christ is in Himself, and of all that He is and does
for us.

It is but a picturesque and condensed way of saying
that Jesus Christ, in the depth of His nature and the
width of His work, stands alone, and is the single,
because the all-sufficient, Object of love and trust and
obedience. There is no need for a forest of little

pillars; as in some great chapter-house one central
shaft, graceful as strong, bears the groined roof, and
makes all other supports unnecessary and impertinent.
There is one Name, and one alone, because in the
depths of that wondrous nature, in the circumference
of that mighty work, there is all that a human heart,
or that all human hearts, can need for peace, for nobleness, for holiness, for the satisfaction of all desires, for
the direction of efforts, for the stability of their being.
The name stands alone, and it will be the only Name
that, at last, shall blaze upon the page of the world's
history when the ages are ended; and the chronicles
of earth, with the brief 'immortality' which they gave
to other names of illustrious men, are moulded into
dust. 'The Name is above every name,' and will out-
last them all, for it is the all-sufficient and encyclopædical embodiment of everything that a single
heart, or the whole race, can require, desire, conceive,
or attain.

So then, brethren, the uniqueness and solitariness
of the name demands an equal and corresponding ex-
clusiveness of devotion and trust in us. 'Hear, O
Israel! The Lord thy God is *one* Lord. Therefore
thou shalt love the Lord thy God with *all* thy heart,
and with all thy soul, and with all thy strength, and
with all thy mind.' And in like manner we may argue
—There is one Christ, and there is none other but He.
Therefore all the current of my being is to set to Him,
and on Him alone am I to repose my undivided weight,
casting all my cares and putting all my trust only on
Him. Lean on none other. You cannot lean too
heavily on that strong arm. Love none other except
in Him; for His heart is wide enough and deep
enough for all mankind. Obey none other, for only His

voice has the right to command. And lifting up our eyes, let us see 'no man any more save Jesus only.' That Name stands alone.

Involved in this, but worthy of briefly putting separately, is this other thought, that the pre-eminent and exclusive mention of the Name carries with it, in fair inference, the declaration of His Divine nature. It seems to me that we have here a clear case in which the Old Testament usage is transferred to Jesus Christ, only, instead of the Name being Jehovah, it is Jesus. It seems to me impossible that a man saturated as this Apostle was with Old Testament teaching, and familiar as he was with the usage which runs through it as to the sanctity of 'the Name of the Lord,' should have used such language as this of my text unless he had felt, as he has told us himself, that 'the Word was God.' And the very incidental character of the allusion gives it the more force as a witness to the commonplaceness which the thought of the divinity of Jesus Christ had assumed to the consciousness of the Christian Church.

II. But passing from that, let me ask you to look, secondly, at the power of the Name to sway the life.

I have explained the full meaning of the preposition in my text in my introductory remarks. It seems to me to cover both the ground of 'on account of,' or ' by reason of,' and 'on behalf of.'

Taking the word in the former of these two senses, note how this phrase, 'for the sake of the Name,' carries with it this principle, that in that Name, explained as I have done, there lie all the forces that are needed for the guidance and the impulses of life. In Him, in the whole fulness of His being, in the wonders of the story of His character and historical manifesta-

E

tion, there lies all guidance for men. He is the Pattern of our conduct. He is the Companion for us in our sorrow. He is the Quickener for us in all our tasks. And to set Him before us as our Pattern, and to walk in the paths that He dictates, is to attain to perfection. Whosoever makes 'for the sake of the Name' the motto of his life will not walk in darkness, but shall have the light of life.

And not only is there guidance, but there is impulse, and that is better than guidance. For what men most of all want is a power that shall help or make them to do the things that they see plainly enough to be right.

And oh, brother, where is there such a force to quicken, to ennoble, to lead men to higher selves than their dead past selves, as lies in the grand sweep of that historical manifestation which we understand by the Name of Jesus? There is nothing else that will go so deep down into the heart and unseal the fountains of power and obedience as that Name. There is nothing else that will so strike the shackles off the prisoned will, and ban back to their caves the wild beasts that tyrannise within, and put the chain round their necks, as the Name of Jesus Christ. That is the Talisman that ennobles everything, that evokes undreamed-of powers, that 'out of these stones,' the hard and unsusceptible and obstinate wills of godless men, will 'raise up children unto Abraham.' This is the secret that turns the heavy lead of our corrupt natures into pure gold.

And where does the impulsive power lie? Where, in that great continent, the whole life and work of Jesus Christ, is the dominant summit from which the streams run down? The Cross! The Cross! The

Love that died for us, individually and singly, as well
as collectively, is the thing that draws out answering
love.   And answering love is the untiring and omnipotent power that transmutes my whole nature into the
humble aspiration to be like Him who has given Himself for me, and to render back myself unto Him for
His gift.   Brother, if you have not known the Name of
Christ as the Name of the Divine Saviour who died on
the Cross for you, you do not yet understand the
power to transform, to ennoble, to energise, to impel
to all self-sacrifice that lies in that Name.   In the fact
of His death, and in the consequent fact of the communication of life from Him to each of us if we will,
lie the great impulses which will blessedly and strongly
carry us along the course which He marks out for us.
And they who can say 'For the sake of the Name' will
live lives calm, harmonious, noble, and in some humble
measure conformed to the serene and transcendent
beauty to which they bow and on which they rest.
The impulse for a life—the only one that will last, and
the only one that will lift—lies in the recognition of
the Name.   And so, let me remind you how our consequent simple duty is honestly, earnestly, prayerfully,
always, to try to keep ourselves under the influence of
that sweet compulsion and mighty encouragement
which lie in the Name of Jesus Christ.   How fragmentary, how interrupted, how imperfect at the best
are our yieldings to the power and the sweetness of
the motives and pattern given to us in Christ's Name!
How much of our lives would be all the same if Jesus
Christ never had come, or if we never had believed in
Him!   Look back over your days, Christian men, and
see how little of them has borne that stamp, and how
slightly it has been impressed upon them.

Our whole life ought to be filled with His Name.
You can write it anywhere. It does not need a gold
plate to carve His Name upon. It does not need to be
set in jewels and diamonds. The poorest scrap of brown
paper, and the bluntest little bit of pencil, and the
shakiest hand, will do to write the Name of Christ;
and all life, the trivialities as well as the crises, may be
flashing and bright with the sacred syllables. Moham-
medans decorate their palaces and mosques with
no pictures, but with the name of Allah, in gilded
arabesques. Everywhere, on walls and roof, and
windows and cornices, and pillars and furniture, the
name is written. There is no such decoration for a
life as that Christ's Name should be inscribed thereon.

III. Lastly, notice the service that even we can do
to the Name.

That, as I said, is the direct idea of the Apostle here.
He is speaking about a very small matter. There
were some anonymous Christian people who had gone
out on a little missionary tour, and in the course of it,
penniless and homeless, they had come to a city the
name of which we do not know, and had been taken
in and kindly entertained by a Christian brother,
whose name has been preserved to us in this one
letter. And, says John, these humble men went out
' on behalf of the Name '—to do something to further
it, to advantage it! Jesus Christ, the bearer of the
Name, was in some sense helped and benefited, if I
may use the word, by the work of these lowly and
unknown brethren.

Now there are one or two other instances in the
New Testament where this same idea of the benefit
accruing to the name of Jesus from His servants on
earth is stated, and I just point to them in a sentence

in order that you may have all the evidence before
you. There is the passage to which I have already
referred, recording the disciples' joy that they were
'accounted worthy to suffer shame on behalf of the
Name.' There are the words of Christ Himself in
reference to Paul at his conversion, 'I will shew him
how great things he must suffer for My Name's sake.'
There is the church's eulogium on Barnabas and Paul,
as 'men that have hazarded their lives for the Name
of our Lord Jesus.' There is Paul's declaration that
he is 'ready, not only to be bound, but to die, on
behalf of the Name of the Lord Jesus.' And in the
introduction of the Epistle to the Romans he connects
his apostleship with the benefit that thereby accrued
to the Name of Christ. If we put all these together
they just come to this, that, wonderful as it is, and
unworthy as we are to take that great Name into our
lips, yet, in God's infinite mercy and Christ's fraternal
and imperial love, He has appointed that His Name
should be furthered by the sufferings, the service, the
life, and the death of His followers.

'He was extolled with my tongue,' says the Psalmist,
in a rapture of wonder that any words of his could
exalt God's Name. So to you Christians is committed
the charge of magnifying the name of Jesus Christ.
You can do it by your lives, and you can do it by your
words, and you are sent to do both. We can 'adorn
the doctrine'; paint the lily and gild the refined gold, and
make men think more highly of our Lord by our example
of faithfulness and obedience. We can do it by our
definite proclamation of His Name, which is laid upon
us all to do, and for which facilities of varying degrees
are granted. The inconsistencies of the professing
followers of Christ are the strongest barriers to the

world's belief in the glory of His Name. The Church
as it is forms the hindrance rather than the help to the
world's becoming a church. If from us sounded out
the Name, and over all that we did it was written,
blazing, conspicuous, the world would look and listen,
and men would believe that there was something in
the Gospel.

If you are a Christian professor, either Christ is
glorified or put to shame in you, His saint; and either
it is true of you that you do all things in the Name of
the Lord Jesus and so glorify His Name, or that
through you the Name of Christ is 'blasphemed
among the nations.' Choose which of the two it
shall be!

FELLOW-WORKERS WITH THE TRUTH

'That we might be fellow-helpers to the truth.'—3 JOHN 8.

'FELLOW-HELPERS to the Truth.' A word or two may
be permitted as to the immediate occasion of the
expression. There seems to have been, as we learn not
only from occasional references in the New Testament,
but from early Christian literature, and very frequent
practice in the primitive churches, of certain members
having, like our friends the Quakers, 'a concern' for
some special ministry, and being loosed from their
ordinary avocations, and sent out with the sanction of
the Church. These travelling evangelists went from
place to place, and sought the hospitality and help of
the Christian communities to which they came. My
text is an exhortation from the aged Apostle to treat

such brethren as they deserved, seeing that they have 'come forth for the sake of the Name'; and should be welcomed and helped as brethren.

Now there are ambiguities about the words, on which I need not dwell. So far as the grammatical construction of the originals are concerned, they may either mean what our Authorised Version takes them to mean, 'fellow-helpers'—or rather 'fellow-*workers*'—*for* the Truth; the co-operation being regarded as confined to the two sets of men, the evangelists and their hospitable receivers—or they may mean, as the Revised Version takes them, 'fellow-workers *with* the Truth'— 'the Truth' and the two sets of human agents being all supposed as co-operating in one common end. The latter is, I presume, the real meaning of the Evangelist. 'The Truth' is supposed to be an active force in the world, which both the men who directly preach it, and the men who sustain and cheer those who do, are co-operating with. Then there is another question as to whether, by 'the Truth' here, we are to understand the whole body of Christian revelation, or whether we are to see shining through the words the august figure of Him who is personally, as He Himself claimed, 'the Way, and the Truth, and the Life.' I believe that the latter explanation is the truer one, and more in accordance with the intense saturation in all John's writings with the words of the Master. I can scarcely think that when he spoke thus about 'the Truth,' or when he spoke in another of his letters about the 'Truth which dwelleth in us, and shall be in us for ever,' he meant only a body of principles. I think he meant Jesus Christ Himself. And so with that sacred and auguster meaning attaching to his words, I wish to look at them with you.

I. The possessors of the Truth are to be workers with the Truth.

I do not say a word about the claim which is made in this expression, that Christian people possess the absolute truth in regard to all matters upon which the revelation made to them in Jesus Christ touches. That is a bold assumption, but I do not need to say a word about it here. I take it for granted that you professing Christians concur in the belief that what you have received about God and Christ and God's will concerning men, and the way of salvation, and the prospects for the future life, stands alone and complete, as 'the Truth,' to which all other conceptions of God and man and duty and destiny are related, but as fragmentary at the highest, and as often perversions, corruptions, and contradictions. Do not let any modern width of thought, or any impressions gathered from the new science of comparative religion, blur the distinctness and the joyousness of your confidence that in Christ we have not a peradventure of men, but the 'Verily! verily!' of heaven: *the* Truth.

And then remember that, according to the representation of my text, this Truth, wherever it enters into a man's heart, lays hold upon him, and makes him its apostle. All moral and spiritual truth has that power. There are plenty of dry statements in various regions of science and thought the reception of which brings with it no compulsion whatever to say a word about them. No man is ever smitten with the conviction that it is his duty to go out into the world and proclaim that 'two and two make four,' or truths of that sort. But once lodge in a man's heart thoughts of a moral, religious, spiritual character, and as soon as he believes them he wakes up to feel 'Then I must—I must proclaim them, and get somebody else to share my convictions.' It is the test of real, deep, vital possession of 'the Truth' that it shall be as a fire shut up in our bones, burning its way necessarily out into the light; and that no man who has it dare wrap it in a napkin and bury it in the ground.

God forbid that I should say that a silent Christian is not a genuine Christian. I know too well how far beneath the ideal we all come, but sure I am that if men have never found that when 'the Truth as it is in Jesus' drew back her veil, and let the lambent beauty of her face blaze in upon their hearts, it made them her slaves and knight-errants for evermore, they have seen very very little of that supreme loveliness. Brethren! the truth that we believe is our mistress, and of the Christian truth that we profess to hold, we are sworn by the very fact to be the apostles and the missioners.

Nor let us forget the solemn and elevating thought which goes along with the imagery of my text; that the Truth, for all its majesty and dignity and divinity, needs men for its helpers. The only way by which it can spread is through us and our fellows. There is no magic by which it can divide and impart itself, apart from the agency of the men who already possess it. The torch has been brought from heaven, and the light with which it blazes is celestial, but in order to enlighten the darkness of the earth it must be passed from hand to hand by a linked chain of men. The lake lies full of possible fertility and promise to flush with green verdure the barren burning desert sands; but it will lie there, its possible good unrealised for ever, unless men with their spades and excavators dig the channels and lead

the heaven-sent blessing that came from the clouds
into all the barren places. The Truth needs us, but
when the work is done that the workers with the Truth
do, it is the Truth and not the workers that have done
the work.

So, Christian men and women, I come to you with
this message—recognise your dignity, the honour that
is laid upon you in being allowed to be co-operators
with the gospel of the glory of the blessed God. Recognise the obligation, solemn and heavy, which is laid
upon you by the very nature of the truth which we
believe, by the common bonds of fellowship between
man and man, to impart the message that has brought
life to us; and recognise it as at once our highest
honour and our widest duty to be 'fellow-workers with
the Truth.'

II. The companions of Christ are to be workers with
Christ.

He, as I have pointed out, is the Incarnate Truth.
And here we come upon the especial peculiarity of
Christianity as a system, considered in its relation to
Jesus Christ, its Founder and its Giver. You can take
Plato's philosophy and do what you like with it, and
treat Plato as a negligible quantity. You can do the
same with all other great teachers, even those of them
who have most impressed their own individuality upon
their thinkings, and theorisings, and teachings, but
you cannot do that with Christianity; you cannot say,
'Never mind who it was that said it. Attend to what
was said.' For Jesus Christ, and His message, are so
interwoven and interlaced in such a fashion as that
you cannot get rid of Him, and keep it. He Himself is
the Truth. Christ is Christianity; and any man that
has ever tried to deal with the teachings of the New

Testament as a body of principles, ignoring the lips from which they came, is left with what they call a *caput mortuum*, a dead mass of impotent generalities. Get Christ into them, and they are all palpitating, and living, and flaming, and have power.

So, then, when I call my brethren, and feel myself bound to the task of being 'workers with the Truth,' it is no mere devotion to the propaganda of a creed that I want to urge, but it is devotion to proclaiming the beloved hand of the person out of whom the creed is carved, and in whom all the truth is shrined and sphered. Every man that is Christ's companion is thereby bound to be a worker with the incarnate Truth. He needs our help. True, he finds all the capital, but we are His partners, His representatives and agents here on earth, as He has taught us in more than one parable. The pound or the talent is His; it is given to me, but it is left with me to determine whether it shall increase and fructify or not. On the Cross He said, 'It is finished,' but all through the ages He is working, and all through the ages His mightiest means of working is through the men by whom He works. The Lord works with them, and they work with the Lord. They are His tools; He makes them, but He cannot do His work without them. And notwithstanding the Cross, notwithstanding the adequate powers for the regeneration of humanity, and the salvation of individuals, which lie in that message of the Gospel, the co-operation of the Church is needed if the world is to be saved. Surely it is constituted in order to fill up that which is behind of the sufferings of Christ, and to carry on the unfinished development of the finished work which, done once for all on the Cross, is not done until it has been applied to the world by

Christ working through His people, and by His people
working with Christ. If there is a flaw in the covering
that enwraps the wire, there will be no message at the
other end. If you and I are non-conductors, no matter
how much power may be flashed into us, that which is
beyond us will want the power. The medium between
Christ and the world that He died and lives to save,
the medium is we Christian people.

'Workers with the Truth.' That is parallel with
what Paul says, in the great word which he ventures
upon when, having just declared that neither he nor
Apollos are anything, he rises to the thought which
balances that of their nothingness: 'We are labourers
together with God.'

Is not that a dignity? And what shall we say of
men who have so little consciousness of union with
Jesus Christ as that they have next to no sympathy
with the things that fill His heart? I plead for no
narrow interpretation of the duties of the 'fellow-
workers with the Truth.' He came to redress all human
misery, sin, and evil. He came not only to speak the
words that save the soul with the everlasting salvation
of sin forgiven, and friendship restored between God
and man, but to carry light and healing and peace and
hope into every region where the darkness broods, to
break every chain and let the oppressed go free. Social
improvements, and all the wider outlooks which Christian benevolence takes in these late years, all come into
the general category of being the carrying out of
Christ's sympathies and purpose, and being part of the
work of those who are 'fellow-workers' with Him in
His toil, and who shall one day hear, 'It is finished!
The kingdoms of this world are the kingdoms of our
Lord and of His Christ.'

III. Further, the workers with Christ are to be workers with one another.

These travelling evangelists had one function. The people in the unknown church in Asia Minor, staying at home and following their secular callings, had another; and that was, to help and to further these peripatetic brethren. Co-operation means diversity of function and identity of aims and ends. For us there remains the duty still, as incumbent as it was in those early days, of recognising our own special task, of cleaving to that, and yet of furthering and helping all our brethren who, in their diverse ways, are engaged in the same great end. The men that take care of the base of operations of that army that is pressing down upon the foe are as truly fighting the enemy as the men that are in the front. It was the old law in Israel, based upon a clear understanding that all who co-operated towards one end, in whatsoever divers ways, are united together; that 'as his part is that goes down into the battle, so shall his part be that abides by the stuff; they shall part alike.'

Brethren, learn your special work. Remember that you have each something to do that nobody can do as well as you. Learn your special work, and beware of narrowing your sympathies to your special work. Let them go out to embrace all, however far apart upon the wall and however different may be their tasks, they are still co-operant to one end. 'He that planteth and he that watereth are one.' Identity of purpose, and wide diversity of method, with as wide charity, and as wide sympathy, ought to mark all Christian workers.

All the thoughts that I have been trying to urge have a very direct bearing upon church as well as upon individual life. Although there is no intention, on our

Apostle's part, of laying down anything like the constitution of a Christian church, in the incidental words of
my text, yet the principles involved in these words do
lie very deep down in the conception of what a Christian church ought to be. They make very short work
of all sacerdotal assumptions. A priest doing a miracle
there at the altar, and the people simple recipients of,
and spectators—that, in many quarters, is the modern
notion of the relation between pastor and people.
John gives the truer one when he says—'fellow-helpers
to the Truth.'

The words bear on a mistake that is more common
in the audience, I suppose, than sacramentarian notion
—namely, that a church is a place where people come
to hear sermons and pay their pew-rents, and there an
end.   There is a dead-weight of idle people clogging
the work of every Christian congregation in England.
Christian professors! what do you do for the Truth, for
your Lord, for your brethren? I, for my part, have to
say with the Apostle, 'not for that we have dominion
over your faith, but are helpers of your joy; for by
faith ye stand.' I decline all responsibility for doing
more than my own share of the evangelistic work of
this church. The Chinese put up mud-forts in which
there is one real cannon that can be fired, and make a
noise, and all the rest are dummies; painted, wooden.
That is a great deal too like what a great many Christian churches are—one piece to fire, and the others for
show.

'Fellow-helpers.' That defines our mutual relation.
But do not be too sure that your work is only the
indirect work of sustaining ' them that are such.' There
is some direct work for *you* to do. And you are shutting
your souls out from a great blessing by not doing it.

Sure I am that whoever is in union with **Jesus Christ** will have his lips touched to proclaim His Name somehow. And sure I am that whoever, smitten by love and loyalty to his Master, by the ardour of affection born of the grasp of the Truth, and by real love for his fellow-men that need it, opens his lips to make Christ known, will find that there is no surer way of increasing his own grasp of the Truth, and deepening his own union with Christ, than to seek to make others share in the blessings which are his life. 'Fellow-helpers to the Truth '—and *with* the Truth—I pray that we may be so more and more for the days or years that may yet remain to us.

THE CHRISTIAN'S WITNESSES TO CHARACTER

'Demetrius hath a good report of all men, and of the truth itself.'—3 JOHN 12.

WHAT a strange fate this Demetrius has had! He has narrowly escaped oblivion, yet he is remembered for ever and his name is known over all the world. But beyond the name nothing is certain. Who he was, where and when he lived, what he had done to earn the old Apostle's commendation are unknown. All his surroundings are swallowed up in darkness, and there shines out only that one little point of light that he 'hath a good report'—or, as the Revised Version better renders it, ' he hath the witness of all men, and of the truth itself.' A great many brilliant reputations might be glad to exchange a fame that has filled the world for a little epitaph like that.

I said we did not know anything about him. What if he should be the Demetrius whose astute appeal to profit and religion roused the shrine-makers at Ephesus

and imperilled Paul's life? Of course, that is mere
conjecture, and the identity of name is not a strong
foundation to build on, for it was a very common one.
If this disciple, thus praised by John, is our old
acquaintance in Acts, what a change had come over
him! Truly, to him, 'old things had passed away, all
things were become new.' If we remember John's
long connection with Ephesus, the conjecture will
perhaps seem reasonable. At all events, we do no
harm if, perhaps led by sentiment, we give as much
weight as we can to the supposition that here we have,
reappearing within the Church, the old antagonist,
and that 'this Paul' had 'persuaded' him, too, that
'they be no gods which are made with hands,' and so
had turned him to Jesus Christ. I wonder what became
of his craft, and his silver shrines, if this is the same
man as he who mustered the Ephesian silversmiths.

But be that as it may, I desire—keeping in mind the
alteration of rendering that I have suggested—'hath
witness of all men,' and of the truth itself—to look at
the sort of witnesses to character that a Christian man
should be able to call.

I. The first witness is Common Opinion.

There is something wrong unless a Christian can put
popular opinion into the witness-box in his favour.
Of course there is a sense in which there is nothing
more contemptible than seeking for that, and in which
no heavier woe can come upon us, and no worse thing
can be said about us, than that all men speak well of
us. But, on the other hand, whether men speak well
of us or not, there should be a distinctive characteristic
plainly visible in us Christians which shall make all
sorts of observers say to themselves, 'Well! that is a
good man anyhow. I may not like him; I may not

want to resemble him; but I cannot help seeing what
sort of a man he is, and that there is no mistake about
his genuine goodness.' That is a testimony which
Christians ought to be more ambitious of possessing
than many of them are, and to lay themselves out
more consciously to get, than most of them do. For
bad men generally know a good one when they see
him, and a great many of them

> ' Compound for sins they are inclined to
> By praising virtues they 've no mind to,'

and substitute admiration of uncongenial goodness for
imitation of it. It is nothing uncommon to find the
drunkard praising the temperate man, and evil-livers
of all sorts recognising the beauty of their own
opposites. The worst man in the world has an ideal
of goodness in his conscience and mind, far purer and
loftier than the best man has realised.

And, again, it is a very righteous and good thing
that people who are not Christians should have such
extremely lofty and strict standards for the conduct
of people that are. We sometimes smile when we see
in the newspapers, for instance, sensational paragraphs
about the crime of some minister, or clergyman, or
some representative religious man. No doubt a dash
of malice is present in these; but they are an unconscious testimony to the high ideal of character which
attaches to the profession of Christianity. No similar
paragraphs appear about the immoralities or crimes of
non-religious men. They are not expected to be saints.
But we are, and it is right that we should be thus expected. The world does not demand of us more than it is
entitled to do, or that our Lord has demanded. There
is nothing more wholesome than that Christian people

F

should feel that there are lynx eyes watching them,
and hundreds who will have a malicious joy if they
defile their garments, and bring discredit on their
profession.

I have not the smallest objection to that; and I
only wish that some of us who talk a great deal about
the depth of our spiritual life could hear what is
thought of us by our next-door neighbours, and our
servants, and the tradesmen that we deal with, and all
those other folk that have no sympathy with our
religion, and are, therefore, rigid judges of our
conduct.

Then there is another consideration which I suggest
—that a great many good people think that it is their
Christianity that makes folk speak ill of them, when
it is their inconsistencies and not their Christianity
that provoke the sarcasm. If you wrap up the
treasure of your Christianity in a rough envelope of
angularity, self-righteousness, sourness, censure, and
criticism, you need not wonder that people do not
think much of your Christianity. It is not because
Christian professors are good, but because they are
not better, that ninety-nine out of a hundred of the
uncharitable things that are said about them are said,
and truly said.

So, dear friends, let us—not in any cowardly spirit
of trying to disarm censure, nor because we have an
itch to be caressed, like a parrot to have its head
scratched, nor because we are pleased that men shall
think well of us, but because the judgment of the
world is, in some degree, a more wholesome tribunal
than the judgment of our own consciences, and is,
in some sense, an anticipation, though with many
mistakes, of the judgment of God—let us try to have a

good report of 'them that are without,' and to be 'living epistles, known and read of all men,' who will recognise the handwriting, and say, 'That is Christ's.'

Remember Daniel in that court where luxury and vice and sensuality, and base intrigues of all sorts rioted, and how they said of him, 'We shall find no occasion against him except it be concerning the law of his God.' And let us try to earn the same kind of reputation; and be sure of this that, unless the world endorses our profession of Christianity, which it may do by *disliking* us—that is as it may be—there is grave reason to doubt whether the profession is a reality or not.

II. Then there is another witness here mentioned— 'the truth itself.'

The Gospel of Jesus Christ witnesses for the man who witnesses for, and lives by it. A law broken testifies against the breaker; a law kept testifies for him. And so, if there be an approximation in the drift of our lives to the great ideal set forth in the law of God, that law will bear witness for us. But there must be in us the things that Christianity plainly requires before 'the truth' can be put into the witness-box for us. There must be manifest self-surrender.

Let us go back to our supposition, which, of course, I freely admit is the only conjecture. If this is the Demetrius of the Acts, and he became a Christian, the first thing that 'the truth' required of him would be to shut up shop, to give up the lucrative occupation by which he had his wealth, and to cast in his lot with the men that were warring against idols. We, in our degree, will have, in some form or other, the same self-surrender to exercise.

I have a letter which tells me the story of a man,

who for years has been trying to serve God, in the
employ of some establishment where they sell wines
and spirits, but now his conscience has smitten him,
and he has had to give it up, and writes to ask me if I
can find him a situation. Well! he is borne witness
to by the truth itself, which he has loyally obeyed.
We all, as Christians, have to do the like, and not only
in the great acts of our lives to rid ourselves of everything that is contrary to the principles and commandments of the Word, but in the small things to be ever
seeking to come nearer and nearer to the ideal which
He requires.

When looking into the perfect law of liberty we see
in its precepts our own characters reflected, if I may so
say; because we keep these we may be sure that we
are right. If we do not, we may be sure that we are
wrong. The truth will bear witness against lives that
are ordered in defiance of it, and for those which are
conformed to it. It is possible that even the lofty and
perfect examples of conduct and character which are in
the history of the Master, and the principles that are
drawn from Him, may testify of us; and if so, what
quiet blessedness will be ours!

III. But there is a last thought here. Christ Himself
will be a witness.

I do not know that in these profound and mystical
letters of the Apostle John, that great designation
'the truth' is ever employed to mean only the body of
teaching contained in what we call the Gospel. I
think that there is always trembling in the expression,
and sometimes predominating in it, in these letters,
the personal application of which our Lord, as reported
by the same Apostle when he was playing the part of
Evangelist, gives us the warrant, when He says, 'I am

the Truth.' And if that personal meaning is, as I
think it is, shimmering through these words, then we
may venture to deal with it separately in conclusion,
and to say that the third witness is Jesus Christ
Himself.

'With me,' said Paul, 'it is a very small matter to be
judged of you, or of man's judgment'; and that
wholesome disregard of opinion is part of the attitude
which we should bear towards popular or any human
estimate—but 'he that judgeth me is the Lord.'

Now, notice Paul's tenses. He does not say, 'He that
is going to judge me,' away out yonder in the indefinite
future, at some great Day of Judgment after death, but
he says, 'He that judgeth me'; and he means us to feel
that, step by step, all through our lives, and in reference to each individual action at the time of its
commission, there is an act of Christ's judgment, in
infallible determination by Him of the moral good or
evil of our deed. So, moment by moment, we are at
that tribunal, and act by act, we please or we displease
Him; and of each feeling and thought, word, and deed,
He says, 'Well,' or 'Ill, is it done.'

We may have Him for our Witness as well as for our
Judge. How does He witness? To-day, and all through
our earthly days, He will witness by His voice in the
inner man, enlightened and made sensitive to evil by
His own gracious presence. I believe that conscience
is always the irradiation of the 'Light that lighteth
every man that cometh into the world'; but I believe
that the conscience of the man who is born again by
faith in Jesus Christ is in a more special manner the
voice of Christ Himself speaking within him. And
when there rises in the heart that quiet glow which
follows His approval, *there* is a Witness that no voices

around, censuring or praising, have the smallest power
to affect.   Never mind what the world says if the
voice within, which is the voice of Jesus Christ, testifies
to integrity and to the desire to serve Him.

And covet this, dear friends, as by far the best and
the happiest thing that we can possess in this world,
when we hear Him, in the recesses of our hearts, saying
to us, 'Well done, good and faithful servant,' then our
thoughts are carried forward still further; and we
may venture, with all our imperfections, to look
onward to the day when again the Judge will be the
Witness for us, even to the surprise of those whose acts
He then attests.   He Himself has taught us so, when He
pictures the wondering servant saying, 'Lord, when
did I do all these things, which Thou hast discovered in
me?'   And He has assured us that 'never will He forget
any of our works,' and that at the last solemn hour,
when we must be manifested before the Judgment-seat
of Christ, He Himself will confess our deeds before the
Father and before His holy angels.   It is well to have
the witness of man; it is heaven to have the witness of
the Truth Himself.

JUDE

THE COMMON SALVATION

'The common salvation.'—JUDE 3.
'The common faith.'—TITUS i. 4.

JUDE was probably one of Christ's brothers, and a man of position and influence in the Church. He is writing to the whole early Christian community, numbering men widely separated from each other by nationality, race, culture, and general outlook on life; and he beautifully and humbly unites himself with them all as recipients of a 'common salvation.' Paul is writing to Titus, the veteran leader to a raw recruit. Wide differences of mental power, of maturity of religious experience, separated the two; and yet Paul beautifully and humbly associates himself with his pupil, as exercising a 'common faith.'

Probably neither of the writers meant more than to bring himself nearer to the persons whom they were respectively addressing; but their language goes a great deal further than the immediate application of it. The 'salvation' was 'common' to Jude and his readers, as 'the faith' was to Paul and Titus, because the salvation and the faith are one, all the world over.

It is for the sake of insisting upon this community, which is universal, that I have ventured to isolate these two fragments from their proper connection, and to bring them together. But you will notice that they take up the same thought at two different stages, as it

were. The one declares that there is but one remedy
and healing for all the world's woes; the other declares
that there is but one way by which that remedy can
be applied. All who possess 'the common salvation'
are so blessed because they exercise 'the common faith.'

I. Note the underlying conception of a universal
deepest need.

That Christian word 'salvation' has come to be
threadbare and commonplace, and slips over people's
minds without leaving any dint. We all think we
understand it. Some of us have only the faintest and
vaguest conception of what it means, and have never
realised the solemn view of human nature and its
necessities which lies beneath it. And I want to press
that upon you now. The word 'to save' means either
of two things—to heal from a sickness, or to deliver
from a danger. These two ideas of sickness to be
healed and of dangers to be secured from enter into
the Christian use of the word. Underlying it is the
implication that the condition of humanity is universally that of needing healing of a sore sickness, and
of needing deliverance from an overhanging and
tremendous danger. *Sin* is the sickness, and the
issues of sin are the danger. And sin is making myself
my centre and my law, and so distorting and flinging
out of gear, as it were, my relations to God.

Surely it does not want many words to show that
that must be the most important thing about a man.
Deep down below all superficialities there lies this
fundamental fact, that he has gone wrong with regard
to God; and no amount of sophistication about
heredity and environment and the like can ever wipe
out the blackness of the fact that men willingly do
break through the law, which commands us all to yield

ourselves to God, and not to set ourselves up as our
own masters, and our own aims and ends, independently of Him. I say that is the deepest wound of
humanity.

In these days of social unrest there are plenty of
voices round us that proclaim other needs as being
clamant, but, oh, they are all shallow and on the surface as compared with the deepest need of all: and the
men that come round the sick-bed of humanity and say,
'Ah, the patient is suffering from a lack of education,'
or 'the patient is suffering from unfavourable environment,' have diagnosed the disease superficially.
There is something deeper the matter than that, and
unless the physician has probed further into the wound
than these surface appearances, I am afraid his remedy
will go as short a way down as his conception of the
evil goes.

Oh, brethren, there is something else the matter
with us than ignorance or unfavourable conditions.
'The whole head is sick, and the whole heart faint.'
The tap-root of all human miseries lies in the solemn
fact of human transgression. That is a universal fact.
Wide differences part us, but there is one thing that
we have all in common: a conscience and a will that
lifts itself against disliked good. Beneath all surface
differences of garb there lies the same fact, the common
sickness of sin. The king's robe, the pauper's uniform,
the student's gown, the mill-hand's fustian, the naked
savage's brown skin, each cover a heart that is evil, and
because it is evil, needs salvation from sickness and
deliverance from danger.

For do not forget that if it is true that men have
driven their rebellious chariots through God's law,
they cannot do that without bringing down God's

hand upon them, and they ought not to be able to do
it; and He would not be a loving God if it were not
so. There are dangers; dangers from the necessary
inevitable consequences, here and yonder, of rebellion
against Him.

Now, do not let us lose ourselves in generalities.
That is the way in which many of us have all our
lives long blunted the point of the message of the
Gospel to our hearts. That is what we do with all
sorts of important moral truths. For instance, I suppose there never was a time in your lives when you
did not believe that all men must die. But I suppose
most of us can remember some time when there came
upon us, with a shock which made some of us cower
before it as an unwelcome thing, the thought, 'And *I*
must.'

The *common* sickness? Yes! 'Thou art the man.'
Oh, brother, whatever you may have or whatever you
may want, be sure of this: that your deepest needs
will not be met, your sorest sickness will not be healed,
your most tremendous peril not secured against, until
the fact of your individual sinfulness and the consequences of that fact are somehow or other dealt with,
stanched, and swept away. So much, then, for the
first point.

II. Now a word as to the common remedy. One
of our texts gives us that—'the common salvation.'

You all know what I am going to say, and so, perhaps, you suppose that it is not worth while for me to
say it. I dare say some of you think that it was not
worth while coming here to hear the whole, threadbare, commonplace story. Well! is it worth while
for me to speak once more to men that have so often
heard and so often neglected? Let me try. Oh, that I

could get you one by one, and drive home to each single soul that is listening to me, or perhaps, that is *not* listening, the message that I have to bring!

'The common salvation.' There is one remedy for the sickness. There is one safety against the danger. There is *only* one, because it is the remedy for all men, and it is the remedy for all men because it is the remedy for each. Jesus Christ deals, as no one else has ever pretended to deal, with this outstanding fact of my transgression and yours.

He, by His death, as I believe, has saved the world from the danger, because He has set right the world's relations to God. I am not going, at this stage of my sermon, to enter upon anything in the nature of discussion. My purpose is an entirely different one. I want to press upon you, dear brethren, this plain fact, that since there is a God, and since you and I have sinned, and since things are as they are, and the consequences will be as they will be, both in this world and in the next, we all stand in danger of death—death eternal, which comes from, and, in one sense, consists of, separation in heart and mind from God.

You believe in a judgment day, do you not? Whether you do or not, you have only to open your eyes, you have only to turn them inwards, to see that even here and now, every sin and transgression and disobedience *does* receive its just recompense of reward. You cannot do a wrong thing without hurting yourself, without desolating some part of your nature, without enfeebling your power of resistance to evil and aspiration after good, without lowering yourself in the scale of being, and making yourself ashamed to stand before the bar of your own conscience. You cannot do some wrong things, that some of you are

fond of doing, without dragging after them consequences, in this world, of anything but an agreeable
kind. Sins of the flesh avenge themselves in kind, as
some of you young men know, and will know better
in the days that are before you. Transgressions which
are plain and clear in the eyes of even the world's
judgment draw after them damaged reputations, enfeebled health, closed doors of opportunity, and a whole
host of such things. And all these are but a kind of
premonitions and overshadowings of that solemn
judgment that lies beyond. For all men will have to
eat the fruit of their doings and drink that which they
have prepared. But on the Cross, Jesus Christ, the
Son of God, bore the weight of the world's sin, yours
and mine and every man's. There is one security
against the danger; and it is that He, fronting the
incidence of the Divine law, says, as He said to His
would-be captors in the garden, 'If ye seek Me, let
these go their way.' And they go their way by the
power of His atoning death.

Further, Jesus Christ imparts a life that cures the
sickness of sin.

What is the meaning of this Whitsuntide that all the
Christian world is professing to keep to-day? Is it
to commemorate a thing that happened nineteen centuries ago, when a handful of Jews for a few minutes
had the power of talking in other languages, and a
miraculous light flamed over their heads and then disappeared? Was that all? Have you and I any share
in it? Yes. For if Pentecost means anything it
means this, that, all down through the ages, Jesus
Christ is imparting to men that cleave to Him the real
gift of a new life, free from all the sickness of the old,
and healthy with the wholesomeness of His own perfect

sinlessness, so that, however inveterate and engrained a man's habits of wrong-doing may have been, if he will turn to that Saviour, and let Him work upon him, he will be delivered from his evil. The leprosy of his flesh, though the lumps of diseased matter may be dropping from the bones, and the stench of corruption may drive away human love and sympathy, can be cleansed, and his flesh become like the flesh of a little child, if only he will trust in Jesus Christ. The sickness can be cured. Christ deals with men in the depth of their being. He will give you, if you will, a new life and new tastes, directions, inclinations, impulses, perceptions, hopes, and capacities, and the evil will pass away, and you will be whole.

Ah, brethren, that is the only cure. I was talking a minute or two ago about imperfect diagnoses; and there are superficial remedies too. Men round us are trying, in various ways, to stanch the world's wounds, to heal the world's sicknesses. God forbid that I should say a word to discourage any such! I would rather wish them ten times more numerous than they are; but at the same time I believe that, unless you deal with the fountain at its head, you will never cleanse the stream, and that you must have the radical change, which comes by the gift of a new life in Christ, before men can be delivered from the sickness of their sins. And so all these panaceas, whilst they may do certain surface good, are, if I may quote a well-known phrase, like 'pills against an earthquake,' or like giving a lotion to cure pimples, when the whole head is sick and the whole heart faint. You will never cure the ills of humanity until you have delivered men from the dominion of their sin.

Jesus Christ heals society by healing the individual.

There is no other way of doing it. If the units are
corrupt the community cannot be pure. And the only
way to make the units pure is that they shall have
Christ on the Cross for their redemption, and Christ in
the heart for their cleansing. And then all the things
that men try to produce in the shape of social good
and the like, apart from Him, will come as a consequence of the new state of things that arises when the
individuals are renewed. Apart from Him all human
attempts to deal with social evils are inadequate.
There is a terrible disillusionising and disappointment
awaiting many eager enthusiasts to-day, who think
that by certain external arrangements, or by certain
educational and cultivated processes, they can mend
the world's miseries. You educate a nation. Well
and good, and one result of it is that your bookshops
get choked with trash, and that vice has a new avenue
of approach to men's hearts. You improve the eco-
nomic condition of the people. Well and good, and
one result of it is that a bigger percentage than ever of
their funds finds its way into the drink-shop. You
give a nation political power. Well and good, and one
result of it is that the least worthy and the least wise
have to be flattered and coaxed, because they are the
rulers. Every good thing, divorced from Christ,
becomes an ally of evil, and the only way by which the
dreams and desires of men can be fulfilled is by the
salvation which is in Him entering the individual
hearts and thus moulding society.

III. Now, lastly, the common means of possessing
the common healing.

My second text tells us what that is—'the common
faith.' That is another of the words which is so
familiar that it is unintelligible, which has been dinned

into your ears ever since you were little children, and
in the case of many of you excites no definite idea, and
is supposed to be an obscure kind of thing that belongs
to theologians and preachers, but has little to do with
your daily lives. There is only one way by which this
healing and safety that I have been speaking about
can possibly find its way into a man's heart. You have
all been trained from childhood to believe that men
are saved by faith, and a great many of you, I dare
say, think that men might have been saved by some
other way, if God had chosen to appoint it so. But
that is a clear mistake. If it is true that salvation is
a gift from God, then it is quite plain that the only
thing that we require is an outstretched hand. If it is
true that Jesus Christ's death on the Cross has brought
salvation to all the world, then it is quite plain that,
His work being finished, we have no need to come in
pottering with any works of ours, and that the only
thing we have to do is to accept it. If it is true that Jesus
Christ will enter men's hearts, and there give a new
spirit and a new life, which will save them from their
sins and make them free from the law of sin and death,
then it is plain that the one thing that we have to do
is to open our hearts and say 'Come in, Thou King of
Glory, come in!' Because salvation is a gift; because
it is the result of a finished work; because it is imparted
to men by the impartation of Christ's own life to them:
for all these reasons it is plain that the only way by
which God can save a man is by that man's putting his
trust in Jesus Christ. It is no arbitrary appointment.
The only possible way of possessing 'the common salvation' is by the exercise of 'the common faith.'

So we are all put upon one level, no matter how
different we may be in attainments, in mental capacity

—geniuses and blockheads, scholars and ignoramuses, millionaires and paupers, students and savages, we are all on the one level. There is no carriage road into heaven. We have all to go in at the strait gate, and there is no special entry for people that come with their own horses; and so some people do not like to have to descend to that level, and to go with the ruck and the undistinguished crowd, and to be saved just in the same fashion as Tom, Dick, and Harry, and they turn away.

Plenty of people believe in a 'common salvation,' meaning thereby a vague, indiscriminate gift that is flung broadcast over the mass. Plenty of people believe in a 'common faith.' We hear, for instance, about a 'national Christianity,' and a 'national recognition of religion,' and 'Christian nations,' and the like. There are no Christian nations except nations of which the individuals are Christians, and there is no ' common faith ' except the faith exercised in common by all the units that make up a community.

So do not suppose that anything short of your own personal act brings you into possession of ' the common salvation.' The table is spread, but you must take the bread into your own hands, and you must masticate it with your own teeth, and you must assimilate it in your own body, or it is no bread for you. The salvation is a 'common,' like one of the great prairies, but each separate settler has to peg off his own claim, and fence it in, and take possession of it, or he has no share in the broad land. So remember that 'the common salvation' must be made the individual salvation by the individual exercise of ' the common faith.' Cry, 'Lord! *I* believe!' and then you will have the right to say, 'The Lord is *my* strength; He also is become *my* salvation.'

KEEPING OURSELVES IN THE LOVE
OF GOD

'But ye, beloved, building up yourselves on your most holy faith, praying in the Holy Ghost, 21. Keep yourselves in the love of God, looking for the mercy of our Lord Jesus Christ unto eternal life.'—JUDE 20, 21.

JUDE has been, in all the former part of the letter, pouring out a fiery torrent of vehement indignation and denunciation against 'certain men' who had 'crept' into the Church, and were spreading gross immorality there. He does not speak of them so much as heretics in belief, but rather as evil-doers in practice; and after the thunderings and lightning, he turns from them with a kind of sigh of relief in this emphatic, '*But*, ye! beloved.' The storm ends in gentle rain; and he tells the brethren who are yet faithful how they are to comport themselves in the presence of prevalent corruption, and where is their security and their peace.

You will observe that in my text there is embedded, in the middle of it, a direct precept: 'Keep yourselves in the love of God'; and that that is encircled by three clauses, like each other in structure, and unlike *it*— 'building,' 'praying,' 'looking.' The great diamond is surrounded by a ring of lesser jewels. Why did Jude put two of these similar clauses in front of his direct precept, and one of them behind it? I think because the two that precede indicate the ways by which the precept can be kept, and the one that follows indicates the accompaniment or issue of obedience to the precept. If that be the reason for the structure of my text, it suggests also to us the course which we had best pursue in the exposition of it.

G

I. So we have, to begin with, the **great direct precept**
for the Christian life.

'Keep yourselves in the love of God.'   Now I need
not spend a moment in showing that ' the love of God '
here means, not ours to Him, but His to us.   It is that
in which, as in some charmed circle, we are to keep
ourselves.   Now that injunction at once raises the
question of the possibility of Christian men being out
of the love of God, straying away from their home,
and getting out into the open.   Of course there is a
sense in which His 'tender mercies are over all His
works.'   Just as the sky embraces all the stars and the
earth within its blue round, so that love of God encom-
passes every creature; and no man can stray so far
away as that, in one profound sense, he gets beyond its
pale.   For no man can ever make God cease to love
him.   But whilst that is quite true, on the other side
it is equally true that contrariety of will and continuance in evil deeds do so alter a man's relation to the
love of God as that he is absolutely incapable of receiving its sweetest and most select manifestations,
and can only be hurt by the incidence of its beams.
The sun gives life to many creatures, but it slays some.
There are crawling things that live beneath a stone,
and when you turn it up and let the arrows of the
sunbeams smite down upon them, they squirm and
die.   It is possible for a man so to set himself in antagonism to that great Light as that the Light shall
hurt and not bless and soothe.

It is also possible for a *Christian* man to step out of
the charmed circle, in the sense that he becomes all
unconscious of that Light.   Then to him it comes to
the same thing that the love shall be non-existent, and
that it shall be unperceived.   If I choose to make my

abode on the northern side of the mountain, my thermometer may be standing at 'freezing,' and I may be
shivering in all my limbs on Midsummer Day at noon-
tide. And so it is possible for us Christian people to
stray away out from that gracious abode, to pass from
the illuminated disc into the black shadow; and
though nothing is 'hid from the heat thereof,' yet we
may derive no warmth and no enlightening from the
all-pervading beams. We have to 'keep ourselves in
the love of God.'

Then that suggests the other more blessed possibility,
that amidst all the distractions of daily duties, and the
solicitations of carking cares, and the oppression of
heavy sorrows, it is possible for us to keep ourselves
perpetually in the conscious enjoyment of the love of
God. I need not say how this ideal of the Christian
life may be indefinitely approximated to in our daily
experiences; nor need I dwell upon the sad contrast
between this ideal unbrokenness of conscious sunning
ourselves in the love of God, and the reality of the
lives that most of us live. But, brethren, if we more
fully believed that we can keep up, amidst all the dust
and struggle of the arena, the calm sweet sense of
God's love, our lives would be different. Nightingales
will sing in a dusty copse by the roadside, however
loud the noise of traffic may be upon the highway.
And we may have, all through our lives, that song, unbroken and melodious. That sub-consciousness underlying our daily work, 'like some sweet beguiling
melody, so sweet, we know not we are listening to it,'
may be ever present with each of us in our daily work,
like some 'hidden brook in the leafy month of June,'
that murmurs beneath the foliage, and yet is audible
through all the wood.

And what a peaceful, restful life ours would be, if we could thus be like John, leaning on the Master's bosom. We might have a secret fortress into the central chamber of which we could go, whither no sound of the war in the plains could ever penetrate. We might, like some dwellers in a mountainous island, take refuge in a central glen, buried deep amongst the hills, where there would be no sound of tempest, though the winds were fighting on the surface of the sea, and the spindrift was flying before them. It is possible to 'keep ourselves in the love of God.' And if we keep in that fortress we are safe. If we go beyond its walls we are sure to be picked off by the well-aimed shots of the enemy. So, then, that is the central commandment for the Christian life.

II. Now let me turn to consider the methods by which we can thus keep ourselves in the love of God.

These are two: one mainly bearing on the outward, the other on the inward, life. By 'building up yourselves on your most holy faith': that is the one. By 'praying in the Holy Ghost': that is the other. Let us look at these two.

'Building up yourselves on your most holy faith.' I suppose that 'faith' here is used in its ordinary sense. Some would rather prefer to take it in the latter, ecclesiastical sense, by which it means, not the act of belief, but the aggregate of the things believed.—'Our most holy faith,' as it is called by quotation—I think misquotation—of this passage. But I do not see that there is any necessity for that meaning. The words are perfectly intelligible in their ordinary meaning. What Jude says is just this: 'Your trust in Jesus Christ has in it a tendency to produce holiness, and that is the foundation on which you are to build a great character. Build up yourselves on your most holy faith.' For although it is not what the world's ethics recognise, the Christian theory of morality is this, that it all rests upon trust in God manifested to us in Jesus Christ. Faith is the foundation of all supreme excellence and nobility and beauty of character; because, for one thing, it dethrones self, and enthrones God in our hearts; making Him our aim and our law and our supreme good; and because, for another thing, our trust brings us into direct union with Him, so that we receive from Him the power thus to build up a character.

Faith is the foundation. Ay! but faith is *only* the foundation. It is 'the potentiality of wealth,' but it is not the reality. 'All things are *possible* to him that believeth'; but all things are not actual except on conditions. A man may have faith, as a great many professing Christians have it, only as a 'fire-escape,' a means of getting away from hell, or have it only as a hand that is stretched out to grasp certain initial blessings of the spiritual life. But that is not its full glory nor its real aspect. It is meant to be the beginning in us of 'all things that are lovely and of good report.' What would you think of a man that carefully put in the foundations for a house, and had all his building materials on the ground, and let them lie there? And that is what a great many of you Christian people do, who 'have fled for refuge,' as you say, 'to the hope set before you in the Gospel'; and who have never wrought out your faith into noble deeds. Remember what the Apostle says, 'Faith which worketh'; and worketh 'by love.' It is the foundation, but only the foundation.

The work of building a noble character on that firm

foundation is never-ending. 'Tis a life-long task 'till
the lump be leavened.' The metaphor of growth by
building suggests effort, and it suggests continuity;
and it suggests slow, gradual rearing up, course
upon course, stone by stone. Some of us have done
nothing at it for a great many years. You will pass,
sometimes, in our suburbs, a row of houses begun by
some builder that has become bankrupt; and there are
mouldering bricks and gaping empty places for the
windows, and the rafters decaying, and stagnant
water down in the holes that were meant for the
cellars. That is like the kind of thing that hosts of
people who call themselves Christians have built.
' But ye, beloved, building up yourselves on your most
holy faith, . . . Keep yourselves in the love.'

Then the other way of building is suggested in the
next clause, 'praying in the Holy Ghost'—that is to
say, prayer which is not mere utterance of my own
petulant desires which a great deal of our 'prayer' is,
but which is breathed into us by that Divine Spirit
that will brood over our chaos, and bring order out of
confusion, and light and beauty out of darkness, and
weltering sea :—

> ' The prayers I make will then be sweet indeed,
>   If Thou the Spirit give by which I pray.'

As Michael Angelo says, such prayer inspired and
warmed by the influences of that Divine Spirit playing
upon the dull flame of our desires, like air injected into
a grate where the fire is half out, such prayers are
our best help in building. For who is there that has
honestly tried to build himself up 'for a habitation of
God' but has felt that it must be 'through a Spirit'
mightier than himself, who will overcome his weak-

nesses and arm him against temptation? No man who honestly endeavours to *re-form* his character but is brought very soon to feel that he needs a higher help than his own. And perhaps some of us know how, when sore pressed by temptation, one petition for help brings a sudden gush of strength into us, and we feel that the enemy's assault is weakened.

Brethren, the best attitude for building is on our knees; and if, like Cromwell's men in the fight, we go into the battle singing,

> ' Let God arise, and scattered
> Let all His enemies be,'

we shall come out victorious. ' Ye, beloved, building and praying, keep yourselves.'

III. Now, lastly, we have here in the final clause the fair prospect visible from our home, in the love of God.

'Looking for the mercy of the Lord Jesus Christ unto eternal life.'

After all building and praying, we need ' the mercy.' Jude has been speaking in his letter about the destruc- tion of evil-doers, when Christ the Judge shall come. And I suppose that that thought of final judgment is still in his mind, colouring the language of my text, and that it explains why he speaks here of ' the mercy of our Lord Jesus Christ' instead of, as is usual in Scripture, 'the mercy of God.' He is thinking of that last Day of Judgment and retribution, wherein Jesus Christ is to be the Judge of all men, saints as well as sinners, and therefore he speaks of mercy as bestowed by Him then on those who have 'kept themselves in the love of God.' Ah! we shall need it. The better we are the more we know how much wood, hay, stubble,

we have built into our buildings; and the more we are
conscious of that love of God as round us, the more
we shall feel the unworthiness and imperfection of
our response to it. The best of us, when we lie down
to die, and the wisest of us, as we struggle on in life,
realise most how all our good is stained and imperfect,
and that after all efforts we have to cry 'God be
merciful to me a sinner.'

Not only so, but our outlook and confident expectation of that mercy day by day, and in its perfect form
at least, depends upon our keeping ourselves 'in the
love of God.' We have to go high up the hill before we
can see far over the plain. Our home in that love commands a fair prospect. When we stray from it, we lose
sight of the blue distance. Our hope of 'the mercy of
God unto eternal life' varies with our present consciousness and experience of His love.

That mercy leads on to eternal life. We get many of
its manifestations and gifts here, but these are but the
pale blossoms of a plant not in its native habitat,
nor sunned by the sunshine which can draw forth all
its fragrance and colour.

We have to look forward for the adequate expression of the mercy of God to all that fulness of perfect
blessedness for all our faculties, which is summed up
in the one great word—'life everlasting.'

So our hope ought to be as continuous as the manifestation of the mercy, and, like it, should last until the
eternal life has come. All our gifts here are fragmentary and imperfect. Here we drink of brooks by the
way. There we shall slake our thirst at the fountain-
head. Here we are given ready money for the day's
expenses. There we shall be free of the treasure-
house, where lie the uncoined and uncounted masses

of bullion, which God has laid up in store for them
that fear Him.   So, brethren, let us hope perfectly for
the perfect manifestation of the mercy.   Let us set
ourselves to build up, however slowly, the fair fabric
of a life and character which shall stand when the
tempest levels all houses built upon the sand.   Let us
open our spirits to the entrance of that Spirit who
helps the infirmities of our desires as well as of our
efforts.   Thus let us keep ourselves in the charmed
circle of the love of God, that we may be safe as a
garrison in its fortress, blessed as a babe on its mother's
breast.

Jude's words are but the echo of the tenderer words
of his Master and ours, when He said, 'As My Father
hath loved Me, so have I loved you.   Abide ye in My
love.   If ye keep My commandments ye shall abide in
My love.'

WITHOUT STUMBLING

'Now unto Him that is able to keep you from falling, and to present you faultless before the presence of His glory with exceeding joy, 25. To the only wise God
our Saviour, be glory and majesty, dominion and power, both now and ever.
Amen.'—JUDE 24, 25.

I POINTED out in a recent sermon on a former verse of
this Epistle that the earlier part of it is occupied with
vehement denunciations of the moral corruptions that
had crept into the Church, and that the writer turns
away from that spectacle earnestly to exhort the
Christian community to 'keep themselves in the love
of God,' by 'building themselves upon their most holy
faith, and praying in the Holy Ghost.'   But that is not
all that Jude has to say.   It is wise to look round on
the dangers and evils that tempt; it is wise to look
inward to the weaknesses that may yield to the temp-

tations. But every look on surrounding dangers, and every look at personal weakness, ought to end in a look upwards ' to Him that is able to keep' the weakest 'from falling' before the assaults of the strongest foes.

The previous exhortation, which I have discussed, might seem to lay almost too much stress on our own strivings—'Keep *yourselves* in the love of God.' Here is the complement to it: 'Unto Him that is able to keep you from falling.' So denunciations, exhortations, warnings, all end in the peaceful gaze upon God, and the triumphant recognition of what He is able to do for us. We have to work, but we have to remember that ' it is He that worketh in us both to will and to do of His own good pleasure.'

I. So I think that, looking at these great words, the first thing to be noted is the solitary, all-sufficient stay for our weakness.

'To the only wise God our Saviour.' Now it is to be noticed, as those of you who use the Revised Version will observe, that the word 'wise' seems to have crept in here by the reminiscence of another similar doxology in the Epistle to the Romans, and was probably inserted by some scribe who had not grasped the great thought of which the text is the expression. It ought to read, 'to the only God, our Saviour.' The writer's idea seems to be just this—he has been massing in a dark crowd the whole multitudinous mob of corruptions and evils that were threatening the faith and righteousness of professing Christians. And he turns away from all that rabble, multitudinous as they are, to look to the One who is all-sufficient, solitary, and enough. ' The only God' is the refuge from the crowds of evils that dog our steps, and from the temptations and foes that assail us at every point.

This is the blessed peculiarity of the Christian faith, that it simplifies our outlook for good, that it brings everything to the one point of possessing the one Person, beyond whom there is never any need that the heart should wander seeking after love, that the mind should depart in its search for truth, or that the will should stray in its quest after authoritative commands. There is no need to seek a multitude of goodly pearls; the gift of Christianity to men's torn and distracted hearts and lives is that all which makes them rich, and all which makes them blessed, is sphered and included in the one transcendent pearl of price, the 'only God.'

I have been in Turkish mosques, the roofs of which are held up by a bewildering forest of slender pillars. I have been in cathedral chapter-houses, where one strong stone shaft in the centre carries all the beauty of the branching roof; and I know which is the highest work and the fairest. Why should we seek in the manifold for what we can never find, when we can find it all in the ONE? The mind seeks for unity in truth; the heart seeks for oneness in love; no man is at rest until he has all his heart's treasures in one person; and no man who foolishly puts all his treasures in one creature-person but is bringing down upon his own head sorrow.

Do you remember that pathetic inscription in one of our country churches, over a little child, whose fair image is left us by the pencil of Reynolds: 'Her parents put all their wealth in one vessel, and the shipwreck was total'? It is madness to trust to but one refuge, unless that refuge is the only God. If we, like the disciples on the Mount of Transfiguration, are wise, we shall lift up our eyes and 'see no man any more, save

Jesus only.' He can be our solitary Stay, Refuge, Wealth, and Companion, because He is sufficient, and He abides for ever.

But there is another peculiarity that I would point out in these words, and that is the unusual attribution to God, the Father, of the name 'Saviour'—'the only God our Saviour.' The same various reading which strikes out ' wise' inserts here, as you will see in the Revised Version, 'through Jesus Christ our Lord.' But although the phraseology is almost unique, the meaning is in full harmony with the scope of New Testament teaching. It is a fault of evangelical and orthodox people that they have too often spoken and thought as if Jesus Christ's work modified and changed the Father's will, and as if God loved men because Christ died for them. The fact is precisely the converse. Christ died because God loved men; and the fontal source of the salvation, of which the work of Jesus Christ is the channel, bringing it to men, is the eternal, unmotived, infinite love of God the Father. Christ is 'the well-beloved Son,' because He is the executor of the Divine purpose, and all which He has done is done in obedience to the Father's will. If I might use a metaphor, the love of God is, as it were, a deep secluded lake amongst the mountains, and the work of Christ is the stream that comes from it, and brings its waters to be life to the world. Let us never forget that, however we love to turn our gratitude and our praise to Christ the Saviour, my text goes yet deeper into the councils of Eternity when it ascribes the praise ' to the only God our Saviour through Jesus Christ our Lord.'

II. And now notice the possibility of firm standing in the slippery present.

'To Him that is able to keep us from falling.' Now

the word that is rendered 'from falling' is even more emphatic, and carries a larger promise.   For it literally means 'without stumbling,' and stumbling is that which precedes falling.   We are not only kept from falling, we are kept even from stumbling over the stumbling-stones that are in the way.   The metaphor, perhaps, was suggested by the words of Isaiah, who, in one of his lovely images, describes God as 'leading Israel through the depths as a horse in the desert, that they stumble not.'   Do you not see the picture?   The nervous, susceptible animal, slipping and sliding over the smooth rock, in a sweat of terror, and the owner laying a kindly hand and a firm one on the bridle-rein, and speaking soothing words of encouragement, and leading it safely, that it stumble not.   So God is able to lay hold of us when we are in perilous places, and when we cry, 'My foot slippeth,' His mercy will hold us up.

Is that rhetoric?   Is that merely pulpit talk?   Brethren, unless we lay firm hold of this faith, that God can and does touch and influence hearts that wait upon Him, so as by His Spirit and by His Word, which is the sword of the Spirit, to strengthen their feeble good, and to weaken their strong evil, to raise what is low, to illumine what is dark, and to support what is weak, we have not come to understand the whole wealth of possible good and blessedness which lies in the Gospel. This generation has forgotten far too much the place which the work of God's Holy Spirit on men's spirits fills in the whole proportioned scheme of New Testament revelation.   It is because we believe that so little, in comparison with the clearness and strength of our faith in the work of Jesus Christ, the atoning sacrifice, that so many of us find it so foreign to our experience that any effluences from God come into our hearts, and that our spirits are conscious of being quickened and lifted by His Spirit! Ah! we might feel, far more than any of us do, His hand on the bridle-rein. We might feel, far more than any of us do, His strong upholding, keeping our feet from *slipping* as well as 'falling.' And if we believed and expected a Divine Spirit to enter into our spirits and to touch our hearts, the expectation would not be in vain.

I beseech you, believe that a solid experience and meaning lies in that word 'able to keep us from stumbling.' If we have that Divine Spirit moving in our spirits, moulding our desires, lifting our thoughts, confirming our wills, then the things that were stumbling-stones—that is to say, that appealed to our worst selves, and tempted us to evil—will cease to be so. The higher desires will kill the lower ones, as the sunshine is popularly supposed to put out household fires. If we have God's upholding help, the stumbling-stone will no more be a stumbling-stone, but a stepping-stone to something higher and better; or like one of those erections that we see outside old-fashioned houses of entertainment, where three or four steps are piled together, in order to enable a man the more easily to mount his horse and go on his way. For every temptation overcome brings strength to the overcomer.

Only let us remember 'Him that is *able* to keep.' Able! What is wanted that the ability may be brought into exercise; that the possibility of which I have spoken, of firm standing amongst those slippery places, shall become a reality? What is wanted? It is of no use to have a stay unless you lean on it. You may have an engine of ever so many horse-power in the engine-house, but unless the power is transmitted by shafts and belting, and brought to the machinery, not a spindle will revolve. He is *able* to keep us from stumbling, and if you trust Him, the ability will become actuality, and you will be kept from falling. If you do not trust Him, all the ability will lie in the engine-house, and the looms and the spindles will stand idle. So the reason why—and the only reason why—with such an abundant, and over-abundant, provision for never falling, Christian men do stumble and fall, is their own lack of faith.

Now remember that this text of mine follows on the heels of that former text which bade us 'build ourselves,' and 'keep ourselves in the love of God.' So you get the peculiarity of Christian ethics, and the blessedness of Christian effort, that it is not effort only, but effort rising from, and accompanied with, confidence in God's keeping hand. There is all the difference between toiling without trust and toiling because we do trust. And whilst, on the one hand, we have to exhort to earnest faith in the upholding hand of God, we have to say on the other, 'Let that faith lead you to obey the apostolic command, "Stand fast in the evil day . . . taking unto you the whole armour of God."'

III. Further, we have here the possible final perfecting in the future.

'To Him that is able . . . to present you faultless before the presence of His glory with exceeding joy.' Now that word rendered 'faultless' has a very beautiful meaning. It is originally applied to the requirement that the sacrificial offerings shall be without blemish. It is then applied more than once to our Lord Himself, as expressive of His perfect, immaculate sinlessness. And it is here applied to the future condition of those who have been kept without stumbling; suggesting at once that they are, as it were, presented before God at last, stainless as the sacrificial lamb; and that they are conformed to the image of the Lamb of God 'without blemish and without spot.' Moral perfectness, absolute and complete; a standing 'before the presence of His glory,' the realisation and the vision of that illustrious light, too dazzling for eyes veiled by flesh to look upon, but of which hereafter the purified souls will be capable, in accordance with that great promise, 'Blessed are the pure in heart, for they shall see God'; 'with exceeding joy,' which refers not to the joy of Him that presents, though that is great, but to the joy of them who are presented. So these three things are the possibilities held out before such poor creatures as we. And miraculous as it is, that all stains should melt away from our characters—though I suppose not the remembrance of them from our consciousness—and be shaken off as completely as the foul water of some stagnant pond drops from the white swan-plumage, and leaves no stain; that perfecting is the natural issue of the present being kept from stumbling.

You have seen sometimes in a picture-dealer's shop window a canvas on which a face is painted, one half of which has been cleaned, and the other half is still covered with some varnish or filth. That is like the Christian character here. But the restoration and the cleansing are going to be finished up yonder; and the great Artist's ideal will be realised, and each redeemed soul will be perfected in holiness.

But as I said about the former point, so I say about this, He is able to do it. What is wanted to make the ability an actuality? Brethren, if we are to stand perfect, at last, and be without fault before the Throne of God, we must begin by letting Him keep us from stumbling here. Then, and only then, may we expect that issue.

Now I was going to have said a word, in the last
place, about the Divine praise which comes from all
these dealings, but your time will not allow me to
dwell upon it.   Only let me remind you that all these
things, which in my text are ascribed to God, 'glory
and majesty, dominion and power,' are ascribed to Him
because He is our Saviour, and able to keep us from
stumbling, and to 'present us faultless before His
glory.' That is to say, the Divine manifestation of
Himself in the work of redemption is the highest of
His self-revealing works. Men are not presumptuous
when they feel that they are greater than sun and
stars; and that there is more in the narrow room of a
human heart than in all the immeasurable spaces of
the universe, if these are empty of beings who can love
and inquire and adore.   And we are not wrong when
we say that the only evil in the universe is sin.   Therefore, we are right when we say that high above all
other works of which we have experience is that
miracle of love and Divine power which can not only
keep such feeble creatures as we are from stumbling,
but can present us stainless and faultless before the
Throne of God.

So our highest praise, and our deepest thankfulness,
ought to arise, and will arise—if the possibility has
become, in any measure, an actuality, in ourselves—to
Him, because our experience will be that of the
Psalmist who sang, 'When I said, my foot slippeth,
Thy mercy, O Lord, held me up.'   Let us take the
comfort of believing, 'He shall not fall, for the Lord
is able to make him stand'; and let us remember the
expansion which another Apostle gives us when, with
precision, he discriminates and says, 'Kept *by* the
power of God *through* faith, *unto* salvation.'

H

REVELATION

THE GIFTS OF CHRIST AS WITNESS, RISEN AND CROWNED

'Grace be unto you, and peace, from . . . 5. Jesus Christ, who is the faithful Witness, and the first begotten of the dead, and the Prince of the kings of the earth.'—REV. i. 4, 5.

So loftily did John in his old age come to think of his Lord. The former days of blessed nearness had not faded from his memory; rather he understood their meaning better than when he was in the midst of their sweetness. Years and experience, and the teaching of God's Spirit, had taught Him to understand what the Master meant when He said :—'It is expedient for you that I go away'; for when He had departed John saw Him a great deal more clearly than ever he had done when he beheld Him with his eyes. He sees Him now invested with these lofty attributes, and, so to speak, involved in the brightness of the Throne of God. For the words of my text are not only remarkable in themselves, and in the order in which they give these three aspects of our Lord's character, but remarkable also in that they occur in an invocation in which the Apostle is calling down blessings from Heaven on the heads of his brethren. The fact that they do so occur points a question: Is it possible to conceive that the writer of these words thought of Jesus Christ as less than divine? Could he have asked for ' grace and peace' to come down on the Asiatic Christians from the divine

114

Father, and an Abstraction, and a Man? A strange
Trinity that would be, most certainly. Rightly or
wrongly, the man that said, 'Grace and peace be unto
you, from Him which is, and which was, and which is
to come, and from the seven Spirits which are before
His Throne, and from Jesus Christ,' believed that the
name of the One God was Father, Son, and Holy
Spirit.

But it is not so much to this as to the connection of
these three clauses with one another, and to the bearing
of all three on our Lord's power of giving grace and
peace to men's hearts, that I want to turn your attention now. I take the words simply as they lie here;
asking you to consider, first, how grace and peace come
to us 'from the faithful Witness'; how, secondly, they
come 'from the first begotten from the dead'; and
how, lastly, they come 'from the Prince of the kings
of the earth.'

I. Now as to the first of these, 'the faithful Witness.'
All of you who have any familiarity with the language
of Scripture will know that a characteristic of all the
writings which are ascribed to the Apostle John, viz.,
his Gospel, his Epistles, and the book of the Revelation,
is their free and remarkable use of that expression,
'Witness.' It runs through all of them, and is one of
the many threads of connection which tie them all
together, and which constitute a very strong argument
for the common authorship of the three sets of writings,
vehemently as that has of late been denied.

But where did John get this word? According to
his own teaching he got it from the lips of the Master,
who began His career with these words, 'We speak
that we do know, and bear witness to that we have
seen,' and who all but ended it with these royal words,

'Thou sayest that I am a King! For this cause came I into the world, that I should bear witness unto the Truth.' Christ Himself, then, claimed to be in an eminent and special sense the witness to the world.

The witness of what? What was the substance of His testimony? It was a testimony mainly about God. The words of my text substantially cover the same ground as His own words, 'I have declared Thy name unto My brethren,' and as those of the Apostle: 'The only begotten Son which is in the bosom of the Father, He hath declared Him.' And they involve the same ideas as lie in the great name by which He is called in John's Gospel, 'the Word of God.'

That is to say, all our highest and purest and best knowledge of God comes from the life and conduct and character of Jesus Christ. His revelation is no mere revelation by words. Plenty of men have talked about God, and said noble and true and blessed things about Him. Scattered through the darkness of heathenism, and embedded in the sinfulness of every man's heart, there are great and lofty and pure thoughts about Him, which to cleave to and follow out would bring strength and purity. It is one thing to speak about God in words, maxims, precepts; it is another thing to show us God in act and life. The one is theology, the other is gospel. The one is the work of man, the other is the exclusive prerogative of God manifested in the flesh.

It is not Christ's words only that make Him the 'Amen,' the 'faithful and true Witness,' but in addition to these, He witnesses by all His deeds of grace, and truth, and gentleness, and pity; by all His yearnings over wickedness, and sorrow, and sinfulness; by all His drawings of the profligate and the outcast and the guilty to Himself, His life of loneliness, His death of shame. In all these, He is showing us not only the sweetness of a perfect human character, but *in* the sweetness of a perfect human character, the sweeter sweetness of our Father, God. The substance of His testimony is the Name, the revelation of the character of His Father and our Father.

This name of 'witness' bears likewise strongly upon the characteristic and remarkable *manner* of our Lord's testimony. The task of a witness is to affirm; his business is to tell his story—not to argue about it, simply to state it. And there is nothing more characteristic of our Lord's words than the way in which, without attempt at proof or argumentation, He makes them stand on their own evidence; or, rather, depend upon His veracity. All His teaching is characterised by what would be insane presumption in any of us, and would at once rule us out of court as unfit to be listened to on any grave subject, most of all on religious truth. For His method is this: 'Verily, verily, I say to you! Take it on My word. You ask Me for proof of My saying: I am the proof of it; I assert it. That is enough for you!' Not so do men speak. So does the faithful Witness speak; and instead of the conscience and common-sense of the world rising up and saying, 'This is the presumption of a religious madman and dictator,' they have bowed before Him and said, 'Thou art fairer than the children of men! Grace is poured into Thy lips.' He is the 'faithful Witness, who lays His own character and veracity as the basis of what He has to say, and has no mightier word by which to back His testimony than His own sovereign 'Verily! verily!'

The name bears, too, on the *ground* of His testimony.

A faithful witness is an eye-witness. And that is what Christ claims when He witnesses about God. 'We speak that we do know, we testify that we have seen.' 'I speak that which I have seen with My Father!' There is nothing more remarkable about the oral portion of our Lord's witness than the absence of any appearance, such as marks all the wisest words of great men, of having come to them as the result of patient thought. We never see Him in the act of arriving at a truth, nor detect any traces of the process of forming opinions in Him. He speaks as if He had seen, and His tone is that of one who is not thinking out truth or grasping at it, but simply narrating that which lies plain and clear ever before His eyes. I do not ask you what that involves, but I quote His own statement of what it involves: 'No man hath ascended up into Heaven save He that came down from Heaven, even the Son of Man which is in Heaven.'

There have been plenty of great and gracious words about God, and there have been plenty of black and blasphemous thoughts of Him. They rise in our own hearts, and they come from our brothers' tongues. Men have worshipped gods gracious, gods loving, gods angry, gods petulant, gods capricious; but God after the fashion of the God whom Jesus Christ avouches to us, we have nowhere else, a God of absolute love, who 'so loved the world'—that is, you and me—'that He gave His only begotten Son, that whosoever believeth in Him should not perish.'

And now I ask, is there not grace and peace brought to us all from that faithful Witness, and from His credible testimony? Surely the one thing that the world wants is to have the question answered whether there really is a God in Heaven that cares anything about me, and to whom I can trust myself wholly; believing that He will lift me out of all my meannesses and sins, and make me clean and pure and blessed like Himself. Surely that is the deepest of all human needs, howsoever little men may know it. And sure I am that none of us can find the certitude of such a Father unless we give credence to the message of Jesus Christ our Lord.

This day needs that witness as much as any other; sometimes in our unbelieving moments, we think *more* than any other. There is a wave—I believe it is only a wave—passing over the cultivated thought of Europe at present which will make short work of all belief in a God that does not grip fast to Jesus Christ. As far as I can read the signs of the times, and the tendency of modern thinking, it is this:—either an absolute Silence, a Heaven stretching above us, blue and clear, and cold, and far away, and *dumb*; or else a Christ that speaks—He or none! The Theism that has shaken itself loose from Him will be crushed, I am sure, in the encounter with the agnosticism and the materialism of this day. And the one refuge is to lay fast hold of the old truth:—'The only begotten Son which is in the bosom of the Father, He hath declared Him.'

Oh! you orphan children that have forgotten your Father, and have turned prodigals and rebels; you that have begun to doubt if there is any one above this low earth that cares for you; you that have got bewildered and befogged amidst the manifold denials and controversies of this day; come back to the one voice that speaks to us in tones of confident certainty as from personal knowledge of a Father. 'He that hath seen Me hath seen the Father,' says Jesus to us all: 'hearken unto Me, and know God, whom to know in

Me is eternal life.' Listen to Him. Without His
testimony you will be the sport of fears, and doubts,
and errors. With it in your hearts you will be at
rest. Grace and peace come from the faithful Witness.

II. We have grace and peace from the Conqueror of
Death.

The 'first *begotten* from the dead' does not precisely
convey the idea of the original, which would be more
accurately represented by 'the first *born* from the
dead'—the resurrection being looked upon as a kind of
birth into a higher order of life. It is, perhaps, scarcely
necessary to observe that the accuracy of this designation, 'the first born from the dead,' as applied to our
Lord, is not made questionable because of the mere
fact that there were others who rose from the dead
before His resurrection, for all of these died again.
What a strange feeling that must have been for Lazarus
and the others, to go twice through the gates of death;
twice to know the pain and the pang of separation!
But these all have been gathered to the dust, and lie
now waiting 'the adoption, that is the resurrection of
the body.' But this Man, being raised, dieth no more,
death hath no more dominion over Him. And how is
it that grace and peace come to us from the risen
Witness? Two or three words may be said about that.

Think how, first of all, the resurrection of Jesus
Christ is the confirmation of His testimony. In it the
Father, to whom He hath borne witness in His life and
death, bears witness to Christ, that His claims were
true and His work well-pleasing. He is 'declared to be
the Son of God by the resurrection from the dead.' If
our Lord did not rise from the dead, as all Christendom to-day[1] has been declaring its faith that He did,

---

[1] Easter Sunday.

then, as it seems to me, there is an end to His claims to be Son of God, and Son of Man, or anything other than a man like the rest of us. If He be no more and naught else than a man, altogether like the rest of us, then there is an end to any special revelation of the Divine nature, heart, purposes, and will, in His works and character. They may still be beautiful, they may still reveal God in the same sense in which the doings of any good man suggest a fontal source of goodness from which they flow, but beyond that they are nothing. So all the truth, and all the peace, all the grace and hope which flow to us from the witness of Jesus Christ to the Father, are neutralised and destroyed unless we believe in the resurrection from the dead. His words may still remain gracious, and true in a measure, only all dashed with the terrible mistake that He asserted that He would rise again, and rose not. But as for His life, it ceases to be in any real sense, because it ceases to be in any unique sense, the revelation to the world of the character of God.

And therefore, as I take it, it is no exaggeration to say that the whole fabric of Christianity, and all Christ's worth as a witness to God, stand or fall with the fact of His resurrection. If you pull out that keystone, down comes the arch. There may still be fair carving on some of the fallen fragments, but it is no longer an arch that spans the great gulf, and has a firm pier on the other side. Strike away the resurrection and you fatally damage the witness of Jesus. You cannot strike the supernatural out of Christianity, and keep the natural. The two are so inextricably woven together that to wrench away the one lacerates the other, and makes it bleed, even to death. If Christ be not risen we have nothing to preach, and you have nothing to believe. Our preaching and your faith are alike vain: ye are yet in your sins. Grace and peace come from faith in the 'first begotten from the dead.'

And that is true in another way too. Faith in the resurrection gives us a living Lord to confide in—not a dead Lord, whose work we may look back upon with thankfulness; but a living one, who works now upon us, and by whose true companionship and real affection strength and help are granted to us every day. The cold frost of death has not congealed that stream of love that poured from His heart while He lived on earth; it flows yet for each of us, for all of us, for the whole world.

My brother, we cannot do without a living Christ to stand beside us, to sympathise, to help, to love. We cannot do without a living Christ with whom we may speak, who will speak to us. And that communion which is blessedness, that communication of power and righteousness which is life, are only possible, if it be true that His death was not the end of His relationship to us, or of His work in the world, but was only a transition from one stage of that work to another. We have to look to Christ, the 'faithful Witness,' the Witness who witnessed when He died; but we have to look to Him that is risen again and takes His place at the right hand of God. And the grace and peace flow to us not only from the contemplation of the past witness of the Lord, but are showered upon us from the open hands of the risen and living Christ.

In still another way do grace and peace reach us, from the 'first begotten from the dead,' inasmuch as in Him and in His resurrection-life we are armed for victory over that foe whom He has conquered. If He be the first born, He will have 'many brethren.' The 'first' implies a second. He has been raised from the dead, therefore death is not the destruction of conscious life. He has been raised from the dead, therefore any other man may be. Like another Samson, He has come forth from the prison-house, with the bars and gates upon His mighty shoulders, and has carried them away up there to the hill-top where He is. And the prison-house door stands gaping wide, and none so weak but he can pass out through the ever open portals. Christ has risen, and therefore if we will trust Him we have conquered that last and grimmest foe. And so for ourselves, when we are trembling, as we all do with the natural shrinking of flesh from the thought of that certain death; for ourselves, in our hours of lonely sorrow, when the tears come or the heart is numbed with pain; for ourselves when we lay ourselves down in our beds to die, grace and peace, like the dove that fell on His sacred head as it rose from the water of the baptism—will come down from His hands who is not only 'the faithful Witness,' but the 'first begotten from the dead.'

III. Lastly, we have grace and peace from the King of kings.

The series of aspects of Christ's work here is ranged in order of time, in so far as the second follows the first, and the third flows from both, though we are not to suppose that our Lord has ceased to be the faithful Witness when He has ascended His Sovereign Throne. His own saying, 'I have declared Thy name, and will declare it,' shows us that His witness is perpetual, and carried on from His seat at the right hand of God.

He is the 'Prince of the kings of the earth,' just because He is 'the faithful Witness.' That is to say: —His dominion is the dominion of the truth; His dominion is a kingdom over men's wills and spirits. Does He rule by force ? No! Does He rule by outward means? No! By terror? No! but because, as He said to the astonished Pilate, He came ' to bear witness to the truth '; therefore is He the King not of the Jews only but of the whole world. A kingdom over heart and conscience, will and spirit, is the kingdom which Christ has founded, and His rule rests upon His witness.

And not only so, He is ' the Prince of the kings of the earth' because in that witness He dies, and so becomes a 'martyr' to the truth—the word in the original conveying both ideas. That is to say, His dominion rests not only upon truth. That would be a dominion grand as compared with the kingdom of this world, but still cold. His dominion rests upon love and sacrifice. And so His Kingdom is a kingdom of blessing and of gentleness ; and He is crowned with the crowns of the universe, because He was first crowned with the crown of thorns. His first regal title was written upon His Cross, and from the Cross His Royalty ever flows. He is the King because He is the sacrifice.

And He is the Prince of the kings of the earth because, witnessing and slain, He has risen again; His resurrection has been the step midway, as it were, between the humiliation of earth and death, and the loftiness of the Throne. By it He has climbed to His place at the right hand of God. He is King and Prince, then, by right of truth, love, sacrifice, death, resurrection.

And King to what end? That He may send grace and peace. Is there no peace for a man's heart in feeling that the Brother that loves him and died for him rules over all the perplexities of life, the confusions of Providence, the sorrows of a world, and the corruptions of his own nature? Is it not enough to drive away fears, to anodyne cares, to disentangle perplexities, to quiet disturbances, to make the coward brave, and the feeble strong, and the foolish wise, and the querulous patient, to think that my Christ is king; and that the hands which were nailed to the Cross wield the sceptre, and that He who died for me rules the universe and rules me?

Oh, brethren! there is no tranquillity for a man anywhere else but in the humble, hearty recognition of that Lord as his Lord. Crown Him with your reverence, with your loyal obedience, with your constant desires; crown Him with your love, the most precious of all the crowns that He wears, and you will find that grace and peace come to you from Him.

Such, then, is the vision that this seer in Patmos had of his Lord. It was to him a momentary opening of the heavens, which showed him his throned Lord; but the fact which was made visible to his inward eye for a moment is an eternal fact. To-day as then, to-morrow as to-day, for Asiatic Greeks and for modern Englishmen, for past centuries, for the present, and for all the future, for the whole world for ever, Jesus Christ is the only witness whose voice breaks the awful silence and tells us of a Father; the only Conqueror of Death who makes the life beyond a firm, certain fact; the King whose dominion it is life to obey. We all need Him. Your hearts have wants which only His grace can supply, your lives have troubles which only His peace can still. Sin and sorrow, change and trial, separation and death, are facts in every man's experience. They are ranked against us in serried battalions. You can conquer them all if you will seek shelter and strength from Him who has died for you, and lives to succour and to save. Trust Him! Let your faith grasp the past fact of the Cross whose virtue never grows old, and the present fact of the Throne from which He bends down with hands full of grace; and on His lips the tender old words: 'Peace I leave with you, My peace give I unto you!'

CHRIST'S PRESENT LOVE AND PAST LOOSING FROM SINS

'Unto Him that loved us, and washed us from our sins in His own blood.'—
REV. i. 5.

THE Revised Version rightly makes two slight but important changes in this verse, both of which are sustained by preponderating authority. For 'loved' it reads 'loveth,' and for 'washed' it reads 'loosed'; the whole standing 'Unto Him that loveth us, loosed us from our sins by His blood.' Now the first of these changes obviously adds much to the force and richness of the representation, for it substitutes for a past a present and timeless love. The second of them, though it seems greater, is really smaller, for it makes no change in the meaning, but only in the figure under which the meaning is represented. If we read 'washed,' the metaphor would be of sin as a stain; if we read 'loosed,' the metaphor is of sin as a 'chain.' Possibly the context may somewhat favour the altera-tion, inasmuch as there would then be the striking contrast between the condition of captives or bonds-men, and the dignity of 'kings and priests unto God,' into which Jesus brings those whom He has freed from the bondage. Taking, then, these changes, and noting the fact that our text is the beginning of a doxology, we have here three points, the present love of Christ, the great past act which is its outcome and proof, and the praise which should answer that great love.

I. We have here that great thought of the present love of Christ.

The words seem to me to become especially beautiful, if we remember that they come from the lips of him whose distinction it was that he was 'the disciple whom Jesus loved.' It is as if he had said, 'I share my privilege with you all. I was no nearer Him than you may be. Every head may rest on the breast where mine rested. Having the sweet remembrance of that early love, these things write I unto you that ye also may have fellowship with me in that which was my great distinction. I, the disciple whom Jesus loved, speak to you as the disciples whom Jesus loves.'

Mark that he is speaking of One who had been dead for half a century, and that he is speaking to people, none of whom had probably ever seen Jesus in His lifetime, and most of whom had not been born when He died. Yet to them all he turns with that profound and mighty present tense, and says, 'He loveth us.' He was speaking to all generations, and telling all the tribes of men of a love which is in active operation towards each of them, not only at the moment when John spoke to Asiatic Greeks, but at the moment when we Englishmen read his words, 'Christ that loveth us.'

Now that great thought suggests two things, one as to the permanence, and one as to the sweep of Christ's love. With regard to the permanence, we have here the revelation of One whose relation to life and death is altogether unique. For though we must believe that the dead do still cherish the love that lighted earth for them, we cannot suppose that their love embraces those whom on earth they did not know, or that for those who are still held in its grasp it can be a potence in active operation to bless them and to do them good. But here is a Man, to the exercise of whose love, to the clearness of whose apprehension and knowledge, to the outgoing of whose warm affection, the active energy of that affection life or death make no difference. The cold which stays the flow of all other human love, like frost laid upon the running streams which it binds in fetters, has no power over the flow of Christ's love, which rolls on, unfrozen and unaffected by it. But not only does Christ's present love require that He should be lifted above death as it affects the rest of us, but it also demands for its explanation that we shall see in Him true Divinity. For this 'loveth' is the timeless present of that Divine nature, of which we cannot properly say either that it was or that it will be, but only that it for ever is, and the outgoings of His love are like the outgoings of that Divine energy of which we cannot properly say that it did or that it will do, but only that it ever does. His love, if I might use such a phrase, is lifted above all tenses, and transcends even the bounds of grammar. He did love. He does love. He will love. All three forms of speech must be combined in setting forth the ever present, because timeless and eternal, love of the Incarnate Word.

Then let me remind you too that this present love of Christ is undiminished by the glory to which He is exalted. We find clear and great differences between the picture of Jesus Christ in the four gospels and the picture of Him drawn in that magnificent vision of this chapter. But the differences are surface, and the identity is deep-lying. The differences affect position

much rather than nature, and as we look upon that
revelation which was given to the seer in his rocky
Patmos, and with him 'in the Spirit' behold 'the
things that are,' we carry into all the glory the thought
'He loveth us'; and the breast girded with the golden
girdle is as loving as that upon which John's happy
head lay, and the hand that holds the seven stars is as
tender as when it was laid on little children in blessing
or on lepers in cleansing; or as when it held up the
sinking Apostle, or lifted the sick from their couches,
or as when it was stretched on the Cross and pierced
with the nails; and the face, 'which is as the sun shineth
in his strength,' is as gracious as when it beamed in
pity upon wanderers and sorrowful ones, and drew by
its beauty and its sweetness the harlots and publicans
to His pity. The exalted Christ loves as did the lowly
Christ on earth.

How different this prosaic, worried present would be
if we could carry with us, as we may if we will, into
all its trivialities, into all its monotony, into all its
commonplace routine, into all its little annoyances
and great sorrows, that one lambent thought as a
source of light and strength and blessing, 'He loveth
us.' Ah! brethren, we lose tremendously of what we
might all possess, because we think so of 'He loved,'
and travel back to the Cross for its proof, and think so
comparatively seldom 'He loveth,' and feel the touch
of His hand on our hearts for its token.

But here we have not only the present and permanent love, but we have the sweep and extent of
it. 'He loveth us.' And though John was speaking
primarily about a little handful of people scattered
through some of the seaboard towns of Asia Minor,
the principle upon which he could make the assertion

I

in regard to them warrants us in extending the assertion not only to men that respond to the love, and
believe in it, but right away over all the generations
and all the successive files of the great army of
humanity, down to the very ends of time, ' He loveth
us.'

That universality, wonderful as it is, and requiring
for its basis the same belief in Christ's Divine nature
which the present energy of His love requires, has to
be translated by each of us into an individualising love
which is poured upon each single soul, as if it were the
sole recipient of the fulness of the heart of Christ.
When we extend our thoughts or our sympathies to a
crowd, we lose the individual. We generalise, as logi-
cians say, by neglecting the particular instances. That
is to say, when we look at the forest we do not see the
trees. But Jesus Christ sees each tree, each stem,
each branch, each leaf, just as when the crowd thronged
Him and pressed Him, He knew when the tremulous
finger, wasted and shrunken to skin and bone, was
timidly laid on the hem of His garment; as there was
room for all the five thousand on the grass, and no
man's plenty was secured at the expense of another
man's penury, so each of us has a place in that heart;
and my abundance will not starve you, nor your feeding full diminish the supplies for me. Christ loves all,
not with the vague general philanthropy with which
men love the mass, but with the individualising knowledge and special direction of affection towards the individual which demands for its fulness a Divine nature
to exercise it. And so each of us may have our own
rainbow, to each of us the sunbeam may come straight
from the sun and strike upon our eye in a direct line,
to each of us the whole warmth of the orb may be con-

veyed, and each of us may say, ' He loved me, and gave Himself for me.' Is that your conception of your relation to Jesus Christ, and of Christ's to you?

II. Notice the great proof and outcome of this present love. Because it is timeless love, and has nothing to do with the distinction of past, present, and future, John lays hold of a past act as the manifestation of a present love. If we would understand what that love is which is offered to each of us in the present, we must understand what is meant and what is involved in that past act to which John points : ' He loosed us from our sins by His own blood.' Christ is the Emancipator, and the instrument by which He makes us free is ' His own blood.'

Now there underlies that thought the sad metaphor that sin is captivity. There may be some kind of allusion in the Apostle's mind to the deliverance from Egyptian bondage; and that is made the more probable if we observe that the next clause, ' hath made us kings and priests unto God,' points back to the great charter of Israel's national existence which was given immediately after the Exodus. But, be that as it may, the notion of bondage underlies this metaphor of loosing a fetter. If we would be honest with ourselves, in our account of our own inward experiences, that bondage we all know. There is the bondage of sin as guilt, the sense of responsibility, the feeling that we have to answer for what we have done, and to answer —as I believe and as I think men's consciences for the most part force them to believe—not only here but hereafter, when we appear before the judgment-seat of Christ. Guilt is a chain. And there is the bondage of habit, which ties and holds us with the cords of our sins, so as that, slight as the fetter may seem at first,

it has an awful power of thickening and becoming
heavier and more pressing, till at last it holds a man
in a grip that he cannot get away from. I know of
nothing in human life more mystically awful than the
possible influence of habit. And you cannot break
these fetters yourselves, brethren, any more than a
man in a dungeon, shackled to the wall, can file through
his handcuffs and anklets with a pin or a broken pen-
knife. You can do a great deal, but you cannot deal
with the past fact of guilt, and you can only very
partially deal with the present fact of tyranny which
the evil habit exercises on you.

'He loosed us from our sins by His own blood.' This
is not the place to enter upon theological speculations,
but I, for my part, believe that, although I may not get
to the bottom of the bottomless, nor speak about the
Divine nature with full knowledge of all that it is,
Scripture is pledged to the fact that the death of Jesus
Christ is the Sacrifice for the world's sin. I admit that
a full theory is not within reach, but I do not admit
that therefore we are to falter in declaring that
Christ's death is indispensable in order that a man's
sin may be forgiven, and the fetters broken, in so far
as guilt and condemnation and Divine disapprobation
are concerned.

But that is only one side of the truth. The other,
and in some aspects a far more important one, is that
that same blood which shed delivers them that trust in
Jesus Christ from the guilt of their sin, imparted to
men, delivers them from the power of their sin. 'The
blood is the life,' according to the simple physiology of
the Old and of the New Testament. When we read in
Scripture that the blood of Jesus Christ cleanses from
all sin, as I believe we are intended to understand that

word, the impartation of Christ's life to us purifies our
nature, and makes us, too, in our degree, and on condition of our own activity, and gradually and successively
free from all evil. So as regards both aspects of the
thraldom of sin, as guilt and as habit: 'He has loosed
us from our sins in His own blood.'

That is the great token and manifestation of His
love. If we do not believe that, how else can we have
any real conviction and proof of anything worth calling
love as being in the heart of Jesus Christ to any of us?
To me it seems that unless a man accepts that great
thought, 'He loved me, and gave Himself for me,' and
is daily working in my nature to make it and me more
like Himself, he has no real proof that Jesus Christ cares
a jot for him, or knows anything about him. But I, for
my part, venture to say that looking on Christ and His
past as this text does, we can look up to Christ in the
present as the seer did, and, behold, enthroned by the
side of the glory, the Man, the Incarnate Word, who
loves with timeless love every single soul of man.

III. So, lastly, let me point you to the praise which
should answer this present love and emancipation.

'Unto Him,' says John, 'be'—or is—'glory and
dominion for ever and ever.' That present love, and
that great past act which is its vindication and manifestation, are the true glory of God. For His glory
lies, not in attributes, as we call them, that distinguish
Him from the limitations of humanity, such as Omniscience and Omnipresence and Eternal Being and the
like; all these are great, but they are not the greatest.
The divinest thing in God is His love, and the true glory
is the glory that rays out from Him whom we behold
'full of grace and truth,' full of love, and dying on
the Cross. When we look at that weak man there

yielding to the last infirmity of humanity, and yet in yielding to it manifesting His dominion over it, there we see God as we do not see Him anywhere besides. To Him is the glory for His love, and His 'loosing' manifest the glory, and from His love and His loosing accrue to Him glory beyond all other revenue of praise which comes to Him from creative and sustaining acts.

'Unto Him be dominion,' for His rule rests on His sacrifice and on His love. The crown of thorns prepared for the 'many crowns' of heaven, the sceptre of reed was the prophecy of the sceptre of the universe. The Cross was the footstool of His Throne. He is King of men because He has loved us perfectly, and given everything for us.

And so, brethren, the question of questions for each of us is, Is Jesus Christ my Emancipator? Do I see in Him He that looses me from my sins, and makes me free indeed, because the Son has made me free and a son? Do I render to Him the love which such a love requires? Do I find in Him my ever-present Lover and Friend, and is His love to me as a stimulus for all service, an amulet against every temptation, a breakwater in all storms, a light in every darkness, the pledge of a future heaven, and the beginning of a heaven even upon earth? I beseech you, recognise your fetters, and do not say 'we were never in bondage to any man.' Recognise your Liberator, put your trust in Him; and then you will be able to join, even here on earth, and more perfectly hereafter, in that great storm and chorus of praise which is in heaven and on the earth, and under the earth, and such as are in the sea, and all that are in them, saying, 'Blessing and honour and glory and power be unto Him that sitteth on the Throne and to the Lamb for ever and ever.'

KINGS AND PRIESTS

'He hath made us kings and priests unto God.'—Rev. 1. 6.

THERE is an evident reference in these words to the original charter of the Jewish nation, which ran, ' If ye will indeed obey My voice and keep My covenant, then shall ye be to Me a kingdom of priests.' That reference is still more obvious if we follow the reading of our text in the Revised Version, which runs, ' He made us to be a kingdom, to be priests.' Now it is unquestionable that, in the original passage, Israel is represented as being God's kingdom, the nation over which He reigned as King. But in John's use of the expression there seems to be a slight modification of meaning, as is obvious in the parallel passage to this, which occurs in a subsequent chapter, where we read in addition, ' They shall reign with Him for ever.' That is to say, in our text we should rather translate the word 'king*ship*' than 'king*dom*,' for it means rather the Royal dominion of the Christian community than its subjection to the reign of God.

So the two dignities, the chief in the ancient world, which as a rule were sedulously kept apart, lest their union should produce a grinding despotism from which there was no appeal, are united in the person of the humblest Christian, and that not merely at some distant future period beyond the grave, but here and now; for my text says, not ' will make,' but 'hath made.' The coronation and the consecration are both past acts, they are the sequel, certain to follow upon the previous act: ' He hath loosed us from our sins in His own blood.' The timeless love of Christ, of which that ' loosing' was the manifestation and the outcome,

is not content with emancipating the slaves; it enthrones and hallows them. 'He lifts the beggar from
the dunghill to set him among princes.' 'He hath
loosed us from our sins,' He hath therein made us
'kings and priests to God.'

I. So, then, we have to consider, first, the Royalty of
the Christian life.

Now as I have already observed, that royalty has two
aspects, a present and a future, and therein the representation coincides with the whole strain of the New
Testament, which never separates the present from
the future condition of Christian people, as if they
were altogether unlike, but lays far more emphasis
upon the point in which they coincide than on the
points in which they differ, and represents that future
as being but the completion and the heightening to a
more lustrous splendour, of that which characterises
Christian life in the present. So there is a present
dominion, notwithstanding all the sorrows and limitations and burdens of life; and there is a future one,
which is but the expansion and the superlative degree
of that which is enjoined in the present. What, then,
is the present royalty of the men that have been loosed
from their sins?

Well, I think that the true kingship, which comes as
the consequence of Christ's emancipation of us from
the guilt and power of sin, is dominion over ourselves.
That is the real royalty, to which every man, whatever
his position, may aspire, and may exercise. Our very
nature shows that we are not, if I might so say, a
republic or a democracy, but a monarchy, for there are
parts of every one of us that are manifestly intended
to be subjected and to obey, and there are parts that
are as manifestly intended to be authoritative and to

command. On the one side are the passions and the
desires that inhere in our fleshly natures, and others,
more refined and sublimated forms of the same, and on
the other, there is will, reason, conscience. And these,
being themselves the authoritative and commanding
parts of our nature, observe a subordination also. For
the will which impels all the rest is but a blind giant
unless it be illumined by reason. And will and
reason alike have to bow to the dictates of that
conscience which is the vicegerent of God in every
man.

But there is rebellion in the monarchy, as we all
know, a revolt that spreads widely. And there is no
power that will enable my will to dominate my baser
part, and no power that will enthrone my reason above
my will, and no power that will give to the empty
voice of conscience force to enforce its decrees, except
the power of Him that 'has loosed us from our sins
in His own blood.' When we bow to Him, then, and,
as I believe in its perfect measure, only then, shall we
realise the dominion over the anarchic, rebellious self,
which God means every man to exercise. Christ, and
Christ alone, makes us fit to control all our nature.
And He does it by pouring into us His own Spirit,
which will subdue, by strengthening all the motives
which should lead men to obedience, by setting before
them the perfect pattern in Himself, and by the communication of His own life, which is symbolised by
His blood cleansing us from the tyranny under which
we have been held. We were slaves, He makes us free,
and making us free He enthrones us. He that is king
over himself is the true king.

Again, the present royalty of the Christian man is
found in his sovereignty over the world. He commands

the world who despises it. He is lord of material
things who bends them to the highest use, the development of his own nature, and the formation in him of a
God-pleasing and Christlike character. He is king of
the material who uses it as men use the leaping-bars
and other apparatus in a gymnasium, for the strengthening of the frame, and the bringing out of the muscles.
He is the king of the world to whom it is all a mirror
that shows God, a ladder by which we can climb to
Him.   And this domination over things visible and
material is possible to us in its superlative degree only
in the measure in which we are united by faith and
obedience to Him who declared, with almost His dying
breath, 'I have overcome the world,' and bade us
therefore 'be of good cheer.'   'This is the victory that
overcometh the world, even our faith,' and He is the
master of all who has submitted himself to the
monarchy of Jesus Christ.   And so the royalty which
begins with ruling my own nature goes on to be master
of all things around me, according to that great saying, the depth of which can be realised only by experience, 'All things are yours, and ye are Christ's.'

There is another department in which the same
kingship is at present capable of being exercised by us
all, and that is that we may become, by faith in Jesus
Christ, independent of men, and lords over them, in
the sense that we shall take no orders from them, nor
hang upon their approbation or disapprobation, nor
depend upon their love for our joy, nor be frightened
or bewildered by their hate, but shall be able to say,
'We are the servants of Christ, therefore we are free
from men.'   The King's servant is everybody else's
master.   In the measure in which we hold ourselves in
close union with that Saviour we are set free from all

selfish dependence on, and regard to, the judgments of perishable and fallible creatures like ourselves.

But the passage to which I have already referred as determining the precise meaning of the ambiguous expression in my text goes a little further. It not only speaks of being kings and priests here and now, but it adds they *shall* 'reign with Him,' and so points us onward to a dim future, in which all that is tendency here, and an imperfect kingship, shall be perfectly realised hereafter. I do not dwell upon that, for we see that future but 'through a glass darkly'; only I remind you of such sayings as 'have thou authority over ten cities,' and the other phrase in one of the letters to the seven churches, in which 'authority over the nations' and 'ruling them with a rod of iron' is promised to Christ's servants. These are promises as dim as they are certain, but they, at least, teach us that they who here, in lowly dependence on the King of kings, have bowed themselves to Him, and, emancipated by Him, have been made to share in some measure in His royalty here, shall hereafter, according to the depth of His own wonderful promise, 'sit with Him on His Throne, as He also hath sat down with the Father on His Throne.'

For indeed this kingship of all Christ's children, like the priesthood with which it is associated in my text, is but one case of the general principle that, by faith in Jesus Christ, we are so united with Him as that where He is, and what He is, there and that 'we shall be also.' He has become like us that we might become like Him. He has taken part of the flesh and blood of which the children are partakers, that they might take part of the Spirit of which He is the Lord. He, the Son, has become the Son of Man that sons of men might

in Him become the sons of God. The branches partake
of the 'fatness' of the vine; and the King who is
Priest makes all to trust Him, not only sons but kings
through Himself.

II. We have here the priesthood of the Christian life.

Now that idea is but a symbolical way of putting
some very great and wondrous thoughts, for what are
the elements that go to make up the idea of a priest.

First, direct access to God, and that is the prerogative
of every Christian. All of us, each of us, may pass
into the secret place of the Most High, and stand there
with happy hearts, unabashed and unafraid, beneath
the very blaze of the light of the Shekinah. And we
can do that, because Jesus Christ has come to us with
these words upon His lips, 'I am the Way; no man
cometh to the Father but by Me.' The path into that
Divine Presence is for every sinful soul blocked by an
immense black rock, its own transgressions; but He
has blasted away the rock, and the path is patent for
all our feet. By His death we have the way made open
into the holiest of all. And so we can come, come with
lowly hearts, come with childlike confidence, come with
the whole burden of our weaknesses and wants and
woes, and can spread them all before Him, and nestle
to the great heart of God the Father Himself. We are
priests to God, and our prerogative is to pass within
the veil by the new and living Way which Christ is
for us.

Again, another idea in the conception of the priest
is that he must have somewhat to offer; and we
Christian people are in that sense priests. Christ has
offered the 'one Sacrifice for sins for ever,' and there
is no addition to that possible or requisite. But after
the offering of the expiatory sacrifice, the ancient

Ritual taught us a deep truth when it appointed that following it there should be the sacrifice of thanksgiving. And these are what we are to bring. You remember the words, 'I beseech you, brethren, by the mercies of God, that ye present'—and that word is the technical one for the offering of sacrifice—'your bodies a living sacrifice, acceptable unto God.' You remember Peter's use of this same expression, 'Ye are a royal priesthood,' and his description of their function to offer up spiritual 'sacrifices.' You remember the other words of the great sacerdotal book of the New Testament, the Epistle to the Hebrews, which claims for Christians all that seemed to be disappearing with the dying Jewish economy, and says, 'By Him, therefore, let us offer the sacrifice of praise unto God . . . that is the fruit of our lips, giving thanks to His Name, and to do good, and to communicate forget not, for with such sacrifices God is well-pleased.' So the sacrifice of myself, moved by the mercies of God as a great thank-offering, and in detail the sacrifice of praise, of good gifts and good deeds, and a life devoted to Him, these are the sacrifices which we have to bring.

I need not remind you of yet another aspect in which the sacrificial idea inheres in the very notion of the Christian life, and that is not only access to God, and the offering of sacrifice, but mediation with man. For the function is laid upon all Christian people by Jesus Christ Himself, that they should represent God and Him in the world, and beseech men, in Christ's stead, to be reconciled to God. And so the priesthood and the kingship both belong to the ideal of the Christian life.

III. In the last place, just a word or two as to the practical conclusions from this idea.

The first of them is one on which I touch very lightly,

but which I cannot well omit, and that is the bearing
of this thought on the relations of the members of the
Christian community to one another. The New Testament knows of two kinds of priesthood, and no third.
It knows of Christ as the High Priest who, by His
great sacrifice for the sins of the world, has made all
other expiation antiquated and impertinent, and has
swept away the whole fabric of ceremonial and sacrificial worship ; and it knows of the derived priesthood
which belongs to every member of Christ's Church.
But it stops there; and there is not a word in the New
Testament which warrants any single member of that
universal priesthood monopolising the title to himself,
and so separating himself from the community of his
brethren. I do not wish to elaborate that point, or to
bring any mere controversial elements into my sermon,
but I am bound to say that if that name of priest be
given to a class, you elevate the class and you degrade
the mass of believers. You take away from the community what you concentrate on the individual. And
historically it has always been the case that wherever
the name of priest has been allotted to the officials, the
ministers of the Church, there the priesthood of the
community has tended to be forgotten.

I do not dwell upon the other great error which goes
along with that name as applied to an officer in any
Christian community. But a priest must have a
sacrifice, and you cannot sustain the sacerdotal idea
except by the help of the sacramentarian idea which,
I venture to say, travesties the simple memorial rite
of the Lord's Supper into what it is called in Roman
Catholic phraseology, ' the tremendous sacrifice.'

Brethren, the hand of the priest paralyses the life
of the Church ; and politically, intellectually, socially,

and above all religiously, it blights whatsoever it
touches. You free Churchmen have laid upon you
this day the imperative duty of witnessing for the two
things, the sole priesthood of Jesus Christ, and the
universal priesthood of all His people.

Let me say again, these thoughts bear upon our individual duty. It is idle, as some of us are too apt to do,
to use them as a weapon to fight ecclesiastical assumptions with, unless they regulate our own lives. Be
what you are is what I would say to all Christian men.
You are a king; see that you rule yourself and the
world. You are a priest; see that the path into the
Temple is worn by your continual feet. See that you
offer yourselves sacrifices to God in the daily work and
self-surrender of life. See that you mediate between
God and man, in such brotherly mediation as is possible
to us.

Above all, dear friends, let us all begin where Christ
begins, where my text begins, and go to Him to have
ourselves 'loosed from our sins in His own blood.'
Then the king's diadem and the priest's mitre will meet
on our happy heads. In plain English, if we want to
govern ourselves and the world, we must let Christ
govern us, and then all things will be our servants.
If we would draw near to God—and to be distant from
Him is misery; and if we would offer to Him the
sacrifices—to refrain from offering which is sin and
sorrow—we must begin with going to Jesus Christ, and
trusting in Him as our Redeemer from sin. And then,
so trusting, He will give us here and now, amid the
sorrows and imperfections of life, and more perfectly
amid the glories and unknown advances in power and
beauty in the heavens, a share in His Royalty and His
unchangeable Priesthood.

THE KING OF GLORY AND LORD OF THE CHURCHES

'I John, who also am your brother, and companion in tribulation, and in the kingdom and patience of Jesus Christ, was in the isle that is called Patmos, for the word of God, and for the testimony of Jesus Christ. 10. I was in the Spirit on the Lord's day, and heard behind me a great voice, as of a trumpet. 11. Saying, I am Alpha and Omega, the first and the last : and, What thou seest, write in a book, and send it unto the seven churches which are in Asia; unto Ephesus, and unto Smyrna, and unto Pergamos, and unto Thyatira, and unto Sardis, and unto Philadelphia, and unto Laodicea. 12. And I turned to see the voice that spake with me. And being turned, I saw seven golden candlesticks; 13. And in the midst of the seven candlesticks one like unto the Son of man, clothed with a garment down to the foot, and girt about the paps with a golden girdle. 14. His head and His hairs were white like wool, as white as snow; and His eyes were as a flame of fire; 15. And His feet like unto fine brass, as if they burned in a furnace; and His voice as the sound of many waters. 16. And He had in His right hand seven stars: and out of His mouth went a sharp two-edged sword: and His countenance was as the sun shineth in his strength. 17. And when I saw Him, I fell at His feet as dead. And He laid His right hand upon me, saying unto me, Fear not; I am the first and the last: 18. I am He that liveth, and was dead; and, behold, I am alive for evermore, Amen; and have the keys of hell and of death. 19. Write the things which thou hast seen, and the things which are, and the things which shall be hereafter; 20. The mystery of the seven stars which thou sawest in My right hand, and the seven golden candlesticks. The seven stars are the angels of the seven churches: and the seven candlesticks which thou sawest are the seven churches.'—REV. i. 9-20.

IN this passage we have the seer and his commission (vs. 9-11); the vision of the glorified Christ (vs. 12-16); His words of comfort, self-revelation, and command (vs. 17-20).

I. The writer does not call himself an apostle, but a brother and sharer in the common good of Christians. He does not speak as an apostle, whose function was to witness to the past earthly history of the Lord, but as a prophet, whose message was as to the future.

The true rendering of verse 9 (R.V.) brings all three words, 'tribulation,' 'kingdom,' and 'patience' into the same relation to 'in Jesus.' Sharing in afflictions which flow from union to Him is the condition of partaking in His kingdom; and tribulation leads to the throne, when it is borne with the brave patience which not only endures, but, in spite of sorrows, goes right onwards, and which is ours if we are in Christ.

Commentators tell us that John was banished to Patmos, an insignificant rock off the Asiatic coast, under Domitian, and returned to Ephesus in the reign of Nerva (A.D. 96). No wonder that all through the book we hear the sound of the sea! It was common for the Romans to dispose of criminals in that fashion, and, clearly, John was shut up in Patmos as a criminal. 'For the word of God, and the testimony of Jesus,' cannot fairly bear any other meaning than that he was sent there as punishment for bearing witness to Jesus. Observe the use of 'witness' or testimony, as connecting the Apocalypse with the Gospel and Epistles of John.

In his rocky solitude the Apostle was 'in the Spirit,' —by which is, of course, not meant the condition in which every Christian should ever be, but such a state of elevated consciousness and communion as Paul was in when he was caught up to the heavens. No doubt John had been meditating on the unforgotten events of that long-past day of resurrection, which he was observing in his islet by solitary worship, as he had often observed it with his brethren in Ephesus; and his devout thoughts made him the more capable of supernatural communications. Whether the name of the first day of the week as 'the Lord's Day' originated with this passage, or had already become common, is uncertain. But, at all events, it was plainly regarded as the day for Christian worship. Solitary souls, far away from the gatherings of Christ's people, may still draw near to Him; and if they turn thought and love towards Him, they will be lifted above this gross earth, and hear that great voice speaking to them, which

K

rose above the dash of waves, and thrilled the inward ear of the lonely exile. That voice, penetrating and clear like a trumpet, gave him his charge, and woke his expectation of visions to follow.

We cannot enter on any consideration of the churches enumerated, or the reasons for their selection. Suffice it to note that their number suggests their representative character, and that what is said to them is meant for all churches in all ages.

II. The fuller consideration of the emblem of the candlesticks will come presently, but we have reverently to gaze upon the glorious figure which flashed on John's sight as he turned to see who spoke to him there in his loneliness. His first glimpse told him that it was 'one like to the Son of man'; for it can scarcely be supposed that the absence of the definite article in the Greek obliges us to think that all that John meant to say was that the form was manlike. Surely it was a more blessed resemblance than that vague one which struck on his heart. It was He Himself ' with His human air,' standing there in the blaze of celestial light. What a rush of memories, what a rapture of awe and surprise would flood his soul, as that truth broke on him! The differences between the form seen and that remembered were startling, indeed, but likeness persisted through them all. Nor is it inexplicable that, when he had taken in all the features of the vision, he should have fallen as one dead; for the truest love would feel awe at the reappearance of the dearest invested with heavenly radiance.

The elements of the description are symbolical, and, in most instances, drawn from the Old Testament. The long robe, girdled high up with a golden girdle, seems to express at once kingly and priestly dignity.

Girded loins meant work.   This girdled breast meant
royal repose and priestly calm.   The whiteness of the
hair (comp. Dan. vii. 9) may indicate, as in Daniel, length
of days; but more probably it expresses 'the transfiguration in light of the glorified person of the
Redeemer' (Trench).   The flaming eyes are the symbol
of His all-seeing wrath against evil, and the feet of
burning brass symbolise the exalted Christ's power to
tread down His enemies and consume them.   His voice
was as the sound of many waters, like the billows that
broke on Patmos, whereby is symbolised the majesty
of His utterance of power, whether for rebuke or
encouragement, but mainly for the former.

Flashing in His hand were seven stars.   The seer
does not stop to tell us how they were disposed there,
nor how one hand could grasp them all; but that right
hand can and does.   What this point of the vision
means we shall see presently.

The terrible power of the exalted Christ's word to
destroy His foes is expressed by that symbol of the
two-edged sword from His mouth, which, like so many
prophetic symbols, is grotesque if pictured, but sublime
when spoken.   The face blazed with dazzling brightness unbearable as the splendours of that southern sun
which poured its rays on the flashing waters round
John's rocky prison.

Is this tremendous figure like the Christ on whose
bosom John had leaned?   Yes; for one chief purpose
of this book is to make us feel that the exalted Jesus
is the same in all essentials as the lowly Jesus.   The
heart that beats beneath the golden girdle is the same
that melted with pity and overflowed with love here.
The hands that bear the seven stars are those that
were pierced with nails.   The eyes that flash fire are

those that dropped tears at a grave and over Jerusalem. The lips from which issues the sharp sword are
the same which said, 'I will give you rest.' He has
carried all His love, His gentleness, His sympathy, into
the blaze of Deity, and in His glory is still our brother.

III. His gracious words to John tell us this and
more. Soothingly He laid the hand with the stars in
it on the terrified Apostle, and gentle words, which he
had heard Him say many a time on earth, came soothingly from the mouth from which the sword proceeded. How the calming graciousness rises into
majesty! 'I am the first and the last.' That is a
Divine prerogative (Isa. xliv. 6). The glorified Christ
claims to have been before all creatures, and to be the
end to which all tend.

Verse 18 should be more closely connected with
the preceding than in Authorised Version. The sentence runs on unbroken, 'and the Living one,' which is
equivalent to the claim to possess life in Himself
(John v. 26), on which follows in majestic continuity,
'and I became dead'—pointing to the mystery of the
Lord of life entering into the conditions of humanity,
and stooping to taste of death—'and, behold, I am
alive for evermore'—the transient eclipse of the grave
is followed by glorious life for ever—'and I have the
keys of death and of Hades'—having authority over
that dark prison-house, and opening and shutting its
gates as I will.

Mark how, in these solemn words, the threefold state
of the eternal Word is set forth, in His pre-incarnate
fulness of Divine life, in His submission to death, in His
resurrection, and in His ascended glory, as Lord of
life and death, and of all worlds. Does our faith grasp
all these? We shall never understand His life and

death on earth, unless we see before them the eternal dwelling of the Word with God, and after them the exaltation of His manhood to the throne of the universe.

The charge to the Apostle, which follows on this transcendent revelation, has two parts—the command to write his visions, and the explanation of the symbols of the stars and the candlesticks. As to the former, we need only note that it extends to the whole book, and that the three divisions of 'what thou seest,' 'the things which are,' and 'the things which shall be here-after,' may refer, respectively, to the vision in this chapter, the letters to the seven churches, and the subsequent prophetic part of the book.

As to the explanation of the symbols, stars are always, in Scripture, emblems of authority, and here they are clearly so. But there is great difference of opinion as to the meaning of the 'angels,' which are variously taken as being guardian angels of each church, or the presiding officers of these, or ideal figures representing each church in its collective aspect. It is impossible to enter on the discussion of these views here, and we can only say that, in our judgment, the opinion that the angels are the bishops of the churches is the most probable. If so, the fact that they are addressed as representing the churches, responsible for and sharing in their spiritual condition, suggests very solemn thoughts as to the weight laid on every one who sustains an analogous position, and the inseparable connection between the spiritual condition of pastor and people.

The seven candlesticks are the seven churches. The formal unity of the ancient church, represented by the one candlestick with its seven branches, is exchanged for the real unity which arises from the presence of Christ in the midst. The old candlestick is at the bottom of the Mediterranean. The unity of the Church does not depend on compression into one organisation, but on all its parts being clustered around Jesus.

The emblem of the candlestick, or lamp-holder, may suggest lessons as to the Church's function. Each church should be light. That light must be derived. There is only one unkindled and unfed light—that of Jesus Christ. Of the rest of us it has to be said, 'He was not that Light, but was sent to bear witness of that Light.' Each church should be, as it were, a clustered light, like those rings of iron, pierced with many little holes, from each of which a tiny jet of gas comes, which, running all together, make one steady lustre. So we should each be content to blend our little twinkle in the common light.

THE THREEFOLD COMMON HERITAGE

'I John, your brother, and partaker with you in the tribulation and kingdom and patience which are in Jesus.'—REV. i. 9 (R.V.).

So does the Apostle introduce himself to his readers; with no word of pre-eminence or of apostolic authority, but with the simple claim to share with them in their Christian heritage. And this is the same man who, at an earlier stage of his Christian life, desired that he and his brother might 'sit on Thy right hand and on Thy left in Thy Kingdom.' What a change had passed over him! What was it that out of such timber made such a polished shaft? I think there is only one answer—the resurrection of Jesus Christ and the gift of God's good Spirit that came after it.

It almost looks as if John was thinking about his
old ambitious wish, and our Lord's answer to it, when
he wrote these words; for the very gist of our Lord's
teaching to him on that memorable occasion is repro-
duced in compressed form in my text. He had been
taught that fellowship in Christ's sufferings must go
before participation in His throne; and so here he puts
tribulation before the kingdom. He had been taught,
in answer to his foolish request, that pre-eminence was
not the first thing to think of, but service; and that
the only principle according to which rank was determined in that kingdom was service. So here he says
nothing about dignity, but calls himself simply a
brother and companion. He humbly suppresses his
apostolic authority, and takes his place, not by the
side of the throne, apart from others, but down among
them.

Now the Revised Version is distinctly an improved
version in its rendering of these words. It reads
'partaker with you,' instead of 'companion,' and so
emphasises the notion of participation. It reads, 'in
the tribulation and kingdom and patience,' instead of
'in tribulation and *in the* kingdom and patience'; and
so, as it were, brackets all the three nouns together
under one preposition and one definite article, and
thus shows more closely their connection. And instead
of 'in the kingdom and patience of Jesus Christ,' it
reads, 'which are in Jesus Christ,' and so shows that
the predicate, 'in Jesus Christ,' extends to all the
three—the 'tribulation,' the 'kingdom,' and the
'patience,' and not only to the last of the three, as
would be suggested to an ordinary reader of our
English version. So that we have here a participation
by all Christian men in three things, all of which are,

in some sense, 'in Christ Jesus.' Note that participation in 'the kingdom' stands in the centre, buttressed, as it were, on the one side by participation 'in the tribulation,' and on the other side by participation 'in the patience.' We may, then, best bring out the connection and force of these thoughts by looking at the common royalty, the common road leading to it, and the common temper in which the road is trodden—all which things do inhere in Christ, and may be ours on condition of our union with Him.

I. So then, first, note the common royalty. 'I John am a partaker with you in the kingdom.'

Now John does not say, 'I am *going to be* a partaker,' but says, 'Here and now, in this little rocky island of Patmos, an exile and all but a martyr, I yet, like all the rest of you, who have the same *weird* to dree, and the same bitter cup to drink, even now *am* a partaker of the kingdom that is in Christ.'

What is that kingdom? It is the sphere or society, the state or realm, in which His will is obeyed; and, as we may say, His writs run. His kingdom, in the deepest sense of the word, is only there, where loving hearts yield, and where His will is obeyed consciously, because the conscious obedience is rooted in love.

But then, besides that, there is a wider sense of the expression in which Christ's kingdom stretches all through the universe, and wherever the authority of God is there is the kingdom of the exalted Christ, who is the right hand and active power of God.

So then the 'kingdom that is in Christ' is yours if you are 'in Christ.' Or, to put it into other words, whoever is ruled *by* Christ has a share in rule *with* Christ. Hence the words in the context here, to which a double meaning may be attached, 'He hath made us to be a kingdom.' We are His kingdom in so far as our wills joyfully and lovingly submit to His authority; and then, in so far as we are His kingdom, we are kings. So far as our wills bow to and own His sway, they are invested with power to govern ourselves and others. His subjects are the world's masters. Even now, in the midst of confusions and rebellions, and apparent contradictions, the true rule in the world belongs to the men and women who bow to the authority of Jesus Christ. Whoever worships Him, saying, 'Thou art the King of Glory, O Christ,' receives from Him the blessed assurance, 'and I appoint unto you a kingdom.' His vassals are altogether princes. He is 'King of kings,' not only in the sense that He is higher than the kings of the earth, but also in the sense, though it be no part of the true meaning of the expression, that those whom He rules are, by the very submission to His rule, elevated to royal dignity.

We rule over ourselves, which is the best kingdom to govern, on condition of saying:—'Lord! I cannot rule myself, do Thou rule me.' When we put the reins into His hands, when we put our consciences into His keeping, when we take our law from His gentle and yet sovereign lips, when we let Him direct our thinking; when His word is absolute truth that ends all controversy, and when His will is the supreme authority that puts an end to every hesitation and reluctance, then we are masters of ourselves. The man that has rule over his own spirit is the true king. He that thus is Christ's man is his own master. Being lords of ourselves, and having our foot upon our passions, and conscience and will flexible in His hand and yielding to

His lightest touch, as a fine-mouthed horse does to the least pressure of the bit, then we are masters of circumstances and the world; and all things are on our side if we are on Christ's side.

So we do not need to wait for Heaven to be heirs, that is possessors, of the kingdom that God hath prepared for them that love Him. Christ's dominion is shared even now and here by all who serve Him. It is often hard for us to believe this about ourselves or others, especially when toil weighs upon us, and adverse circumstances, against which we have vainly striven, tyrannise over our lives. We feel more like powerless victims than lords of the world. Our lives seem concerned with such petty trivialities, and so absolutely lorded over by externals, that to talk of a present dominion over a present world seems irony, flatly contradicted by facts. We are tempted to throw forward the realisation of our regality to the future. We are heirs, indeed, of a great kingdom, but for the present are set to keep a small huckster's shop in a back street. So we faithlessly say to ourselves; and we need to open our eyes, as John would have his brethren do, to the fact of the present participation of every Christian in the present kingdom of the enthroned Christ. There can be no more startling anomalies in our lots than were in his, as he sat there in Patmos, a solitary exile, weighed upon with many cares, ringed about with perils not a few. But in them all he knew his share in the kingdom to be real and inalienable, and yielding much for present fruition, however much more remained over for hope and future possession. The kingdom is not only 'of' but 'in' Jesus Christ. He is, as it were, the sphere in which it is realised. If we are 'in Him' by that faith which engrafts us into Him, we shall ourselves both be and possess that kingdom, and *possess* it, because we *are* it.

But while the kingdom is present, its perfect form is future. The crown of righteousness is laid up for God's people, even though they are already a kingdom, and already (according to the true reading of Rev. v. 10) 'reign upon the earth.' Great hopes, the greater for their dimness, gather round that future when the faithfulness of the steward shall be exchanged for the authority of the ruler, and the toil of the servant for the joy of the Lord. The presumptuous ambition of John in his early request did not sin by setting his hopes too high; for, much as he asked when he sought a place at the right hand of his Master's throne, his wildest dreams fell far below the reality, reserved for all who overcome, of a share in that very throne itself. There is room there, not for one or two of the aristocracy of heaven, but for all the true servants of Christ.

They used to say that in the days of the first Napoleon every French soldier carried a field-marshal's baton in his knapsack. That is to say, every one of them had the chance of winning it, and many of them did win it. But every Christian soldier carries a crown in his, and that not because he perhaps may, but because he certainly will, wear it, when the war is over, if he stands by his flag, and because he has it already in actual possession, though for the present the helmet becomes his brow rather than the diadem. On such themes we can say little, only let us remember that the present and the future life of the Christian are distinguished, not by the one possessing the royalty which the other wants, but as the partial and perfect forms of the same kingdom, which, in both forms

alike, depends on our true abiding in Him. That
kingdom is *in* Him, and is the common heritage of all
who are in Him, and who, on earth and in heaven,
possess it in degrees varying accurately with the
measure in which they are in Christ, and He in them.

II. Note, secondly, the common road to that common
royalty.

As I have remarked, the kingdom is the central
thought here, and the other two stand on either side as
subsidiary: on the one hand, a common 'tribulation';
on the other, a common 'patience.' The former is the
path by which all have to travel who attain the
royalty; the latter is the common temper in which all
the travellers must face the steepnesses and rough-
nesses of the road.

'Tribulation' has, no doubt, primarily reference to
actual persecution, such as had sent John to his exile
in Patmos, and hung like a threatening thunder-cloud
over the Asiatic churches. But the significance of the
word is not exhausted thereby. It is always true that
'through much tribulation we must enter the kingdom.'
All who are bound to the same place, and who start
from the same place, must go by the same road. There
are no short-cuts nor by-paths for the Christian
pilgrim. The only way to the kingdom that is in
Christ is the road which He Himself trod. There is
'tribulation in Christ,' as surely as in Him there are
peace and victory, and if we are in Christ we shall be
sure to get our share of it. The Christian course brings
new difficulties and trials of its own, and throws those
who truly out-and-out adopt it into relations with the
world which will surely lead to oppositions and pains.
If we are in the world as Christ was, we shall have to
make up our minds to share 'the reproach of Christ'

until Egypt owns Him, and not Pharaoh, for its King. If there be no such experience, it is much more probable that the reason for exemption is the Christian's worldliness than the world's growing Christlikeness.

No doubt the grosser forms of persecution are at an end, and no doubt multitudes of nominal Christians live on most amicable terms with the world, and know next to nothing of the tribulation that is in Christ. But that is not because there is any real alteration in the consequences of union with Jesus, but because their union is so very slight and superficial. The world 'loves its own,' and what can it find to hate in the shoals of people, whose religion is confined to their tongues mostly, and has next to nothing to do with their lives? It has not ceased to be a hard thing to be a real and thorough Christian. A great deal in the world is against us when we try to be so, and a great deal in ourselves is against us. There will be ' tribulation ' by reason of self-denial, and the mortification and rigid suppression or regulation of habits, tastes, and passions, which some people may be able to indulge, but which we must cast out, though dear and sensitive as a right eye, if they interfere with our entrance into life. The law is unrepealed—' If we suffer with Him, we shall also reign with Him.'

But this participation in the tribulation that is in Christ has another and gentler aspect. The expression points to the blessed softening of our hardest trials when they are borne in union with the Man of Sorrows. The sunniest lives have their dark times. Sooner or later we all have to lay our account with hours when the heart bleeds and hope dies, and we shall not find strength to bear such times aright unless we bear them in union with Jesus Christ, by which our darkest sorrows are turned into the tribulation that is in Him, and all the bitterness, or, at least, the poison of the bitterness, taken out of them, and they almost changed into a solemn joy. Egypt would be as barren as the desert which bounds it, were it not for the rising of the Nile; so when the cold waters of sorrow rise up and spread over our hearts, if we are Christians, they will leave a precious deposit when they retire, on which will grow rich harvests. Some edible plants are not fit for use till they have had a touch of frost. Christian character wants the same treatment. It is needful for us that the road to the kingdom should often run through the valley of weeping. Our being in the kingdom depends upon the bending of our wills in submission to the King; then surely nothing should be more welcome to us, as nothing can be more needful, than anything which bends them, even if the fire which makes their obstinacy pliable, and softens the iron so that it runs in the appointed mould, should have to be very hot. The soil of the vineyards on the slopes of Vesuvius is disintegrated lava. The richest grapes, from which a precious wine is made, grow on the product of eruptions which tore the mountain-side and darkened all the sky. So our costliest graces of character are grown in a heart enriched by losses and made fertile by convulsions which rent it and covered smiling verdure with what seemed at first a fiery flood of ruin. The kingdom is reached by the road of tribulation. Blessed are they for whom the universal sorrows which flesh is heir to become helps heavenwards because they are borne in union with Jesus, and so hallowed into 'tribulation that is in Him.'

III. We note the common temper in which the common road to the common royalty is to be trodden.

'Tribulation' refers to circumstances—'patience' to disposition. We shall certainly meet with tribulation if we are Christians, and if we are, we shall front tribulation with patience. Both are equally, though in different ways, characteristics of all the true travellers to the kingdom. Patience is the link, so to speak, between the kingdom and the tribulation. Sorrow does not of itself lead to the possession of the kingdom. All depends on the disposition which the sorrow evokes, and the way in which it is borne. We may take our sorrows in such a fashion as to be driven by them out of our submission to Christ, and so they may lead us away from and not towards the kingdom. The worst affliction is an affliction wasted, and every affliction is wasted, unless it is met with patience, and that in Christ Jesus. Many a man is soured, or paralysed, or driven from his faith, or drowned in self-absorbed and self-compassionating regret, or otherwise harmed by his sorrows, and the only way to get the real good of them is to keep closely united to our Lord, that in Him we may have patience as well as peace.

Most of us know that the word here translated 'patience' means a great deal more than the passive endurance which we usually mean by that word, and distinctly includes the notion of active perseverance. That active element is necessarily implied, for instance, in the exhortation, 'Let us run with patience the race that is set before us.' Mere uncomplaining passive endurance is not the temper which leads to running any race. It simply bears and does nothing, but the persistent effort of the runner with tense muscles calls for more than patience. A vivid metaphor underlies the word—that of the fixed attitude of one bearing up a heavy weight or pressure without yielding or being crushed. Such immovable constancy is more than passive. There must be much active exercise of power to prevent collapse. But all the strength is not to be exhausted in the effort to bear without flinching. There should be enough remaining for work that remains over and above the sorrow. The true Christian patience implies continuance in well-doing, besides meek acceptance of tribulation. The first element in it is, no doubt, unmurmuring acquiescence in whatsoever affliction from God or man beats against us on our path. But the second is, continual effort after Christian progress, notwithstanding the tribulation. The storm must not blow us out of our course. We must still 'bear up and steer right onward,' in spite of all its force on our faces, or, as 'birds of tempest-loving kind' do, so spread our pinions as to be helped by it towards our goal.

Do I address any one who has to stagger along the Christian course under some heavy and, perhaps, hopeless load of sorrow? There is a plain lesson for all of us in such circumstances. It is not less my duty to seek to grow in grace and Christlikeness because I am sad. That is my first business at all times and under all changes of fortune and mood. My sorrows are meant to help me to that, and if they so absorb me that I am indifferent to the obligation of Christian progress, then my patience, however stoical and uncomplaining it may be, is not the 'perseverance that is in Christ Jesus.' Nor does tribulation absolve from plain duties. Poor Mary of Bethany sat still in the house, with her hands lying idly in her lap, and her regrets busy with the most unprofitable of all occupations—fancying how different all would have been if one thing had been different. Sorrow is excessive and misdirected and selfish, and therefore hurtful, when for the sake of indulgence in it we fling up plain tasks. The glory of the kingdom shining athwart the gloom of the tribulation should help us to be patient, and the patience, laying hold of the tribulation by the right handle, should convert it into a blessing and an instrument for helping us to a fuller possession of the kingdom.

This temper of brave and active persistence in the teeth of difficulties will only be found where these other two are found—in Christ. The stem from which the three-leaved plant grows must be rooted in Him. He is the King, and in Him abiding we have our share of the common royalty. He is the forerunner and pathfinder, and, abiding in Him, we tread the common path to the common kingdom, which is hallowed at every rough place by the print of His bleeding feet. He is the leader and perfecter of faith, and, abiding in Him, we receive some breath of the spirit which was in Him, who, for the joy that was set before Him, endured the Cross, despising the shame. Abiding in Him, we shall possess in our measure all which is in Him, and find ourselves partakers with an innumerable company 'in the tribulation and kingdom and patience which are in Christ Jesus,' and may hope to hear at last, 'Ye are they which have continued with Me in My temptations, and I appoint unto you a Kingdom, as My Father hath appointed unto Me.'

L

THE LIVING ONE WHO BECAME DEAD

'I am He that liveth, and was dead; and, behold, I am alive for evermore, Amen; and have the keys of hell and of death.'—REV. i. 18.

IF we had been in 'the isle which is called Patmos' when John saw the glorified Lord, and heard these majestic words from His mouth, we should probably have seen nothing but the sunlight glinting on the water, and heard only the wave breaking on the shore. The Apostle tells us that he 'was in the Spirit'; that is, in a state in which sense is lulled to sleep, and the inner man made aware of supersensual realities. The communication was none the less real because it was not perceived by the outward eye or ear. It was not born in, though it was perceived by, the Apostle's spirit. We must hold fast by the objective reality of the communication, which is not in the slightest degree affected by the assumption that sense had no part in it.

Further what John once saw always is; the vision was a transient revelation of a permanent reality. The snowy summits are there, behind the cloud-wrack that hides them, as truly as they were when the sunshine gleamed on their peaks. The veil has fallen again, but all behind it is as it was. So this revelation, both in regard of the magnificent symbolic image imprinted on the Apostle's consciousness, and in regard of the words which he reports to us as impressed upon him by Christ Himself, is meant for us just as it was for him, or for those to whom it was originally transmitted. 'He that hath an ear, let him hear what the Spirit saith to the churches.' And as we meditate upon this proclamation by the kingly Christ Himself of His own style and titles, I think we shall

best gain its full sublimity and force if we simply take
the words, clause by clause, as they stand in the text.

I. First, then, the royal Christ proclaims His absolute
life.

Observe that, as the Revised Version will show those
who use it, there is a much closer connection between
the words of our text and those of the preceding verse
than our Authorised Version gives. We must strike
out that intrusive and wholly needless supplement, ' I
am,' and read the sentence unbrokenly : ' I am the first,
and the last and the living One.'

Now that close connection of clauses in itself sug·
gests that this expression, 'the Living One,' means
something more than the mere declaration that He was
alive. That follows appropriately, as we shall see, in
the last clause of the verse, which cannot be cleared
from the charge of tautology, unless we attach a far
deeper meaning than the mere declaration of life to
this first solemn clause. What can stand worthily by
the side of these majestic words, ' I am the first and
the last'?   These claim a Divine attribute and are a
direct quotation from ancient prophecy, where they
are spoken as by the great Jehovah of the old covenant,
and appear in a connection which makes any tamper-
ing with them the more impossible. For there follow
upon them the great words, 'and beside Me there is no
God.' But this royal Christ from the heavens puts out
an unpresumptuous hand, and draws to Himself, as
properly belonging to Him, the very style and signature
of the Divine nature, 'I am the first'—before all
creatural being, 'and the last,' as He to whom it all
tends—its goal and aim. And therefore I say that this
connection of clauses, apart altogether from other consideration, absolutely forbids our taking this great

word, 'the Living One,' as meaning less than the similar
lofty and profound signification. It means, as I
believe, exactly what Jesus Christ meant when, in the
hearing of this same Apostle, He said upon earth, 'As
the Father hath life in Himself so hath He given '—
strange paradox—'so hath He given to the Son to have
life in Himself.' A life which, considered in contrast
with all the life of creatures, is underived, independent,
self-feeding, and, considered in contrast with the life
of the Father with whom that Son stands in ineffable
and unbroken union, is bestowed. It is a paradox, I
know, but until we assume that we have sounded all
the depths and climbed all the heights, and gone round
the boundless boundaries of the circumference of that
Divine nature, we have no business to say that it is
impossible. And this, as I take it, is what the great
words that echoed from Heaven in the Apostle's hearing upon Patmos meant—the claim by the glorified
Christ to possess absolute fontal life, and to be the
Source of all creation, ' in whom was life.' He was not
only ' the Living One,' but, as Himself has said, He was
' the Life.' And so He was the agent of all creation,
as Scripture teaches us.

Now I am not going to dwell upon this great thought,
but I simply wish, in one sentence, to leave with you
my own earnest conviction that it is the teaching of
all Scripture, that it is distinctly the teaching of Christ
Himself when on earth; that it is repeated in a real
revelation from Himself to the recipient seer in this
vision before us, that it is fundamental to all true
understanding of Christ's person and work, since none
of His acts on earth shine in their full lustre of beauty
unless the thought of His pre-incarnate and essential
life is held fast to heighten all the marvels of His

condescension, and to invest with power all the sweetness of His pity. 'I am the first, and the last, and the Living One.'

II. Secondly, the royal Christ proclaims His submission to death.

The language of the original is, perhaps, scarcely capable of smooth transference into English, but it is to be held fast notwithstanding, for what is said is not 'I *was* dead,' as describing a past condition, but 'I *became* dead,' as describing a past act. There is all the difference between these two, and avoidance of awkwardness is dearly purchased by obliteration of the solemn teaching of that profound word ' became.'

I need not dwell upon this at any length, but I suggest to you one or two plain considerations. Such a statement implies our Lord's assumption of flesh. The only possibility of death, for 'the Living One,' lies in His enwrapping Himself with that which can die. As you might put a piece of asbestos into a twist of cotton wool, over which the flame could have power, or as a sun might plunge into thick envelopes of darkness, so this eternal, absolute Life gathered to itself by voluntary accretion the surrounding which was capable of mortality. It is very significant that the same word which the seer in Patmos employs to describe the Lord's submission to death is the word which, in his character of evangelist, he employs to describe the same Lord's incarnation: 'The Word became flesh,' and so the Life ' became dead.' And this expression implies, too, another thing, on which I need not dwell, because I was touching on it in a previous sermon, and that is the entirely voluntary character of our Lord's submission to the great law of mortality. He ' became' dead, and it was His act that He became so.

Thus we are brought into the presence of the most stupendous fact in the world's history. Brethren, as I said that the firm grasp of the other truth of Christ's absolute life was fundamental to all understanding of His earthly career, so I say that this fundamental truth of His voluntarily becoming dead is fundamental to all understanding of His Cross. Without that thought His death becomes mere surplusage, in so far as His power over men is concerned. With it, what adoration can be too lowly, what gratitude can be disproportionate? He arrays Himself in that which can die, as if the sun plunged into the shadow of eclipse. Let us bow before that mystery of Divine love, the death of the Lord of Life. The motive which impelled Him, the consequences which followed, are not in view here. These are full of blessedness and of wonder, but we are now to concentrate our thoughts on the bare fact, and to find in it food for endless adoration and for perpetual praise.

But there is another consideration that I may suggest. The eternal Life became dead. Then the awful solitude—awful when we think of it for ourselves, awful when we stand by the bed, and feel so near, and yet so infinitely remote from the dear one that may be lying there—the awful solitude is solitary no longer. 'All alone, so Heaven has willed, we die'; but as travellers are cheered on a solitary road when they see the footprints that they know belonged to loved and trusted ones who have trodden it before, that desolate loneliness is less lonely when we think that He became dead. He will come to the shrinking, single soul as He joined Himself to the sad travellers on the road to Emmaus, and 'our hearts' may burn within us, even in that last hour of their beating, if we can remember who has become dead and trodden the road before us.

III. The royal Christ proclaims His eternal life in glory.

'Behold!'—as if calling attention to a wonder—'I am alive for evermore.' Again, I say, we have here a distinctly Divine prerogative claimed by the exalted Christ, as properly belonging to Himself. For that eternal life of which He speaks is by no means the communicated immortality which He imparts to them that in His love go down to death, but it is the inherent eternal life of the Divine nature.

But, mark, who is the 'I' that speaks ? The seer has told us : 'One like unto the Son of Man'—which title, whether it repeats the name which our Lord habitually used, or whether, as some persons suppose, it should be read ' a Son of Man,' and merely declares that the vision of the glorified One was manlike, is equally relevant for my present purpose. For that is to ask you to mark that the 'I' of my text is the Divine-human Jesus. The manhood is so intertwined with the Deity that the absolute life of the latter has, as it were, flowed over and glorified the former ; and it is a Man who lays His hand upon the Divine prerogative, and says, 'I live for evermore.'

Now why do I dwell upon thoughts like this ? Not for the purpose merely of putting accurately what I believe to be the truth, but for the sake of opening out to you and to myself the infinite treasures of consolation and strength which lie in that thought that He who ' is alive for evermore' is not merely Divine in His absolute life, but, as Son of Man, lives for ever. And so, ' because I live, ye shall live also.' We cannot die as long as Christ is alive. And if we knit our hearts to

Him, the Divine glory which flows over His Manhood will trickle down to ours, and we, too, though by derivation, shall possess as immortal — and, in its measure, as glorious—a life as that of the Brother who reigns in Heaven, the Man Christ Jesus.

His resurrection is not only the demonstration of what manhood is capable*of, and so, as I believe, the one irrefragable and all-satisfying proof of immortality, but it is also the actual source of that immortal life to all of us, if we will trust ourselves to Him. For it is only because ' He both died and rose and revived' that He, in the truest and properest sense, becomes the gift of life to us men. The alabaster box was broken, and the house was filled with the odour of the ointment. Christ's death is the world's life. Christ's resurrection is the pledge and the source of eternal life for us.

IV. And so, lastly, the royal Christ proclaims His authority over the dim regions of the dead.

Much to be regretted are two things in our Authorised Version's rendering of the final words of our text. One is the order in which, following an inferior reading, it has placed the two things specified. And the other is that deplorable mistranslation, as it has come to be, of the word *hades* by the word 'hell.' The true original does not read 'hell and death,' but 'death and *hades*,' the dim unseen regions in which *all* the dead, whatsoever their condition may be, are gathered. The *hades* of the New Testament includes the paradise into which the penitent thief was promised entrance, as well as the *gehenna* which threatened to open for the impenitent.

Here it is figured as being **a** great gloomy fortress, with **bars** and gates and locks, of which that 'shadow feared of man' is the warder, and keeps the portals. But he does not keep the keys. The kingly Christ has these in His own hand. So, brethren, He has authority to open and to shut; and death is not merely a terror nor is it altogether accounted for, when we say either that it is the fruit of sin, or that it is the result of physical laws. For behind the laws is the will—the will of the loving Christ. It is His hand that opens the dark door, and they who listen aright may hear Him say, when He does it, 'Come! My people; enter thou into thy chamber until these calamities be overpast.' 'He openeth, and no man shutteth; He shutteth, and no man openeth.' So is not the terror gone; and 'the raven plumes of that darkness smoothed until it smiles'?

If we believe that He has the keys, how shall we dread when ourselves or our dear ones have to enter into the portal? There are two gates to the prison-house, and when the one that looks earthwards opens, the other, that gives on the heavens, opens too, and the prison becomes a thoroughfare, and the light shines through the short tunnel even to the hither side.

Because He has the keys, He will not leave His holy ones in the fetters. And for ourselves, and for our dearest, we have the right to think that the darkness is so short as to be but like an imperceptible wink of the eye; and ere we know that we have passed into it, we shall have passed out.

'This is the gate of the Lord, into which the righteous shall enter.' And it may be with us as it was with the Apostle who was awakened out of his sleep by the angel—only we shall be awakened out of ours by the angel's Master—and who did not come to himself, and know that he had been delivered, until he had passed through the iron gate 'that opened to him of its own accord'; and then, bewildered, he recovered himself when he found that, with the morning breaking over his head, he stood, delivered, in the city.

THE SEVEN STARS AND THE SEVEN CANDLESTICKS

'. . . He that holdeth the seven stars in His right hand, who walketh in the midst of the seven golden candlesticks.'—REV. ii. 1.

IT is one of the obligations which we owe to hostile criticism that we have been forced to recognise with great clearness the wide difference between the representation of Christ in John's Gospel and that in the Apocalypse. That there is such a contrast is unquestionable. The Prince of all the kings of the earth, going forth conquering and to conquer, strikes one at once as being unlike the Christ whom the Evangelist painted weeping at the grave of Lazarus. We can afford to recognise the fact, though we demur to the inference that both representations cannot have proceeded from one pen. Surely that is not a necessary conclusion unless the two pictures are contradictory. Does the variety amount to discordance? Unless it do, the variety casts no shadow of suspicion on the common authorship. I, for my part, see no inconsistency in them, and thankfully accept both as completing each other.

This grand vision, which forms the introduction to the whole Book of the Apocalypse, gives us indeed the Lord Jesus clothed with majesty and wielding supreme power, but it also shows us the old love and tenderness. It was the old voice which fell on John's ear, in words heard from Him before, 'Fear not.' It was the same hand as he had often clasped that was lovingly laid upon him to strengthen him. The assurance which He gives His Apostle declares at once the change in the circumstances of His Being, and in the functions which He discharges, and the substantial identity of His Being through all the changes: 'I am the first, and the last. . . . I am the Living One, who was dead, and behold I am alive for evermore.' This vision and the whole book calls to us, ' Behold the Lion of the Tribe of Judah'; and when we look, 'Lo, in the midst of the throne, stands a Lamb as it had been slain '—the well-known meek and patient Jesus, the suffering Redeemer—'the Lamb of God which taketh away the sins of the world.'

Still further, this vision is the natural introduction to all that follows, and indeed defines the main purpose of the whole book, inasmuch as it shows us Christ sustaining, directing, dwelling, in His Churches. We are thus led to expect that the remainder of the prophecy shall have the Church of Christ for its chief subject, and that the politics of the world, and the mutations of nations, shall come into view mainly in their bearing upon that.

The words of our text, then, which resumes the principal emblem of the preceding vision, are meant to set forth permanent truths in regard to Christ's Churches, His relation to them, and theirs to the world, which I desire to bring to your thoughts now. They speak to us of the Churches and their servants, of the Churches and their work, of the Churches and their Lord.

I. We have in the symbol important truths concerning the Churches and their servants.

The seven stars are the angels of the seven Churches. Now I need not spend time in enumerating all the

strange and mystical interpretations which have been
given to these angels of the Churches. I see no need
for taking them to have been anything but men; the
recognised heads and representatives of the respective
communities. The word 'angel' means messenger.
Those superhuman beings who are usually designated
by it are so called, not to describe their nature, but
their function. They are 'God's messengers,' and their
name means only that. Then the word is certainly
used, both in its Hebrew and Greek forms, in reference
to men. It is applied to priests, and even in one
passage, as it would appear, to an officer of the
synagogue. If here we find that each Church had its
angel, who had a letter addressed to him, who is
spoken to in words of rebuke and exhortation, who
could sin and repent, who could be persecuted and die,
who could fall into heresies and be perfected by suffering, it seems to me a violent and unnecessary hypothesis that a superhuman being is in question. And
the name by which he is called need not imply more
than his function,—that of being the messenger and
representative of the Church.

Believing this as the more probable meaning of the
phrase, I see in the relations between these men and
the little communities to which they belonged an
example of what should be found existing between all
congregations of faithful men and the officers whom
they have chosen, be the form of their polity what it
may. There are certain broad principles which must
underlie all Christian organisations, and are incomparably more important than the details of Church
government.

Note then, first, that the messengers are rulers. They
are described in a double manner—by a name which

expresses subordination, and by a figure which expresses authority. I need not do more than remind
you that throughout Scripture, from the time when
Balaam beheld from afar the *star* that should come
out of Jacob and the sceptre that should rise out of
Israel, that has been the symbol for rulers. It is so
notably in this Book of Revelation. Whatever other
ideas, then, are connected with its use here, this leading one of authority must not be lost sight of.

But this double representation of these persons as
being in one aspect servants and in another rulers,
perfectly embodies the very essential characteristic
of all office and power in Christ's Church. It is a
repetition in pictorial form of the great principle, so
sadly forgotten, which He gave when He said, 'He
that is greatest among you, let him be your servant.'
The higher are exalted that they may serve the lower.
Dignity and authority mean liberty for more and more
self-forgetting work. Power binds its possessor to toil.
Wisdom is stored in one, that from him it may flow to
the foolish; strength is given that by its holder feeble
hands may be stayed. *Noblesse oblige.* The King Himself has obeyed the law. 'Jesus, knowing the Father
had given all things into His hands, took a towel, and
girded Himself.' We are redeemed because He came
to minister, and to give His life a ransom for many.
He is among us 'as He that serveth.' God Himself
has obeyed the law. He is above all that He may bless
all. He, the highest, stoops the most deeply. His
dominion is built on love, and stands in giving. And
that law which makes the throne of God the refuge
of all the weak, and the treasury of all the poor, is
given for our guidance in our humble measure. Wheresoever Christian men think more of themselves and of

their dignity than of their brethren and their work; wheresoever gifts are hoarded selfishly or selfishly squandered; wheresoever the accidents of authority, its baubles and signature, its worldly consequences, and its pride of place, bulk larger in its possessors' eyes than its solemn obligations;—there the law is broken, and the heathen devilish notion of rule lays waste the Church of God.

The true idea is not certain to be held, nor its tempting counterfeit to be avoided, by any specific form of organisation. Wherever there are offices, there will be danger of officialism. Where there are none, that will not drive out selfishness. Quakerism and Episcopacy, with every form of Church government that lies between, are in danger from the same source—our forgetfulness that in Christ's kingdom to rule is to serve. All Churches have shown that their messengers could become 'lords over God's heritage.' The true spirit of Christ's servants is not secured by any theory about the appointment or the duties of the servants, but only by fellowship and sympathy with the Master who helps us all, and cares nothing for any glory which He cannot share with His disciples.

But to be servant of all does not mean to do the bidding of all. The service which imitates Christ is helpfulness, not subjection. Neither the Church is to lord it over the messenger, nor the messenger over the Church. The true bond is broken by official claims of dominion; it is broken just as much by popular claims to control. All alike are to stand free from all men— in independence of will, thought, and action; shaping their lives and moulding their beliefs, according to Christ's will and Christ's word; and repelling all coercion, from whatsoever quarter it comes. All alike are by love to serve one another; counting every possession, material, intellectual, and spiritual, as given for the general good.   The one guiding principle is, 'He that is chiefest among you, let him be your servant,' and the other, which guards this from misconstruction and abuse from either side, 'One is your Master, even Christ, and all ye are brethren.'

Another point to be observed in this symbol is, that the messengers and the churches have at bottom the same work to do.

Stars shine, so do lamps.   Light comes from both, in different fashion indeed, and of a different quality, but still both are lights.   These are in the Saviour's hands, those are by His side; but each is meant to stream out rays of brightness over a dark night.   So, essentially, all Christian men have the same work to do.   The ways of doing it differ, but the thing done is one. Whatever be the difference between those who hold offices in God's Church and the bulk of their brethren, there is no difference here.   The loftiest gifts, the most conspicuous position, the closest approach to the central sun, have no other purpose than that which the lowliest powers, in the obscurest corner, are meant to subserve.   The one distributing Spirit divides to each man severally as He will; and whether He endows him with starlike gifts, which soar above and blaze over half the world with lustre that lives through the centuries, or whether He sets him in some cottage window to send out a tiny cone of light, that pierces a little way into the night for an hour or two, and then is quenched—it is all one.   The manifestation of the Spirit is given to every man for the same purpose—to do good with.   And we have all one office and function to be discharged by each in his own fashion—namely,

to give the light of the knowledge of the glory of God
in the face of Christ Jesus.

Again, observe, the Churches and their messengers are
alike in their religious condition and character. The
successive letters treat his strength or weakness, his
fervour or coldness, his sin or victory over evil, as
being theirs. He represents them completely. And
that representative character seems to me to be the
only reason worth considering for supposing that these
angels are superhuman beings, inasmuch as it seems
that the identification is almost too entire to be applicable to the relation of any man to the community.
But, perhaps, if we think of the facts which every
day's experience shows us, we may see even in this
solemn paralleling of the spiritual state of the Churches
and of their servants, a strong reason for holding to
our interpretation, as well as a very serious piece of
warning and exhortation for us all.

For is it not true that the religious condition of a
Church, and that of its leaders, teachers, pastors, ever
tend to the same, as that of the level of water in two
connected vessels? There is such a constant inter-
action and reciprocal influence that uniformity results.
Either a living teacher will, by God's grace, quicken a
languid Church, or a languid Church will, with the
devil's help, stifle the life of the teacher. Take two balls
of iron, one red hot, and one cold, and put them down
beside each other. How many degrees of difference
between them, after half an hour, will your thermometer show? Thank God for the many instances in
which one glowing soul, all aflame with love of God,
has sufficed to kindle a whole heap of dead matter, and
send it leaping skyward in ruddy brightness! Alas!
for the many instances in which the wet, green wood

has been too strong for the little spark, and has
not only obstinately resisted, but has ignominiously
quenched its ineffectual fire! Thank God, that when
His Church lives on a high level of devotion, it has
never wanted for single souls who have towered even
above that height, and have been elevated by it, as the
snowy Alps spring not from the flats of Holland, but
from the high central plateau of Europe. Alas! for
the leaders who have rayed out formalism, and have
chilled down the Church to their own coldness, and
stiffened to their own deadness!

Let us, then, not bandy reproaches from pulpit to
pew, and from pew to pulpit; but remembering that
the spiritual character of each helps to determine the
condition of the whole, and the general condition of
the body determines the vigour of each part, let us go
together to God with acknowledgments of common
faithlessness, and of our individual share in it, and let
us ask Him to quicken His Church, that it may yield
messengers who in their turn shall be the helpers of
His people and the glory of God.

II. The text brings before us the Churches and their
work.

Of course, you understand that what the Apostle
saw was not seven candlesticks, which are a modern
piece of furniture, but seven lamps. There is a distinct
reference in this, as in all the symbols of the Apocalypse, to the Old Testament. We know that in the
Jewish Temple there stood, as an emblem of Israel's
work in the world, the great seven-branched candlestick, burning for ever before the veil and beyond the
altar. The difference between the two symbols is
as obvious as their resemblance. The ancient lamp
had all the seven bowls springing from a single stem.

M

It was a formal unity. The New Testament seer saw not one lamp with seven arms rising from one pillar, but seven distinct lamps—the emblems of a unity which was not formal, but real. They were one in their perfect manifoldness, because of Him who walked in the midst. In which difference lies a representation of one great element in the superiority of the Church over Israel, that for the hard material oneness of the separated nation there has come the true spiritual oneness of the Churches of the saints ; one not because of any external connection, but by reason that Christ is in them. The seven-branched lamp lies at the bottom of the Tiber. There let it lie. We have a better thing, in these manifold lights, which stand before the Throne of the New Temple, and blend into one, because lighted from one Source, fed by one Spirit, tended and watched by one Lord.

But looking a little more closely at this symbol, it suggests to us some needful thoughts as to the position and work of the Church, which is set forth as being light, derived light, clustered light.

The Church is to be light. That familiar image, which applies, as we have seen, to stars and lamps alike, lends itself naturally to point many an important lesson as to what we have to do, and how we ought to do it. Think, for instance, how spontaneously light streams forth. 'Light is light, which circulates.' The substance which is lit cannot but shine ; and if we have any real possession of the truth, we cannot but impart it ; and if we have any real illumination from the Lord, who is the light, we cannot but give it forth. There is much good done in the world by direct, conscious effort. There is perhaps more done by spontaneous, unconscious shining, by the involuntary influence of character, than by the lip or the pen. We need not balance the one form of usefulness against the other. We need both. But, Christian men and women, do you remember that from you a holy impression revealing Jesus ought to flow as constantly, as spontaneously, as light from the sun! Our lives should be like the costly box of fragrant ointment which that penitent, loving woman lavished on her Lord, the sweet, penetrating, subtle odour of which stole through all the air till the house was filled. So His name, the revelation of His love, the resemblance to His character, should breathe forth from our whole being; and whether we think of it or no, we should be unto God a sweet savour of Christ.

Then think again how *silent* and gentle, though so mighty, is the action of the light. Morning by morning God's great mercy of sunrise steals upon a darkened world in still, slow, self-impartation; and the light which has a force that has carried it across gulfs of space that the imagination staggers in trying to conceive, yet falls so gently that it does not move the petals of the sleeping flowers, nor hurt the lids of an infant's eyes, nor displace a grain of dust. Its work is mighty, and done without 'speech or language.' Its force is gigantic, but, like its Author, its gentleness makes its dependents great. So should we live and work, clothing all our power in tenderness, doing our work in quietness, disturbing nothing but the darkness, and with silent increase of beneficent power filling and flooding the dark earth with healing beams.

Then think again that heaven's light is itself *invisible*, and, revealing all things, reveals not itself. The source you can see, but not the beams. So we are to shine, not showing ourselves but our Master—not coveting fame or conspicuousness—glad if, like one to whom He bore testimony that he was a light, it be said of us to all that ask who we are, 'He was not that Light, but was sent to bear witness of that Light,' and rejoicing without stint or reservation that for us, as for John the Baptist, the necessity is, that we must decrease and Christ must increase.

We may gather from this emblem in the text the further lesson that the Church's light is derived light. Two things are needed for the burning of a lamp: that it should be lit, and that it should be fed. In both respects the light with which we shine is derived. We are not suns, we are moons; reflected, not self-originated, is all our radiance. That is true in all senses of the figure: it is truest in the highest. It is true about all in every man which is of the nature of light. Christ is the true light which lighteth every man that cometh into the world. Whatsoever beam of wisdom, whatsoever ray of purity, whatsoever sunshine of gladness has ever been in any human spirit, from Him it came, who is the Light and Life of men: from Him it came, who brings to us in form fitted for our eyes, that otherwise inaccessible light of God in which alone we see light. And as for the more special work of the Church (which chiefly concerns us now), the testimony of Christ to John, which I have just quoted in another connection, gives us the principle which is true about all. 'He was not that light,' the Evangelist said of John, denying that in him was original and native radiance. 'He was a lamp burning'—where the idea is possibly rather 'lighted' or made to burn—and therefore shining, and in whose light men could rejoice for a little while. A derived and transient light is all that any man can be. In ourselves we are darkness, and only as we hold fellowship with Him do we become capable of giving forth any rays of light. The condition of all our brightness is that Christ shall give us light. He is the source, we are but reservoirs. He the fountain, we only cisterns. He must walk amidst the candlesticks, or they will never shine. He must hold the stars in His hand, or they will drop from their places and dwindle into darkness. Therefore our power for service lies in reception; and if we are to live *for* Christ, we must live *in* Christ.

But there is still another requisite for the shining of the light. The prophet Zechariah once saw in vision the great Temple lamp, and by its side two olive trees from which golden oil flowed through golden pipes to the central light. And when he expressed his ignorance of the meaning of the vision, this was the interpretation by the angel who talked with him: 'Not by might, nor by power, but by My Spirit, saith the Lord of Hosts.' The lamp that burns must be kept fed with oil. Throughout the Old Testament the soft, gracious influences of God's Spirit are symbolised by oil, with which therefore prophets, priests, and kings were designated to their office. Hence the Messiah in prophecy says, 'The Spirit of the Lord is upon me, because He hath anointed me.' Thus the lamp too must be fed, the soul which is to give forth the light of Christ must first of all have been kindled by Him, and then must constantly be supplied with the grace and gift of His Divine Spirit. Solemn lessons, my friends, gather round that thought. What became of those who had lamps without oil? Their lamps had gone out, and their end was darkness. Oh! let us beware lest by any sloth and sin we choke the golden pipes, through which there steals into our tiny lamps the soft flow of that Divine oil which alone can keep up the flame. The wick, untrimmed and unfed, may burn for a little while, but it soon chars, and smokes, and goes out at last in foul savour offensive to God and man. Take care lest you resist the Holy Spirit of God. Let your loins be girt and your lamps burning; and that they may be, give heed that the light caught from Jesus be fed by the pure oil which alone can save it from extinction.

Again, the text sets before us the Church's light as blended or clustered light.

Each of these little communities is represented by one lamp. And that one light is composed of the united brightness of all the individuals who constitute the community. They are to have a character, an influence, a work as a society, not merely as individuals. There is to be co-operation in service, there is to be mingling of powers, there is to be subordination of individuals to the whole, and each separate man and his work is to be gladly merged in the radiance that issues from the community. A Church is not to be merely a multitude of separate points of brilliancy, but the separate points are to coalesce into one great orbed brightness. You know these lights which we have seen in public places, where you have a ring pierced with a hundred tiny holes, from each of which bursts a separate flame; but when all are lit, they run into one brilliant circle, and lose their separateness in the rounded completeness of the blended blaze. That is like what Christ's Church ought to be. We each by our own personal contact with Him, by our individual communion with our Saviour, become light in the Lord, and yet we joyfully blend with our brethren, and, fused into one, give forth our mingled light. We

unite our voices to theirs, knowing that all are needed
to send out the Church's choral witness and to hymn
the Church's full-toned praise. The lips of the multitude thunder out harmony, before which the melody of
the richest and sweetest single voice is thin and poor.

Union of heart, union of effort is commended to us
by this symbol of our text. The great law is, work
together if you would work with strength. To separate
ourselves from our brethren is to lose power. Why,
half-dead brands heaped close will kindle one another,
and flame will sparkle beneath the film of white ashes
on their edges. Fling them apart and they go out.
Rake them together and they glow. Let us try not to
be little feeble tapers, stuck in separate sockets, and
each twinkling struggling rays over some inch or so of
space; but draw near to our brethren, and be workers
together with them, that there may rise a glorious
flame from our summed and collective brightness
which shall be a guide and hospitable call to many a
wandering and weary spirit.

III. Finally, the text shows us the Churches and their
Lord.

He it is who holds the stars in His right hand, and
walks among the candlesticks. That strong grasp of
that mighty hand—for the word in the original conveys
more than 'holds,' it implies a tight and powerful grip
—sustains and guards His servants, whose tasks need
special grace, and whose position exposes them to
special dangers. They may be of good cheer, for none
shall pluck them out of His hand. That strengthening
and watchful presence moves among His Churches,
and is active on their behalf. The symbols are but the
pictorial equivalent of His own parting promise, 'Lo, I
am with you always!'

That presence is a plain literal fact, however feebly we lay hold of it. It is not to be watered down into a strong expression for the abiding influence of Christ's teaching or example, nor even to mean the constant benefits which flow to us from His work, nor the presence of His loving thoughts with us. All these things are true and blessed, but none of them, nor all of them taken together, reach to the height of this great promise. He is absent in body, He is present in person. Talk of a 'real presence'! This is *the* real presence: 'I will not leave you orphans, I will come unto you.' Through all the ages, in every land wheresoever two or three are gathered in His name, there is He in the midst of them. The presence of Christ with His Church is analogous to the Divine presence in the material universe. As in it, the presence of God is the condition of all life; and if He were not here, there were no beings and no 'here': so in the Church, Christ's presence constitutes and sustains it, and without Him it would cease. So St. Augustine says, 'Where Christ, there the Church.'

I know what wild absurdities these statements appear to many men who have no faith in the true Divinity of our Lord. Of course the belief of His perpetual presence with His people implies the belief that He possesses Divine attributes. This mysterious Person, who lived among men the exemplar of all humility, departing, leaves a promise which is either the very acme of insane arrogance, or comes from the consciousness of indwelling Divinity. He declares that, from generation to generation, He will in very deed be with all who in every place call upon His name. Who does He thereby claim to be?

For what purpose is He there with His Churches?

The text assures us that it is to hold up and to bless. His unwearied hand sustains, His unceasing activity moves among them. But beyond these purposes, or rather included in them, the vision of which the text is the interpretation brings into great prominence the thought that He is with us to observe, to judge, and, if need be, to punish. Mark how almost all the attributes of that majestic figure suggest such thoughts. The eyes like a flame of fire, the feet glowing as if in a furnace, hot to burn, heavy to tread down all evil where He walks, from the lips a two-edged sword to smite, and, thank God, to heal, the countenance as the sun shineth in his strength—this is the Lord of the Churches. Yes, and this is the same loving and forbearing Lord whom the Apostle had learned to trust on earth, and found again revealed from heaven.

Brethren! He dwells with us; He guards and protects His Churches to the end, else they perish. He rules all the commotions of earth, all the errors of His people, all the delusions of lies, and overrules them all for the strengthening and purifying of His Church. But He dwells with us likewise as the watchful observer, out of these eyes of flame, of all our faults; as the merciful destroyer, with the sword of His mouth, of every error and every sin. Thank God for the chastising presence of Christ. He loves us too well not to smite us when we need it. He will not be so cruelly kind, so foolishly fond, as in anywise to suffer sin upon us. Better the eye of fire than the averted face. Better the sharp sword than His holding His peace as He did with Caiaphas and Herod. Better the Judge in our midst, though we should have to fall at His feet as dead, than that He should say, 'I will go and return to My place.' Pray Him not to depart, and

submit to the merciful rebukes and effectual chastise-
ment which prove that, for all our unworthiness, He
loves us still, and has not cast us away from His
presence.

Nor let us forget how much of hope and encouragement lies in the examples, which these seven Churches
afford, of His long-suffering patience. That presence
was granted to them all, the best and the worst—the
decaying love of Ephesus, the licentious heresies of
Pergamos and Thyatira, the all but total deadness of
Sardis, and the self-satisfied indifference of Laodicea,
concerning which even He could say nothing that was
good. All had Him with them as really as the faithful
Smyrna and the steadfast Philadelphia. We have no
right to say with how much of theoretical error and
practical sin the lingering presence of that patient pitying Lord may consist. For others our duty is the widest
charity — for ourselves the most careful watchful-
ness.

For these seven Churches teach us another lesson—
the possibility of quenched lamps and ruined shrines.
Ephesus and her sister communities, planted by Paul,
taught by John, loved and upheld by the Lord, warned
and scourged by Him—where are they now? Broken
columns and roofless walls remain; and where Christ's
name was praised, now the minaret rises by the side of
the mosque, and daily echoes the Christless proclamation, 'There is no God but God, and Mahomet is His
prophet.' 'The grace of God,' says Luther somewhere,
'is like a flying summer shower.' It has fallen upon
more than one land, and passed on. Judæa had it, and
lies barren and dry. These Asiatic coasts had it and
flung it away. Let us receive it, and hold it fast, lest
our greater light should bring greater condemnation,

and here, too, the candlestick should be removed out of its place.

Remember that solemn, strange legend which tells us that, on the night before Jerusalem fell, the guard of the Temple heard through the darkness a voice mighty and sad, saying, 'Let us depart,' and were aware as of the sound of many wings passing from out of the Holy Place; and on the morrow the iron heels of the Roman legionaries trod the marble pavement of the innermost shrine, and heathen eyes gazed upon the empty place where the glory of the God of Israel should have dwelt, and a torch, flung by an unknown hand, burned with fire the holy and beautiful house where He had promised to put His name for ever. And let us learn the lesson, and hold fast by that Lord whose blood has purchased, and whose presence preserves through all the unworthiness and the lapses of men, that Church against which the gates of hell shall not prevail.

I.—THE VICTOR'S LIFE-FOOD

'. . . To him that overcometh will I give to eat of the tree of life, which is in the midst of the paradise of God.'—REV. ii. 7.

THE sevenfold promises which conclude the seven letters to the Asiatic Churches, of which this is the first, are in substance one. We may, indeed, say that the inmost meaning of them all is the gift of Christ Himself. But the diamond flashes variously coloured lights according to the angle at which it is held, and breaks into red and green and white. The one great thought may be looked at from different points of view, and sparkle into diversely splendid rays. The reality is single and simple, but so great that our best

way of approximating to the apprehension of that
which we shall never comprehend till we possess it is
to blend various conceptions and metaphors drawn
from different sources.

I have a strong conviction that the Christianity of
this day suffers, intellectually and practically, from its
comparative neglect of the teaching of the New Testament as to the future life. We hear and think a great
deal less about it than was once the case, and we are
thereby deprived of a strong motive for action, and a
sure comfort in sorrow. Some of us may, perhaps, be
disposed to look with a little sense of lofty pity at
the simple people who let the hope of heaven spur, or
restrain, or console. But if there is a future life at all,
and if the characteristic of it which most concerns us is
that it is the reaping, in consequences, of the acts of
the present, surely it cannot be such superior wisdom,
as it sometimes pretends to be, to ignore it altogether;
and perhaps the simplicity of the said people is more
in accordance with the highest reason than is our
attitude.

Be that as it may, believing, as I do, that the hope of
immortality is meant to fill a very large place in the
Christian life, and fearing, as I do, that it actually does
fill but a very small one with many of us, I have thought
that it might do us all good to turn to this wealth of
linked promises and to consider them in succession, so
as to bring our hearts for a little while into contact
with the motive for brave fighting which does occupy
so large a space in the New Testament, however it may
fail to do so in our lives.

I. I ask you to look first at the Gift.

Now, of course, I need scarcely remind you that this
first promise, in the last book of Scripture, goes back

to the beginning, to the old story in Genesis about
Paradise and the Tree of Life. We may distinguish
between the substance of the promise and the highly
metaphorical form into which it is here cast. The
substance of the promise is the communication of life;
the form is a poetic and imaginative and pregnant
allusion to the story on the earliest pages of Revelation.

Let me deal first with the substance. Now it seems
to me that if we are to pare down this word 'life' to
its merely physical sense of continuous existence, this
is not a promise that a man's heart leaps up at the
hearing of. To anybody that will honestly think, and
try to realise, in the imperfect fashion in which alone
it is possible for us to realise it, that notion of an
absolutely interminable continuance of being, its
awfulness is far more than its blessedness, and it
overwhelms a man. It seems to me that the 'crown
of life,' if life only means conscious existence, would
be a crown of thorns indeed.

No, brethren, what our hearts crave, and what
Christ's heart gives, is not the mere bare, bald, continuance of conscious being. It is something far deeper
than that. That is the substratum, of course; but it
is only the substratum, and not until we let in upon
this word, which is one of the key-words of Scripture,
the full flood of light that comes to it from John's
Gospel, and its use on the Master's lips there, do we begin
to understand the meaning of this great promise.
Just as we say of men who are sunk in gross animalism, or whose lives are devoted to trivial and transient
aims, that theirs is not worth calling life, so we say
that the only thing that deserves, and that in Scripture
gets, the august name of 'life,' is a condition of exist-

ence in conscious union with, and possession of, God,
who is manifested and communicated to mortals
through Jesus Christ His Son. 'In Him was life, and
the life was manifested.' Was that bare existence?
And the life was not only manifested but communicated, and the essence of it is fellowship with God
through Jesus Christ. The possession of 'the Spirit
of life which was in Christ,' and which in heaven will
be perfectly communicated, will make men 'free,' as
they never can be upon earth whilst implicated in
the bodily life of this material world, 'from the law of
sin and death.' The gift that Christ bestows on him
that 'overcometh' is not only conscious existence, but
existence derived from, and, so to speak, embraided
with the life of God Himself, and therefore blessed.

For such a life, in union with God in Christ, is the
only condition in which all a man's capacities find
their fitting objects, and all his activity finds its
appropriate sphere, and in which, therefore, to live
is to be blessed, because the heart is united with the
source and fountain of all blessedness. Here is the
deepest depth of that promise of future blessedness.
It is not mainly because of any changes, glorious as
these must necessarily be, which follow upon the
dropping away of flesh, and the transportation into
the light that is above, that heaven is a place of
blessedness, but it is because the saints that are there
are joined to God, and into their recipient hearts
there pours for ever the fulness of the Divine life.
That makes the glory and the blessedness.

But let us remember that all which can come hereafter of that full and perfect life is but the continuance, the development, the increase, of that
which already is possessed. Here it falls in drops;

there in floods. Here it is filtered; there poured.
Here, the plant, taken from its native climate and soil,
puts forth some pale blossoms, and grows but to a
stunted height; there, set in their deep native soil,
and shone upon by a more fervent sun, and watered
by more abundant warm rains and dews, 'they that'
on earth 'were planted in the house of the Lord shall,'
transplanted, 'flourish in the courts of our God.' The
life of the Christian soul on earth and of the Christian
soul in heaven is continuous, and though there is a
break to our consciousness looking from this side—the
break of death—the reality is that without interrup-
tion, and without a turn, the road runs on in the same
direction. We begin to live the life of heaven here,
and they who can say, 'I was dead in trespasses and
sins, but the life which I live in the flesh I live by
the faith of the Son of God,' have already the germs of
the furthest development in the heavens in their
hearts.

Notice, for a moment, the form that this great
promise assumes here. That is a very pregnant and
significant reference to the Tree of Life in the paradise
of God. The old story tells how the cherub with the
flaming sword was set to guard the way to it. And
that paradise upon earth faded and disappeared. But
it reappears. 'Then comes a statelier Eden back to
man,' for Jesus Christ is the restorer of all lost
blessings; and the Divine purpose and ideal has not
faded away amidst the clouds of the stormy day of
earth's history, like the flush of morning from off the
plains. Christ brings back the Eden, and quenches the
flame of the fiery sword; and instead of the repellent
cherub, there stands Himself with the merciful invitation upon His lips: 'Come! Eat; and live for ever.'

'There never was one lost good; what was shall live as before.

On the earth the broken arcs ; in heaven the perfect round.'

Eden shall come back ; and the paradise into which the victors go is richer and fuller, by all their conflict and their wounds, than ever could have been the simpler paradise of which souls innocent, because untried, could have been capable. So much for the gift of life.

II. Notice, secondly, the Giver.

This is a majestic utterance ; worthy of coming from the majestic Figure portrayed in the first chapter of this book. In it Jesus Christ claims to be the Arbiter of men's deserts and Giver of their rewards. That involves His judicial function, and therefore His Divine as well as human nature. I accept these words as truly His words. Of course, if you do not, my present remarks have no force for you; but if you do not, you ought to be very sure of your reasons for not doing so; and if you do, then I see not how any man who believes that Jesus Christ has said that He will give to all the multitude of faithful fighters, who have brought their shields out of the battle, and their swords undinted, the gift of life eternal, can be vindicated from the charge of taking too much upon him, except on the belief of His Divine nature.

But I observe, still further, that this great utterance of the Lord's, paralleled in all the other six promises, in all of which He is represented as the bestower of the reward, whatever it may be, involves another thing, viz., the eternal continuance of Christ's relation to men as the Revealer and Mediator of God. 'I will give'—and that not only when the victor crosses the threshold and enters the Capitol of the heavens, but all through its ceaseless ages Christ is the Medium by which the Divine life passes into men. True, there is a sense in which He shall deliver up the kingdom to His Father, when the partial end of the present dispensation has come. But He is the Priest of mankind for ever; and for ever is His kingdom enduring. And through all the endless ages, which we have a right to hope we shall see, there will never come a point in which it will not remain as true as it is at this moment: 'No man hath seen God at any time, nor can see Him; the only begotten Son, which is in the bosom of the Father, He hath declared Him.' Christ is for ever the Giver of life in the heavens as on earth.

Another thing is involved which I think also is often lost sight of. The Bible does not know anything about what people call 'natural immortality.' Life here is not given to the infant once for all, and then expended through the years, but it is continually being bestowed. My belief is that no worm that creeps, nor angel that soars, nor any of the beings between, is alive for one instant except for the continual communication from the fountain of life, of the life that they live. And still more certainly is it true about the future, that there all the blessedness and the existence, which is the substratum and condition of the blessedness, are only ours because, wavelet by wavelet, throbbing out as from a central fountain, there flows into the Redeemed a life communicated by Christ Himself. If I might so say—were that continual bestowment to cease, then heaven, like the vision of a fairy tale, would fade away; and there would be nothing left where the glory had shone. 'I will give' through eternity.

III. Lastly, note the Recipients.

'To him that overcometh.' Now I need not say, in

N

more than a sentence, that it seems to me that the
fair interpretation of this promise, as of all the other
references in Scripture to the future life, is that the
reward is immediately consequent upon the cessation
of the struggle. 'To depart' is 'to be with Christ,' and
to be with Christ, in regard of a spirit which has
passed from the bodily environment, is to be conscious
of His presence, and lapt in His robe, feeling the
warmth and the pressure of His heart. So I believe
that Scripture teaches us that at one moment there
may be the clash of battle, and the whiz of the arrows
round one's head, and next moment there may be the
laurel-crowned quiet of the victor.

But that does not enter so much into our consideration now. We have, rather, here to think of just
this one thing, that the gift is given to the victor because
only the victor is capable of receiving it; that future
life, interpreted as I have ventured to interpret it in
this sermon, is no arbitrary bestowment that could be
dealt all round miscellaneously to everybody, if the
Giver chose so to give. Here on earth many gifts are
bestowed upon men, and are neglected by them, and
wasted like water spilled upon the ground; but this
elixir of life is not poured out so. It is only poured
into vessels that can take it in and hold it.

Our present struggle is meant to make us capable of
the heavenly life. And that is—I was going to say the
only, but at all events—incomparably the chiefest, of
the thoughts which make life not only worth living,
but great and solemn. Go into a mill, and in a quiet
room, often detached from the main building, you will
find the engine working, and seeming to do nothing
but go up and down. But there is a shaft which goes
through the wall and takes the power to the looms.

We are working here, and we are making the cloth that we shall have to own and say, 'Yes, it *is* my manufacture!' when we get yonder. According to our life to-day will be our destiny in the great to-morrow. Life is given to the victor, because the victor only is capable of possessing it.

But the victor can only conquer in one way. 'This,' said John, when he was not an apocalyptic seer, but a Christian teacher to the Churches of Asia, 'this is the victory that overcometh the world, even our faith.' If we trust in Christ we shall get His power into our hearts, and if we get His power into our hearts, then 'we shall be more than conquerors through Him that loved us.' Christ gives life eternal, gives it here in germ and yonder in fulness. In its fulness only those who overcome are capable of receiving it. Those only who fight the good fight by His help overcome. Those only who trust in Him fight the good fight by His help. He gives to eat of the Tree of Life; He gives it to faith, but faith must be militant. He gives it to the conqueror, but the conqueror must win by faith in Him who overcame the world for us, who will help us to overcome the world by Him.

Help us, O our God, we beseech Thee; 'teach our hands to war, and our fingers to fight.' Give us grace to hold fast by the life which is in Jesus Christ; and living by Him the lives which we live in the flesh, may we be capable, by the discipline of earth's sorrows, of that rest and fuller 'life which remaineth for the people of God.'

II.—THE VICTOR'S LIFE-CROWN

'. . . He that overcometh shall not be hurt of the second death.'—Rev. ii. 11.

Two of the seven Churches, viz., Smyrna, to which our text is addressed, and Philadelphia—offered nothing, to the pure eyes of Christ, that needed rebuke. The same two, and these only, were warned to expect persecution. The higher the tone of Christian life in the Church, the more likely it is to attract dislike and, if circumstances permit, hostility. Hence the whole gist of this letter is to encourage to steadfastness, even if the penalty is death.

That purpose determined at once the aspect of Christ which is presented in the beginning, and the aspect of future blessedness which is held forth at the close. The aspect of Christ is—'these things saith the First and the Last, which was dead and is alive'; a fitting thought to encourage the men who were to be called upon to die for Him. And, in like manner, the words of our text naturally knit themselves with the previous mention of death as the penalty of the Smyrneans' faithfulness.

Now this promise is sharply distinguished from those to the other Churches by two peculiarities: one, that it is merely negative, whilst all the rest are radiantly positive; the other, that there is no mention of our Lord in it, whilst in all the others He stands forth with His emphatic and majestic '*I* will give'; '*I* will write upon him My new Name'; '*I* will make him a pillar in the temple of My God.' The first peculiarity may partially account for the second, because the Giver is naturally more prominent in a promise of positive gifts, than in one of a merely negative exemption. But another reason is to be found for the omission of the mention of our Lord in this promise. If you will refer to the verse immediately preceding my text, you will find the missing positive promise with the missing reference to Jesus Christ: 'I will give thee a crown of life.' So that we are naturally led to link together both these statements when taking account of the hopes that were held forth to animate the Christians of Smyrna in the prospect of persecution even to the death; and we have to consider them both in conjunction now. I think I shall best do so by simply asking you to look at these two things: the Christian motive contained in the victor's immunity from a great evil, and the Christian motive contained in the victor's possession of a great good. 'He shall not be hurt of the second death.' 'I will give thee a crown of life.'

I. The Christian motive contained in the victor's immunity from a great evil.

Now that solemn and thrilling expression 'the second death' is peculiar to this book of the Apocalypse. The *name* is peculiar; the *thing* is common to all the New Testament writers. Here it comes with especial appropriateness, in contrast with the physical death which was about to be inflicted upon some members of the Smyrnean Church. But beyond that there lies in the phrase a very solemn and universally applicable meaning. I do not feel, dear brethren, that such a thing ought to be made matter of pulpit rhetoric. The bare vagueness of it seems to me to shake the heart a great deal more than any weakening expansion of it that we can give.

But yet, let me say one word. Then, behind that grim figure, the shadow feared of man that waits for all at some turn of their road, cloaked and shrouded, there rises a still grimmer and more awful form, 'if form it can be called which form hath none.' There *is* something, at the back of physical death, which can lay its grip upon the soul that is already separated from the body; something running on the same lines somehow, and worthy to bear that name of terror and disintegration—'the second death.' What can it be? Not the cessation of conscious existence; that is never the meaning of death. But let us apply the key which opens so many of the locks of the New Testament sayings about the future that the true and deepest meaning of *death* is separation from Him who is the fountain of life, and in a very deep sense is the only life of the universe. Separation from God; *that* is death. What touches the surface of mere bodily life is but a faint shadow and parable, and the second death, like a second tier of mountains, rises behind and above it, sterner and colder than the lower hills of the foreground. What desolation, what unrest, what blank misgivings, what pealing off of capacities, faculties, opportunities, delights, may be involved in that solemn conception, we never can tell here—God grant that we may never know! Like some sea-creature, cast high and dry on the beach, and gasping out its pained being, the men that are separated from God die whilst they live, and live a living death. The second is the comparative degree, of which the first is the positive.

Now note again that immunity from this solemn fate is no small part of the victor's blessedness. At first sight we feel as if the mere negative promise of my text stands on a lower level than what I have called the radiantly positive ones in the other letters; but it is worthy to stand beside these. Gather them to-

gether, and think of how manifold and glorious the
dim suggestions which they make of felicity and progress are, and then set by the side of them this one of
our text as worthy to stand there.   To eat of the Tree
of Life; to have power over the nations; to rule them
with a rod of iron; to blaze with the brightness of the
morning star; to eat of the hidden manna; to bear the
new name known only to those who receive it; to have
that name confessed before the Father and His angels;
to be a pillar in the Temple of the Lord; to go no
more out; and to sit with Christ on His throne:—these
are the positive promises, along with which this barely
negative one is linked, and is worthy to be linked:
'He shall not be hurt of the second death.'

If this immunity from that fate is fit to stand in
line with these glimpses of an inconceivable glory, how
solemn must be the fate, and how real the danger of our
falling into it!   Brethren, in this day it has become
unfashionable to speak of that future, especially of its
sterner aspects.   The dimness of the brightest revelations in the New Testament, the unwillingness to accept
it as the source of certitude with regard to the future,
the recoil from the stern severity of Divine retribution,
the exaggerated and hideous guise in which that great
truth was often presented in the past, the abounding
worldliness of this day, many of its best tendencies and
many of its worst ones concur in making some of us
look with very little interest, and scarcely credence, at
the solemn words of which the New Testament is full.
But I, for my part, accept them; and I dare not but,
in such proportion to the rest of revelation as seems to
me to be right, bring them before you.   I beseech you,
recognise the solemn teaching that lies in this thought,
that this negative promise of immunity from the second

death stands parallel with all these promises of felicity and blessedness.

Further, note that such immunity is regarded here as the direct outcome of the victor's conduct and character. I have already pointed out the peculiarities marking our text. The omission of any reference to our Lord in it is accounted for, as suggested, by that reference occurring in the immediately preceding context, but it may also be regarded as suggesting—when considered in contrast with the other promises, where He stands forward as the giver of heavenly blessedness— that that future condition is to be regarded not only as retribution, which implies the notion of a judge, and a punitive or rewarding energy on his part, but also as being the necessary result of the earthly life that is lived ; a harvest of which we sow the seeds here.

Transient deeds consolidate into permanent character. Beds of sandstone rock, thousands of feet thick, are the sediment dropped from vanished seas, or borne down by long dried-up rivers. The actions which we often so unthinkingly perform, whatever may be the width and the permanency of their effects external to us, react upon ourselves, and tend to make our permanent bent or twist or character. The chalk cliffs at Dover are the skeletons of millions upon millions of tiny organisms, and our little lives are built up by the recurrence of transient deeds, which leave their permanent marks upon us. They make character, and character determines position yonder. As said the Apostle, with tender sparingness, and yet with profound truth, ' he went to *his own place*,' wherever that was. The surroundings that he was fitted for came about him, and the company that he was fit for associated themselves with him. So in another part of this book where the same solemn expression, 'the second death,' is employed, we read, 'These shall have their *part* in . . . the second death': the lot that belongs to them. Character and conduct determine position. However small the lives here, they settle the far greater ones hereafter, just as a tiny wheel in a machine may, by cogs and other mechanical devices, transmit its motion to another wheel at a distance, many times its diameter. You move this end of a lever through an arc of an inch, and the other end will move through an arc of yards. The little life here determines the sweep of the great one that is lived yonder. The victor wears his past conduct and character, if I may so say, as a fireproof garment, and if he entered the very furnace, heated seven times hotter than before, there would be no smell of fire upon him. 'He that overcometh shall not be hurt of the second death.'

II. Now note, secondly, the Christian motive contained in the victor's reception of a great good.

'I will give him a crown of life.' I need not remind you, I suppose, that this metaphor of 'the crown' is found in other instructively various places in the New Testament. Paul, for instance, speaks of his own personal hope of 'the crown of righteousness.' James speaks, as does the letter to the Smyrnean Church, of 'the crown of life.' Peter speaks 'of the crown of glory.' Paul, in another place, speaks of 'the crown incorruptible.' And all these express substantially the one idea. There may be a question as to whether the word employed here for the crown is to be taken in its strictly literal acceptation as meaning, not a kingly coronal, but a garland. But seeing that, although that is the strict meaning of the word, it is employed in a subsequent part of the letter to designate what must

evidently be kingly crowns—viz., in the fourth chapter
—there seems to be greater probability in the supposition that we are warranted in including under the
symbolism here both the aspects of the crown as royal,
and also as laid upon the brows of the victors in the
games or the conflict. I venture to take it in that
meaning. Substantially the promise is the same as
that which we were considering in the previous letter,
'I will give him to eat of the Tree of Life'; the promise
of life in all the depth and fulness and sweep of that
great encyclopædical word. But it is life considered
from a special point of view that is set forth here.

It is a *kingly* life. Of course that notion of regality
and dominion, as the prerogative of the redeemed and
glorified servants of Jesus Christ, is for ever cropping
up in this book of the Revelation. And you remember
how our Lord has set the example of its use when
He said, 'Have thou authority over ten cities.'
What may lie in that great symbol it is not for us
to say. The rule over ourselves, over circumstances,
the deliverance from the tyranny of the external, the
deliverance from the slavery of the body and its lusts
and passions, these are all included. The man that can
will rightly, and can do completely as he rightly wills,
that man is a king. But there is more than that.
There is the participation in wondrous, and for us inconceivable, ways, in the majesty and regality of the
King of kings and Lord of lords. Therefore did the
crowned elders before the throne sing a new song to the
Lamb, who made redeemed men out of every tribe and
tongue, to be to God a kingdom, and priests who should
reign upon the earth.

But, brethren, remember that this conception of a
kingly life is to be interpreted according to Christ's

own teaching of that wherein royalty in His kingdom consists. For heaven, as for earth, the purpose of dominion is service, and the use of power is beneficence. 'He that is chiefest of all, let him be servant of all,' is the law for the regalities of heaven as well as for the lowliness of earth.

That life is a *triumphant* life. The crown was laid on the head of the victor in the games. Think of the victor as he went back, flushed and modest, to his village away up on the slopes of some of the mountain-chains of Greece. With what a tumult of acclaim he would be hailed! If we do our work and fight our fight down here as we ought, we shall enter into the great city not unnoticed, not unwelcomed, but with the praise of the King and the pæans of His attendants. 'I will confess his name before My Father and the holy angels.'

That life is a *festal* life. The garlands are twined on the heated brows of revellers, and the fumes of the wine and the closeness of the chamber soon make them wilt and droop. This amaranthine crown fadeth never. And the feast expresses for us the felicities, the abiding satisfactions without satiety, the blessed companionship, the repose which belong to the crowned. Royalty, triumph, festal goodness, all fused together, are incomplete, but they are not useless symbols. May we experience their fulfilment!

Brethren, the crown is promised not merely to the man that says, 'I have faith in Jesus Christ,' but to him who has worked out his faith into faithfulness, and by conduct and character has made himself capable of the felicities of the heavens. If that immortal crown were laid upon the head of another, it would be a crown of thorns; for the joys of that future require the fitness which comes from the apprenticeship to faith and faithfulness here on earth. We evangelical preachers are often taunted with preaching that future blessedness comes as the result of the simple act of belief. Yes; but only if, and when, the simple act of faith, which is more than belief, is wrought out in the loveliness of faithfulness. 'We are made partakers of Christ, if we hold fast the beginning of our confidence firm unto the end.'

Now, dear friends, I dare say that some of you may be disposed to brush aside these fears and hopes as very low motives, unworthy to be appealed to; but I cannot so regard them. I know that the appeal to fear is directed to the lower order of sentiments, but it is a legitimate motive. It is meant to stir us up to gird ourselves against the dangers which we wisely dread. And I, for my part, believe that we preachers are going aside from our Pattern, and are flinging away a very powerful weapon, in the initial stages of religious experience, if we are afraid to bring before men's hearts and answering consciences the solemn facts of the future which Jesus Christ Himself has revealed to us. We are no more to be blamed for it than the signalman for waving his red flag. And I fancy that there are some of my present hearers who would be nearer the love of God if they took more to heart the fear of the Lord and of His judgment.

Hope is surely a perfectly legitimate motive to appeal to. We are not to be good because we thereby escape hell and secure heaven. We are to be good, because Jesus Christ wills us to be, and has won us to love Him, or has sought to win us to love Him, by His great sacrifice for us. But that being the basis, men can be brought to build upon it by the compulsion of fear and by the attraction of hope. And that being the deepest motive, there is a perfectly legitimate and noble sphere for the operation of these two other lower motives, the consideration of the personal evils that attend the opposite course, and of the personal good that follows from cleaving to Him. Am I to be told that Polycarp, Bishop of Smyrna, who went to his martyrdom, and was 'faithful unto death,' with the words on his lips: 'Eighty-and-six years have I served Him, and He has done me nothing but good; how shall I deny my King and my Saviour!' was yielding to a low motive when to him the crown that the Master promised to the Church of which he was afterwards bishop floated above the head that was soon to be shorn off, and on whose blood-stained brows it was then to fall? Would that we had more of such low motives! Would that we had more of such high lives as fear nothing because they 'have respect to the recompense of the reward,' and are ready for service or martyrdom, because they hear and believe the crowned Christ saying to them: 'Be thou faithful unto death, and I will give thee a crown of life.'

III.—THE VICTOR'S LIFE-SECRET

'... To him that overcometh will I give to eat of the hidden manna, and will give him a white stone, and in the stone a new name written, which no man knoweth saving he that receiveth it.'—REV. ii. 17.

THE Church at Pergamos, to which this promise is addressed, had a sharper struggle than fell to the lot of the two Churches whose epistles precede this. It was set 'where Satan's seat is.' Pergamos was a special centre of heathen worship, and already the blood of a faithful martyr had been shed in it. The severer the struggle, the nobler the reward. Consequently the promise given to this militant Church surpasses, in some respects, those held out to the former two. They were substantially promised that life eternal, which indeed includes everything; but here some of the blessed contents of that life are expanded and emphasised.

There is a threefold promise given: 'the hidden manna,' 'the white stone,' a 'new name' written. The first and the last of these are evidently the most important. They need little explanation; of the central one 'the white stone,' a bewildering variety of interpretations—none of them, as it seems to me, satisfactory—have been suggested. Possibly there may be an allusion to the ancient custom of dropping the votes of the judges into an urn—a white pebble meaning innocence and acquittal; black meaning guilty—just as we, under somewhat similar circumstances, talk about 'blackballing.' But the objection to that interpretation lies in the fact that the 'white stone' of our text is *given* to the person concerned, and not deposited elsewhere. There may be an allusion to a practice, which antiquarians have hunted out, of conferring upon the victors in the games a little tile with a name inscribed upon it, which gave admission to the public festivals. But all the explanations are so doubtful that one hesitates to accept any of them. There remains one other alternative, which seems to me to be suggested by the very language of the text, viz., that the 'white stone' is here named—with possibly some subsidiary thought of innocence and purity—merely as the vehicle for the name. And so I dismiss it from further consideration, and concentrate our thoughts on the remaining two promises.

I. We have the victor's food, the manna.

That seems, at first sight, a somewhat infelicitous symbol, because manna was wilderness food. But that characteristic is not to be taken into account. Manna, though it fell in the wilderness, came from heaven, and it is the heavenly food that is suggested by the symbol. When the warrior passes from the fight into the city, the food which came down from heaven will be given to him in fulness. It is a beautiful thought that as soon as the man, 'spent with changing blows,' and weary with conflict, enters the land of peace, there is a table spread for him; not, as before, in 'the presence of his enemies,' but in the presence of the companions of his repose. One moment hears the din of the battlefield, the next moment feels the refreshment of the heavenly manna.

But now there can be little need for dealing, by way of exposition, with this symbol. Let us rather try to lay it upon our hearts.

Now the first thing that it plainly suggests to us is the absolute satisfaction of all the hunger of the heart. It is possible, and for those that overcome it will one day be actual experience, that a man shall have everything that he wishes the moment that he wishes it. Here we have to suppress desires, sometimes because they are illegitimate and wrong, sometimes because circumstances sternly forbid their indulgence. There, to desire will be to have, and partly by the rectifying of the appetite, partly by the fulness of the supply, there will be no painful sense of vacuity, and no clamouring of the unsubdued heart for good that is beyond its reach. They — and you and I may be amongst them, and so we may say '*we*'—'shall hunger no more, neither thirst any more.' Oh, brethren! to us who are driven into activity by desires, half of which go to water and are never fulfilled—to us who know what it is to try to tame down the hungering, yelping wishes and longings of our souls—to us who have so often spent our 'money for that which is not bread, and our labour for that which satisfieth not,' it ought to be a Gospel: 'I will give him to eat of the hidden manna.' Is it such to you? Do you believe it possible, and are you addressing yourselves to make the fulfilment of it actual in your case?

Then there is the other plain thing suggested here, that that satisfaction does not dull the edge of appetite or desire. Bodily hunger is fed, is replete, wants nothing more until the lapse of time and digestion have intervened. But it is not so with the loftiest satisfactions. There are some select, noble, blessed desires even here, concerning which we know that the more we have, the more we hunger with a hunger which has no pain in it, but is only the greatened capacity for greater enjoyment. You that know what happy love is know what that means—a satisfaction which never approaches satiety, a hunger which has in it no gnawing. And in the loftiest and most perfect of all realms, that co-existence of perfect fruition and perfect desire will be still more wondrously and blessedly manifest. At each moment the more we have, the wider will our hearts be expanded by possession, and the wider they are expanded the more will they be capable of receiving, and the more they are capable of receiving the more deep and full and blessed and all-covering will be the inrush of the river of the water of life. Satisfaction without satiety, food which leaves him blessedly appetised for larger bestowments, belong to the victor.

Another thing to be noticed here is what we have already had occasion to point out in the previous promises: 'I will give him.' Do you remember our Lord's own wonderful words: 'Blessed are those servants, whom the Lord when He cometh shall find watching: verily I say unto you, that He shall gird Himself, and shall come forth and serve them'? The victor is seated at the board, and the Prince, as in some earthly banquet to a victorious army, Himself moves up and down amongst the tables, and supplies the wants of the guests. There was an old Jewish tradition, which perhaps may have influenced the form of this promise, to the effect that the Messiah, when He came, would bring again to the people the gift of the manna, and men should once more eat angels' food. Whether there is any allusion to that poetic fancy or no in the words of my text, the reality infinitely transcends it. Christ Himself bestows upon His servants the sustenance of their spirits in the realm above. But there is more than that. Christ is not only the Giver, but He is Himself the Food. I believe that the deepest meaning of this sevenfold cluster of jewels, the promises to these seven Churches, is in each case Christ. He is the Tree of Life; He is the Crown of Life, He *is* —as well as *gives*—'the hidden manna.' You will remember how He Himself gives us this interpretation when, in answer to the Jewish taunt, 'Our fathers did eat manna in the wilderness. What dost Thou work?' He said, 'I am that Bread of God that came down from heaven.'

So, then, once more, we come back to the all-important teaching that, whatever be the glories of the perfected flower and fruit in heaven, the germ and root of it is already here. The man who lives upon

o

the Christ by faith, love, obedience, imitation, communion, aspiration, here on earth, has already the earnest of that feast. No doubt there will be aspects and sweetnesses and savours and sustenance in the heavenly form of our possession of, and living on, Him, which we here on earth know nothing about. But no doubt also the beginning and positive degree of all these sweetnesses and savours and sustenances yet to be revealed is found in the experience of the man who has listened to the cry of that loving voice, 'Eat, and your souls shall live'; and has taken Jesus Christ Himself, the living Person, to be not only the source but the nourishment of his spiritual life.

So, brethren, it is of no use to pretend to ourselves that we should like—as they put it in bald, popular language—to 'go to heaven,' unless we are using and relishing that of heaven which is here to-day. If you do not like the earthly form of feeding upon Jesus Christ, which is trusting Him, giving your heart to Him, obeying Him, thinking about Him, treading in His footsteps, you would not like, you would like less, the heavenly form of that feeding upon Him. If you would rather have the strong-smelling garlic and the savoury leeks—to say nothing about the swine's trough and the husks—than 'this light bread,' the 'angels' food,' which your palates cannot stand and your stomachs cannot digest, you could not swallow it if it were put into your lips when you get beyond the grave; and you would not like it if you could. Christ forces this manna into no man's mouth; but Christ gives it to all who desire it and are fit for it. As is the man's appetite, so is the man's food; and so is the life that results therefrom.

II. Note the victor's new name.

I have often had occasion to point out to you that
Scripture attaches, in accordance with Eastern habit,
large importance to names, which are intended to be
significant of character, or circumstances, or parental
hopes or desires. So that, both in reference to God
and man, names come to be the condensed expression
of the character and the personality. When we read,
'I will give him a stone, on which there is a new name
written,' we infer that the main suggestion made in
that promise is of a change in the self, something new
in the personality and the character. I need not dwell
upon this, for we have no material by which to expand
into detail the greatness of the promise. I would only
remind you of how we are taught to believe that the
dropping away of the corporeal and removal from
this present scene carries with it, in the case of those
who have here on earth begun to walk with Christ,
and to become citizens of the spiritual realm, changes
great, ineffable, and all tending in the one direction of
making the servants more fully like their Lord. What
new capacities may be evolved by the mere fact of
losing the limitations of the bodily frame; what new
points of contact with a new universe; what new
analogues of what we here call our senses and means
of perception of the external world may be the accom-
paniments of the disembarrassment from 'the earthly
house of this tabernacle,' we dare not dream. We
could not, if we were told, rightly understand. But,
surely, if the tenant is taken from a clay hut and set
in a royal house, eternal, not made with hands, its
windows must be wider and more transparent, and
there must be an inrush of wondrously more brilliant
light into the chambers.

But whatsoever be these changes, they are changes

that repose upon that which has been in the past.
And so the second thought that is suggested by this
new name is that these changes are the direct results
of the victor's course. Both in old times and in the
peerage of England you will find names of conquerors,
by land or by water, who carry in their designations
and transmit to their descendants the memorial of
their victories in their very titles. In like manner as a
Scipio was called Africanus, as a Jervis became Lord
St. Vincent, so the victor's 'new name' is the concen-
tration and memorial of the victor's conquest. And
what we have wrought and fought here on earth we
carry with us, as the basis of the changes from glory
to glory which shall come in the heavens. 'They rest
from their labours; their works do follow them,' and,
gathering behind the laurelled victor, attend him as he
ascends the hill of the Lord.

But once more we come to the thought that whatever there may be of change in the future, the main
direction of the character remains, and the consolidated
issues of the transient deeds of earth remain, and the
victor's name is the summing up of the victor's life.

But, further, Christ gives the name. He changed
the names of His disciples. Simon He called Cephas,
James and John He called 'Sons of Thunder.' The act
claimed authority, and designated a new relation to
Him. Both these ideas are conveyed in the promise:
'I will give him . . . a new name written.' Only,
brethren, remember that the transformation keeps
true to the line of direction begun here, and the process of change has to be commenced on earth. They
who win the new name of heaven are they of whom it
would be truly said, while they bore the old name of
earth, 'If any man be in Christ he is a new creature.'

'Old things are passed away; behold, all things are become new.'

III. Lastly, note the mystery of both the food and the name.

'I will give him the hidden manna . . . a new name . . . which no man knoweth saving he that receiveth it.' Now we all know that the manna was laid up in the Ark, beneath the Shekinah, within the curtain of the holiest place. And, besides that, there was a Jewish tradition that the Ark and its contents, which disappeared after the fall of Jerusalem and the destruction of the first Temple, had been buried by the prophet Jeremiah, and lay hidden away somewhere on the sacred soil, until the Messiah should return. There may be an allusion to that here, but it is not necessary to suppose it. The pot of manna lay in the Ark of the Covenant, of which we hear in another part of the symbolism in this book, within the veil in the holiest of all. And Christ gives the victor to partake of that sacred and secret food. The name which is given 'no man knoweth saving he that receiveth it.' Both symbols point to the one thought, the impossibility of knowing until we possess and experience.

That impossibility besets all the noblest, highest, purest, divinest emotions and possessions of earth. Poets have sung of love and sorrow from the beginning of time; but men must love to know what love means. Every woman has heard about the sweetness of maternity, but not till the happy mother holds her infant to her breast does she understand it. And so we may talk till Doomsday, and yet it would remain true that we must eat the manna, and look upon the white stone for ourselves, before we can adequately comprehend.

Since, then, experience alone admits to the know-

ledge, how vulgar, how futile, how absolutely destructive of the very purpose which they are intended to
subserve are all the attempts of men to forecast that
ineffable glory. It is too great to be understood. The
mountains that ring us round keep the secret well of
the fair lands beyond. There are questions that bleeding hearts sometimes ask, questions which prurient
curiosity more often ask, and which foolish people to-
day are taking illegitimate means of solving, about
that future life, which are all left—though some of
them might conceivably have been answered — in
silence. Enough for us to listen to the voice that says,
'In My Father's house are many mansions'—room for
you and me—' if it were not so I would have told you.'
For the silence is eloquent. The curtain is the picture.
The impossibility of telling is the token of the greatness of the thing to be told. Hope needs but little yarn
to weave her web with. I believe that the dimness is
part of the power of that heavenly prospect. Let us
be reticent before it. Let us remember that, though
our knowledge is small and our eyes dim, Christ knows
all, and we shall be with Him; and so say, with no
sense of pained ignorance or unsatisfied curiosity,
'It doth not yet appear what we shall be, but we know
that when He shall appear we shall be like Him, for
we shall see Him as He is.' Cannot our hearts add, 'It
is enough for the servant that he be as his master'?

An old commentator on this verse says, 'Wouldst
thou know what manner of new name thou shalt bear?
Overcome. It is vain for thee to ask beforehand. Hereafter thou shalt soon see it written on the white stone.'

Help us, O Lord, to fight the good fight of faith, in
the sure confidence that Thou wilt receive us, and re-
fresh us, and renew us.

THE FIRST AND LAST WORKS

' I know thy last works . . . to be more than the first.'—REV. ii. 19.

IT is beautiful to notice that Jesus Christ, in this letter, says all He can of praise before He utters a word of blame. He is glad when His eye, which is as a flame of fire, sees in His children that which He can commend. Praise from Him is praise indeed ; and it does not need that the act should be perfect in order to get His commendation. The main thing is, which way does it look ? Direction, and not attainment, is what He commends. And if the deed of the present moment be better than the deed of the last, though there be still a great gap between it and absolute completeness, the commendation of my text applies, and is never grudgingly rendered. 'I know thy last done works to be more than the first.'

There is blame in plenty, grave, and about grave matters, following in this letter, but that is not permitted in the slightest degree to diminish the warmth and heartiness of the commendation.

I. So these words tell us, first, what every Christian life is meant to be.

A life of continual progress, in which each 'to-morrow shall be as this day, and much more abundant,' in reference to all that is good and noble and true is the ideal after which every Christian man, by his profession, is bound to aim, because in the gospel that we say we believe there lie positively infinite powers to make us perfectly pure and noble and complete all round. And in it there lie, if we lay them upon our hearts, and let them work, positively omnipotent motives, to impel us with unwearied and ever-growing earnestness towards likeness to the Master whom we say we love and serve. A continuous progress towards and in all good of every sort is the very law of the Christian life.

The same law holds good in regard to all regions of life. Everybody knows, and a hundred commonplace proverbs tell us, that practice makes perfect, that the man who carries a little weight to-day will be able to carry a bigger one to-morrow; that powers exercised are rewarded by greater strength; that he that begins by a short march, though he is wearied after he has walked a mile or two, will be able to walk a great deal farther the next day. In all departments of effort it is true that the longer we continue in a course, the easier ought it be to do the things, and the larger ought to be the results. The fruit tree does not begin to bear for a year or two, and when it does come the crop is neither in size nor in abundance anything to compare with that which is borne afterwards.

In the same way, for the Christian course, continual progress and an ever-widening area of the life conquered for and filled with Christ, manifestly ought to be the law. 'Forgetting the things that are behind, reaching forth toward the things that are before, we press toward the mark.' Every metaphor about the life of the Christian soul carries the same lesson. Is it a building? Then course by course it rises. Is it a tree? Then year by year it spreads a broader shadow, and its leafy crown reaches nearer heaven. Is it a body? Then from childhood to youth, and youth to manhood, it grows. Christianity is growth, continual, all-embracing, and unending.

II. The next remark that I make is this, the com-

mendation of Christ describes what a sadly large proportion of professedly Christian lives are not.

Do you think, brethren, that if He were to come
amongst us now with these attributes which the context
gives us, with His 'eyes like unto a flame of fire' to
behold, and His 'feet like unto fine brass' to tread
down all opposition and evil, He would find amongst
us what would warrant His pure lips in saying this
about us, either as a community or as individuals—'I
know that thy last works are more than thy first'?

What is the ordinary history of the multitudes of
professing Christians? Something which they call—
rightly or wrongly is not the question for the moment
—'conversion,' then a year or two, or perhaps a month
or two, or perhaps a week or two, or perhaps a day or
two, of profound earnestness, of joyful consecration,
of willing obedience—and then back swarm the old
ties, and habits, and associations. Many professing
Christians are cases of arrested development, like some
of those monstrosities that you see about our pavements—a full-grown man in the upper part with no
under limbs at all to speak of, aged half a century, and
only half the height of a ten-year-old child. Are there
not multitudes of so-called Christian people, in all our
churches and communities, like that? I wonder if
there are any of them here to-night, that have not
grown a bit for years, whose deeds yesterday were just
the same as their deeds to-day, and so on through a
long, dreary, past perspective of unprogressive life,
the old sins cropping up with the old power and venom,
the old weak bits in the dyke bursting out again every
winter, and at each flood, after all tinkering and mend-
ing, the old faults as rampant as ever, the new life as
feeble, fluttering, spasmodic, uncertain. They grow, if

at all, by fits and starts, after the fashion, say, of a tree that every winter goes to sleep, and only makes wood for a little while in the summer time. Or they do not grow even as regularly as that, but there will come sometimes an hour or two of growth, and then long dreary tracts in which there is no progress at all, either in understanding of Christian doctrine or in the application of Christian precept; no increase of conformity to Jesus Christ, no increase of realising hold of His love, no clearer or more fixed and penetrating contemplation of the unseen realities, than there used to be long, long ago. How many of us are babes in Christ when we have grey hairs upon our heads, and when for the time we ought to be teachers have need that one should teach us again which be the first principles of the oracles of God?

Oh! dear friends, it seems to me sometimes that that notion of the continuous growth in Christian understanding and feeling and character, as attaching to the very essence of the Christian life, is clean gone out of the consciousness of half the professing Christians of this day. How far our notions about Church fellowship, and reception of people into the Church, and the like, have to do with it, is not for me to discuss here. Only this I cannot help feeling, that if Jesus Christ came into most of our congregations nowadays He would not, and could not, say what He said to these poor people at Thyatira, 'I know thy last works are more than thy first.'

Well, then, let us remember that if He cannot say that, He has to say the opposite. I take it that the words of my text are a distinct allusion to other words of His, when He spoke the converse, about the 'last state of that man as worse than the first.' The allusion

is obvious, I think, and it is also made in the Second
Epistle of Peter, where we find a similar description of
the man who has fallen away from Jesus Christ. Let us
learn the lesson that either to-day is better than yesterday or it is worse. If a man on a bicycle stands still,
he tumbles. The condition of keeping upright is to
go onwards. If a climber on an Alpine ice-slope does
not put all his power into the effort to ascend, he cannot stick at the place, at an angle of forty-five degrees
upon ice, but down he is bound to go. Unless, by effort,
he overcomes gravitation, he will be at the bottom very
soon. And so, if Christian people are not daily getting
better, they are daily getting worse. And this will be
the end of it, the demon that was cast out will go back
to his house, which he finds 'swept and garnished'
indeed, but 'empty,' because there is no all-filling
principle of love to Jesus Christ living in it. He finds
it empty. Nature abhors a vacuum; and in he goes
with his seven friends; and 'the last of that man is
worse than the first.'

There are two alternatives before us. I would that
I could feel for myself always, and that you felt for
yourselves, that one or other of them must describe us
as professing Christians. Either we are getting more
Christlike or we are daily getting less so.

III. Lastly, my text, in its relation to this whole
letter, suggests how this commendation may become
ours.

Notice the context. Christ says, according to the
improved reading which will be found in the Revised
Version : 'I know thy works, and love, and faith, and
service' (or ministry), 'and patience, and that thy last
works are more than the first.' That is to say, the great
way by which we can secure this continual growth in the

manifestations of Christian life is by making it a habit to cultivate what produces it, viz., these two things, charity (or love) and faith.

These are the roots; they need cultivating. A Christian man's love to Jesus Christ will not grow of itself any more than his faith will. Unless we make a conscience by prayer, by reading of the Scriptures, by subjecting ourselves to the influences provided for the purpose in His word, of strengthening our faith and warming our love, both will dwindle and become fruitless, bearing 'nothing but leaves' of barren though glittering profession. You need to cultivate faith and love just as much as to cultivate any other faculty or any other habit. Neglected, they are sure to die. If they are not cultivated, then their results of 'service' (or 'ministry') and 'patience' are sure to become less and less.

These two, faith and love, are the roots; their vitality determines the strength and abundance of the fruit that is borne. And unless you dig about them and take care of them, they are sure to die in the unkindly soil of our poor rocky hearts, and blown upon by the nipping winds that howl round the world. If we want our works to increase in number and to rise in quality, let us see to it that we make an honest habit of cultivating that which is their producing cause—love to Jesus Christ and faith in Him.

And then the text still further suggests another thought. At the end of the letter I read: 'He that overcometh and keepeth My works to the end, to him will I give,' etc.

Now mark what were called 'thy works' in the beginning of the letter are called 'My works' in its close. And it is laid down here that the condition of victory, and the prerequisite to a throne and dominion, is the persevering and pertinacious keeping unto the end of these which are now called 'Christ's works' —that is to say, if we want that the Master shall see in us a continuous growth towards Himself, then, in addition to cultivating the habit of faith and love, we must cultivate the other habit of looking to Him as the source of all the work that we do for Him. And when we have passed from the contemplation of our deeds as ours, and come to look upon all that we do of right and truth and beauty as Christ working in us, then there is a certainty of our work increasing in nobility and in extent. The more we lose ourselves and feel ourselves to be but instruments in Christ's hands, the more shall we seek to fill our lives with all noble service ; the more shall we be able to adorn them with all beauty of growing likeness to Him who is their source.

There is still another thing to be remembered, and that is, that if we are to have this progressive godliness we must put forth continuous effort right away to the very close.

We come to no point in our lives when we can slack off in the earnestness of our endeavour to make more and more of Christ's fulness our own. But to the very last moment of life there is a possibility of still larger victories, and the corresponding possibility of defeat. And, therefore, till the very last, effort, built upon faith and made joyous by love and strong by the grasp of His hand, must be the law for us. It is the man that 'keeps His works' and persistently strives to do them 'to the' very 'end' that 'overcomes.' And if he slacks one moment before the end he loses the blessing that he otherwise would have attained.

'Forgetting the things that are behind, and reaching

forth unto the things that are before,' must be our
motto till the last. We must ever have shining far
before us the unattained heights which it may yet be
possible for our feet to tread. We must never let habit
stiffen us in any one attitude of obedience, nor past
failures set a bound to our anticipations of what it is
possible for us to become in the future. We must never
compare ourselves with ourselves, or with one another.
We must never allow low thoughts, and the poor
average of Christian life, in our brethren, to come
between us and that lofty vision of perfect likeness to
Jesus Christ, which should burn before us all as no
vain dream, but as the will of God in Christ Jesus
concerning us.

And if, smitten by its beauty, and drawn by its
power, and daily honestly submitting ourselves to the
accumulating influences of Christ's long experienced
love, and enlisting habit upon the side of godliness,
and weakening opposition and antagonism by long
discipline and careful pruning, 'we press toward the
mark for the prize of the higher calling of God in
Jesus Christ,' we shall be like the wise householder that
keeps the best wine until the last,

> 'And in old age, when others fade,
> We fruit still forth shall bring.'

And then death itself will but continue the process that
has blessed and ennobled life, and will lead us up into
another state, whereof 'the latest works shall be more
than the first.'

IV.—THE VICTOR'S LIFE-POWER

'He that overcometh, and keepeth My works unto the end, to him will I give power over the nations: 27. And he shall rule them with a rod of iron; as the vessels of a potter shall they be broken to shivers: even as I received of My Father. 28. And I will give him the morning star.'—REV. ii. 26-28.

THIS promise to the victors in Thyatira differs from the preceding ones in several remarkable respects. If you will observe, the summons to give ear to 'what the Spirit saith to the churches' *precedes* the promises in the previous letters; here it follows that promise, and that order is observed in the three subsequent epistles. Now the structure of all these letters is too careful and artistic to allow of the supposition that the change is arbitrary or accidental. There must be some significance in it, but I do not profess to be ready with the explanation, and I prefer acknowledging perplexity to pretending enlightenment.

Then there is another remarkable peculiarity of this letter, viz., the expansion which is given to the designation of the victor as 'He that overcometh and keepeth My works unto the end.' Probably not unconnected with that expansion is the other peculiarity of the promise here, as compared with its precursors, viz., that they all regard simply the individual victor and promise to him 'partaking of the tree of life'; a 'crown of life'; immunity from 'the second death'; 'the hidden manna'; the 'white stone'; and the 'new name written'; which, like all the rest of the promises there, belonged to Himself alone; but here the field is widened, and we have others brought in on whom the victor is to exercise an influence. So, then, we enter upon a new phase of conceptions of that future life in these words, which not only dwell upon the sustenance, the repose, the glory that belong to the man himself, but look upon him as still an instrument in Christ's hands, and an organ for carrying out, by His activities, Christ's purposes in the world. So, then, I want you to look with me very simply at the ideas suggested by these words.

I. We have the victor's authority.

Now the promise in my text is moulded by a remembrance of the great words of the second psalm. That psalm stands at the beginning of the Psalter as a kind of prelude; and in conjunction with its companion psalm, the first, is a summing up of the two great factors in the religious life of the Hebrews, viz., the blessedness in the keeping of the law, and the brightness of the hope of the Messiah. The psalm in question deals with that Messianic hope under the symbols of an earthly conquering monarch, and sets forth His dominion as established throughout the whole earth. And our letter brings this marvellous thought, that the spirits of just men made perfect are, somehow or other, associated with Him in that campaign of conquest.

Now, there is much in these words which, of course, it is idle for us to attempt to expand or expound. We can only wait, as we gaze upon the dim brightness, for experience to unlock the mystery. But there is also much which, if we will reverently ponder it, may stimulate us to brave conflict and persistent diligence in keeping Christ's commandments. I, for my part, believe that Scripture is the only source of such knowledge as we have of the future life; and I believe, too, that the knowledge, such as it is, which we derive from Scripture *is* knowledge, and can be absolutely trusted. And so, though I abjure all attempts at rhetorical

setting forth of the details of this mysterious symbol,
I would lay it upon our hearts. It is not the less
powerful because it is largely inconceivable; and the
mystery, the darkness, the dimness, may be, and are
part of the revelation and of the light. '*There* was the
hiding of His power.'

And so, notice that whatever may be the specific
contents of such a promise as this, the general form
of it is in full harmony with the words of our Lord
whilst He was on earth. Twice over, according to the
gospel narratives—once in connection with Peter's
foolish question, 'What shall *we* have therefore?' and
once in a still more sacred connection, at the table on
the eve of Calvary—our Lord gave His trembling disciples this great promise: 'In the regeneration, when
the Son of man shall sit on the throne of His glory, ye
also shall sit on twelve thrones, judging the twelve
tribes of Israel.' Make all allowance that you like for
the vesture of symbolism, the reality that lies beneath
is that Jesus Christ, the truth, has pledged Himself
to this, that His servants shall be associated with Him
in the activity of His royalty. And the same great
thought, which we only spoil when we try to tear
apart the petals which remain closed until the sun
shall open them, underlies the twin parables of the
pounds and the talents, in regard to each of which we
have, 'Thou hast been faithful over a few things; I
will make thee ruler over many things'; and, linked
along with the promise of authority, the assurance of
union with the Master, 'Enter thou into the joy of thy
Lord.' So this book of the Revelation is only following
in the footsteps and expanding the hints of Christ's
own teaching when it triumphs in the thought that we
are made kings and priests to God; when it points

P

onwards to a future wherein—we know not how, but we know, if we believe Him when He speaks, that it shall be so—they shall reign with Him for ever and ever.

My text adds further the image of a conquering campaign, of a sceptre of iron crushing down antagonism, of banded opposition broken into shivers, 'as a potter's vessel' dashed upon a pavement of marble. And it says that in that final conflict and final conquest they that have passed into the rest of God, and have dwelt with Christ, shall be with Him, the armies of heaven following Him, clad in white raiment pure and glistening, and with Him subduing, ay! and converting into loyal love the antagonisms of earth. I abjure all attempts at millenarian prophecy, but I point to this, that all the New Testament teaching converges upon this one point, that the Christ who came to die shall come again to reign, and that He shall reign, and His servants with Him. That is enough; and that is all. For all the rest is conjecture and fancy and sometimes folly; and details minimise, and do not magnify, the great, undetailed, magnificent fact.

But all the other promises deal not with something in the remoter future, but with something that begins to take effect the moment the dust, and confusion, and garments rolled in blood, of the battlefield are swept away. At one instant the victors are fighting, at the next they are partaking of the Tree of Life, and on their locks lies the crown, and their happy lips are feeding upon 'the hidden manna.' And so, I think, that though, no doubt, the main stress of the promise of authority here points onwards, as our Lord Himself has taught us, to the time of 'the regeneration, when the Son of man shall sit on the throne of His glory,'

the incidence of the promise is not to be exclusively
confined thereto. There must be something in the
present for the blessed dead, as well as for them in the
future. And this is, that they are united with Jesus
Christ in His present activities, and through Him, and
in Him, and with Him, are even now serving Him.
The servant, when he dies, and has been fitted for it,
enters at once on his government of the ten cities.

Thus this promise of my text, in its deepest meaning,
corresponds with the deepest needs of a man's nature.
For we can never be at rest unless we are at work; and
a heaven of doing nothing is a heaven of *ennui* and
weariness. Whatever sneers may have been cast at
the Christian conception of the future, which find
vindication, one is sorry to say, in many popular
representations and sickly bits of hymns, the New
Testament notion of what that future life is to be is
noble with all energy, and fruitful with all activity,
and strenuous with all service. This promise of my
text comes in to supplement the three preceding. They
were addressed to the legitimate, wearied longings for
rest and fulness of satisfaction for oneself. This is
addressed to the deeper and nobler longing for larger
service. And the words of my text, whatever dim
glory they may partially reveal, as accruing to the
victor in the future, do declare that, when he passes
beyond the grave, there will be waiting for him nobler
work to do than any that he ever has done here.

But let us not forget that all this access of power
and enlargement of opportunity are a consequence of
Christ's royalty and Christ's conquering rule. That is
to say, whatever we have in the future we have
because we are knit to Him, and all our service there,
as all our blessedness here, flows from our union with

that Lord. So when He says, as in the words that I
have already quoted, that His servants shall sit on
thrones, He presents Himself as on the central throne.
The authority of the steward over the ten cities is but
a consequence of the servant's entrance into the joy
of the Lord. Whatever there lies in the heavens, the
germ of it all is this, that we are as Christ, so closely
identified with Him that we are like Him, and share
in all His possessions. He says to each of us, 'All
Mine is thine.' He has taken part of our flesh and
blood that we may share in His Spirit. The bride is
endowed with the wealth of the bridegroom, and the
crowns that are placed on the heads of the redeemed
are the crown which Christ Himself has received as
the reward of His Cross—'even as I have received of
My Father.'

II. Note the victor's starry splendour.

The second symbol of my text is difficult of interpretation, like the first: 'I will give him the morning
star.' Now, no doubt, throughout Scripture a star is a
symbol of royal dominion; and many would propose
so to interpret it in the present case. But it seems to
me that whilst that explanation—which makes the
second part of our promise simply identical with the
former, though under a different garb—does justice to
one part of the symbol, it entirely omits the other.
For the emphasis is here laid on 'morning' rather
than on 'star.' It is 'the morning star,' not any star
that blazes in the heavens, that is set forth here as
a symbolical representation of the victor's condition.
Then another false scent, as it were, on which interpretations have gone, seems to me to be that, taking into
account the fact that in the last chapter of the Revelation our Lord is Himself described as 'the bright and

morning star,' they bring this promise down simply to mean, 'I will give him Myself.' Now though it is quite true that, in the deepest of all views, Jesus Christ Himself is the gift as well as the giver of all these seven-fold promises, yet the propriety of representation seems to me to forbid that He should here say, 'I will give them Myself!'

So I think we must fall back upon what any touch of poetic imagination would at once suggest to be the meaning of the promise, that it is the dawning splendour of that planet of hope and morning, the harbinger of day, which we are to lay hold of. Hebrew prophets, long before, had spoken of Lucifer, 'light-bringer,' 'the son of the morning.' Many a poet sang of it before Milton with his

> ' Hesperus, that led the starry host,
> Rode brightest.'

So that I think we are just to lay hold of the thought that the starry splendour, the beauty and the lustre that will be poured upon the victor is that which is expressed by this symbol here. What that lustre will consist in it becomes us not to say. That future keeps its secret well, but that it shall be the perfecting of human nature up to the most exquisite and consummate height of which it is capable, and the enlargement of it beyond all that human experience here can conceive, we may peaceably anticipate and quietly trust.

Only, note the advance here on the previous promises is as conspicuous as in the former part of this great promise. There the Christian man's influence and authority were set forth under the emblem of regal dominion. Here they are set forth under the emblem of lustrous splendour. It is the spectators that see the glory of the beam that comes from the star. And this promise, like the former, implies that in that future there will be a sphere in which perfected spirits may ray out their light, and where they may gladden and draw some eyes by their beams. I have no word to say as to the sky in which the rays of that star may shine, but I do feel that the very essence of this great representation is that Christian souls in the future, as in the present, will stand forth as the visible embodiments of the glory and lustre of the unseen God.

Further, remember that this image, like the former, traces up the lustre, as that traced the royalty, to communion with Christ, and to impartation from Him. '*I* will *give* him the morning star.' We shall shine as the 'brightness of the firmament, and as the stars for ever,' as Daniel said—not by inherent but by reflected light. We are not suns, but planets, that move round the Sun of Righteousness, and flash with His beauty.

III. Lastly, mark the condition of the authority and of the lustre.

Here I would say a word about the remarkable expansion of the designation of the victor, to which I have already referred: 'He that overcometh, and keepeth My works unto the end.' We do not know why that expansion was put in, in reference to Thyatira only, but if you will glance over the letter you will see that there is more than usual about works—works to be repented of, or works which make the material of a final retribution and judgment.

Whatever may be the explanation of the expanded designation here, the lesson that it reads to us is a very significant and a very important one. Bring the metaphor of a victor down to the plain, hard, prose fact

of doing Christ's work right away to the end of life.
Strip off the rhetoric of the fight, and it comes down
to this—dogged, persistent obedience to Christ's commandments. 'He that keepeth My works' does not
appeal to the imagination as 'He that overcometh'
does. But it is the explanation of the victory, and one
that we all need to lay to heart.

'My works': that means the works that He enjoins.
No doubt; but look at a verse before my text: 'I will
give unto every one of you according to *your* works.'
That is, the works that yo. *do*, and Christ's works are
not only those which He enjo. ʒ, but those of which He
Himself set the pattern. He will 'give according to
works'; He will give authority; give the morning star.
That is to say, the life which has been moulded according to Christ's pattern, and shaped in obedience to
Christ's commandments is the life which is capable of
being granted participation in His dominion, and invested with reflected lustre. If here we do His work
we shall be able to do it more fully yonder. 'The
works that I do shall he do also.' That is the law for
life—ay, and it is the promise for heaven. 'And greater
works than these shall he do, because I go to My
Father.' When we have come to partial conformity
with Him here we may hope—and only then have we
the right to hope—for entire assimilation to Him hereafter. If here, from this dim spot which men call earth,
and amid the confusion and dust and distances of this
present life, we look to Him, and with unveiled faces
behold Him, and here, in degree and part, are being
changed from glory to glory, there He will turn His
face upon us, and, beholding it, in righteousness, 'we
shall be satisfied when we awake with His likeness.'

Brethren, it is for us to choose whether we shall share

in Christ's dominion or be crushed by His iron sceptre.
It is for us to choose whether, moulding our lives after
His will and pattern, we shall hereafter be made like
Him in completeness. It is for us to choose whether,
seeing Him here, we shall, when the brightness of His
coming draws near, be flooded with gladness, or
whether we shall call upon the rocks and the hills to
cover us from the face of Him that sitteth on the
Throne. Time is the mother of Eternity. To-day
moulds to-morrow, and when all the to-days and
to-morrows have become yesterdays, they will have
determined our destiny, because they will have settled
our characters. Let us keep Christ's commandments,
and we shall be invested with dignity and illuminated
with glory, and entrusted to work, far beyond anything
that we can conceive here, though, in their farthest reach
and most dazzling brightness, these are but the continuation and the perfecting and the feeble beginnings
of earthly conflict and service.

THE LORD OF THE SPIRITS AND THE STARS

'. . . These things saith He that hath the seven Spirits of God, and the seven
stars.'—Rev. iii. 1.

THE titles by which our Lord speaks of Himself in the
letters to the seven churches are chosen to correspond
with the spiritual condition of the community addressed. The correspondence can usually be observed
without difficulty, and in this case is very obvious.
The church in Sardis, to which Christ is presented
under this aspect as the possessor of ' the seven Spirits
of God and the seven stars,' had no heresies needing
correction. It had not life enough to produce even
such morbid. secretions. Neither weeds nor flowers

grow in winter.   There may be a lower depth than the
condition of things when people are all thinking, and
some of them thinking wrongly, about Christian truth.
Better the heresies of Ephesus and **Thyatira** than the
acquiescent deadness of Sardis.

It had no immoralities.   The gross corruptions of
some in Pergamum had no parallel there.   Philadelphia
had none, for it kept close to its Lord, and Sardis is
rebuked for none, because its evil was deeper and
sadder.   It was not flagrantly corrupt, it was only—
dead.

Of course it had no persecutions.   Faithful Smyrna
had tribulation unto death, hanging like a thunder-
cloud overhead, and Philadelphia, beloved of the Lord,
was drawing near its hour of trial.   But Sardis had
not life enough to be obnoxious.   Why should the
world trouble itself about a dead church?   It exactly
answers the world's purpose, and is really only a bit
of the world under another name.

To such a church comes flaming in upon its stolid
indifference this solemn and yet glad vision of the Lord
of the 'seven Spirits of God,' and of 'the seven stars.'

I. Let us think of the condition of the church which
especially needs this vision.

It is all summed up in that judgment, pronounced
by Him who 'knows its works': 'Thou hast a name
that thou livest, and art dead.'   No works either good
or bad are enumerated, though there were some, which
He gathers together in one condemnation, as 'not
perfect before God.'

We are not to take that word 'dead' in the fullest
sense of which it is capable, as we shall see presently.
But let us remember how, when on earth, the Lord,
whose deep words on that matter we owe mainly to

John, taught that all men were either living, because
they had been made alive by Him, or dead—how He
said, 'Except ye eat the flesh and drink the blood of
the Son of man, ye have no life in you,' and how one
of the main ideas of John's whole teaching is, 'He that
hath the Son hath life.' This remembrance will help
us to give the words their true meaning. Death is the
condition of those who are separated from Him, and
not receiving from Him the better life into their spirits
by communion and faith.

Into this condition the church in Sardis had fallen.
People and bishop had lost their hold on Him. Their
hearts beat with no vigorous love to Him, but only
feebly throbbed with a pulsation which even His hand
laid on their bosoms could scarcely detect. Their
thoughts had no clear apprehension of Him or of His
love. Their communion with Him had ceased. Their
lives had no radiant beauty of self-sacrifice for Christ's
sake. Their Christianity was dying out.

But this death was not entire, as is seen from the
fact that in the next verse 'ready to die' is the expression applied to some among them, or perhaps to
some lingering works which still survived. They were
at the point of death, moribund, with much of their
spiritual life extinct, but here and there a spark among
the ashes, which His eye saw, and His breath could
fan into a flame. Some works still survived, though
not 'perfect,' shrunken and sickly like the blanched
shoots of a plant feebly growing in a dark cellar.

In some animals of low organisation you may see
muscular movements after life is extinct. So churches
and individual Christians may keep on performing
Christian work for a time after the true impulse that
should produce it has ceased. A train will run for some

distance after the steam has been shut off. Institutions last after the life is out of them, for use and wont keeps up a routine of action, though the true motive is dead, and men may go on for long, nominal adherents of a cause to which they are bound by no living conviction. How much of your Christian activity is the manifestation of life, and how much of it is the ghastly twitchings of a corpse under galvanism?

This death was unseen but by the flame-eyed Christ. These people in Sardis had 'a name to live.' They had a high reputation among the Asiatic churches for vigorous Christian character. And they themselves, no doubt, would be very much astonished at the sledge-hammer blow of this judgment of their state. One can fancy them saying—'We dead! Do not we stand high among our brethren, have we not this and the other Christian work among us? Have we not pro-phesied in Thy name?' Yes, and the surest sign of spiritual death is unconsciousness. Paralysis is not felt. Mortification is painless. Frost-bitten limbs are insensitive. They only tingle when life is coming back to them. When a man says I am asleep, he is more than half awake.

One characteristic of their death is that they have forgotten what they were in better and happier times, and therefore need the exhortation, 'Remember how thou hast received and didst hear.' They have fallen so far that the height on which they once stood is out of their sight, and they are content to lie on the muddy flat at its base. No stings from conscious decline disturb them. They are too far gone for that. The same round of formal Christian service which marked their decline from their brethren hid it from themselves.

That is a solemn fact worth making very clear to

ourselves, that the profoundest spiritual decline may
be going on in us, and we be all unconscious of it.
'Samson wist not that his strength was departed from
him,' and in utter ignorance he tried to perform his
old feats, only to find his weakness. So the life of our
spirits may have ebbed away, and we know not how
much blood we have lost until we try to raise ourselves
and sink back fainting. Like some rare essence in a
partially closed vessel, put away in some drawer, we
go to take it out and find nothing but a faint odour,
a rotten cork, and an empty phial. The sure way to
lose the precious elixir of a Christian life is to shut
it up in our hearts. No life is maintained without
food, air, and exercise. We must live on the
bread of God which came down from heaven, and
breathe the breath of His life-giving Spirit, and use
all our power for Him, or else, for all our name to live,
and our shrunken, feeble imitations of the motions of
life, the eyes which are as a flame of fire will see the
sad reality, and the lips into which grace is poured
will have to speak over us the one grim word—*dead*.

II. Notice now the thought of Christ presented to
such a church. 'He that hath the seven Spirits of God
and the seven stars.'

The greater part of the attributes with which our
Lord speaks of Himself in the beginnings of the seven
letters to the churches are drawn from the features of
the majestic vision of the Christ in the first chapter of
this book. But nothing there corresponds to the first
clause of this description, and so far this designation
is singular. There are, however, three other places in
the Apocalypse which throw much light on it, and to
these we may turn for a moment. In the apostolic
salutation at the beginning of the book (i. 4) John in-

vokes mercy and grace on the Asiatic churches from
the Eternal Father, 'and from the seven Spirits which
are before the throne,' and from Christ, the faithful
witness.   In the grand vision of heavenly realities
(ch. iv.) the seer beholds burning before the throne
seven lamps of fire, 'which are the seven Spirits of
God,' and when, in the later portion of the same, he
beholds the conquering Lamb, who looses the seals of
the book of the world's history, he sees Him having
'seven eyes which are the seven Spirits of God, sent
forth into all the earth,' an echo of old words of the
same prophet who had been John's precursor in the
symbolic use of the ' candlestick,' as representing the
Church, and who speaks of ' the seven eyes of the Lord
which run to and fro throughout the whole earth '
(Zech. iv. 10).

Clearly in all these passages we have the same idea
presented of the Holy Spirit of God in the completeness
and manifoldness of its sevenfold energies, conceived
of as possessed and bestowed by the Lamb of God, the
Lord of all the churches.   The use of the plural and
the number seven is remarkable, but quite explicable,
on the ground of the sacred number expressing perfection, and not inconsistent with personal unity,
underlying the variety of manifestations.   The personality of the Spirit is sufficiently set forth by that
refrain in each epistle, ' Let him hear what the Spirit
saith to the churches.'   The divinity of the Spirit is
plainly involved in the triple benediction at the beginning of the letter, and by the sacred place in which
there the Spirit is invoked, midmost between the Father
and the Son.   The seven lamps before the throne speak
of the flaming perfection of that Spirit of burning
conceived of as 'immanent' in the Divine nature.   The

seven eyes sent forth into all the earth speak of the
perfectness of the energies of that same Spirit, conceived of as flashing and gleaming through all the
world. And the great words of our text agree with
that vision of these seven as being the eyes of the
Lamb slain, in telling us that that fiery Spirit is poured
out on men by the Lord, who had to die before He
could cast fire on earth.

This is the thought which a dead or decaying church
needs most. There is a Spirit which gives life, and
Christ is the Lord of that Spirit. The whole fulness
of the Divine energies is gathered in the Holy Spirit,
and this is His chiefest work—to breathe into our
deadness the breath of life. Many other blessed offices
are His, and many other names belong to Him. He is
'the Spirit of adoption,' He is ' the Spirit of Supplication,' He is 'the Spirit of Holiness,' He is ' the Spirit of
Wisdom,' He is 'the Spirit of Power and of Love and
of a sound mind,' He is 'the Spirit of Counsel and
Might'; but highest of all is the name which expresses
His mightiest work, 'the Spirit of Life.' The flaming
lamps tell of His flashing brightness; the seven eyes
of His watchful Omniscience, and other symbols witness
the various sides of His gracious activity on men's
hearts. The anointing oil was consecrated from gold
to express His work of causing men's whole powers to
move sweetly and without friction in the service of
God, and of feeding the flame of devotion in the heart.
The 'water' spoke of cleansing efficacy, as 'fire' of
melting, transforming, purifying power. But the
'rushing mighty wind,' blowing where it listeth, un-
sustained, and free, visible only in its effects, and yet
heard by every ear that is not deaf, sometimes soft and
low, as the respiration of a sleeping child, sometimes

loud and strong as the storm, is His best emblem. The
very name 'the Spirit' emphasises that aspect of His
work in which He is conceived of as the source of life.
This is the thought of His working which comes with
most glad yet solemn meaning to Christian people
who feel how low their life has sunk. This is the true
antidote to the deadness, so real and common among
all communions now, however it is skimmed over and
hidden by a kind of film of activity.

Christ has this sevenfold Spirit. That means first that
the same peaceful dove which floated down from the
open heavens on His meek head, just raised from the
baptismal stream, fills now and for ever His whole
humanity with its perfect energies. 'God giveth not
the Spirit by measure unto him.' How marvellous
that there is a manhood to which the whole fulness of
the Spirit of God can be imparted, an 'earthen vessel,'
capacious enough to hold this 'treasure'! How marvellous that there is a Son of man, who is likewise Son
of God, and has the Spirit, not only for His own human
perfecting, but to shed it forth on all who love Him!
It is the slain Lamb, who has the seven Spirits of God.
That is to say, it was impossible that the fulness of
spiritual influence could be poured out quickening on
men until Christ had died, and by His death He has
become the dispenser to the world of the principle of
life. In His hands is the gift. He is the Lord of the
Spirit, ascended up to give to men according to the
measure of their capacity, of that Spirit which He has
received, until we all come to the measure of the
stature of the fulness of Christ. How unlike the relation
of other teachers to their disciples! Their spirit is the
very thing they cannot give. They can impart teaching, they can give a method and principles, and a certain

direction to the mind. They can train imitators. But
they are like Elijah, knowing not if their spirit will
rest on their successors, and sure that, if it do, it has
not been their gift. The departing prophet had to say
to the petition for an elder son's legacy of his spirit,
'Thou hast asked a hard thing,' but Christ ascending
let that gift fall from His uplifted hands of blessing,
and the dove that abode on Him fluttered downwards
from the hiding cloud, to rest on the Apostles' heads,
as they steadfastly gazed up into heaven. Therefore
they went back to Jerusalem with joy, even before the
fuller gift of Pentecost.

Pentecost was but a transitory sign of a perpetual
gift. The rushing wind died into calm, and the flicker-
ing tongues of fire had faded before the spectators
reached the place. Nor did the miracle of utterance
last either. But whilst all that is past, the substance
remains. The fire of Pentecost has not died down into
chilly embers, nor have the 'rivers of living water,'
promised by the lips of incarnate truth, been swallowed
up in the sands or failed at their source. He is perpetually bestowing the Spirit of God upon His Church.
We are only too apt to forget the present activity of
our ascended Lord. We think of His mighty work as
'finished' on the Cross, and do not conceive clearly and
strongly enough His continuous work which is being
done, now and ever, on the throne. That work is not
only His priestly intercession and representation of us
in heaven, but is also His working on earth in the
bestowal on all His followers of that Divine Spirit to
be the life of their lives and the fountain of all their
holiness, wisdom, strength, and joy. For ever is He
near us, ready to quicken and to bless. He will breathe
in silent ways grace and power into us, and when life

is low, He will pour a fuller tide into our veins. He knows all our deadness and He can cure it all. He is Himself the life, and He is the Lord and giver of life, because the seven Spirits of God sent forth into all the earth are the seven eyes of the slain Lamb.

One great channel through which spiritual life is imparted to a dying church is suggested by the other part of the description of our Lord here as having 'the seven stars.' The 'stars' are the 'angels of the churches,' by whom we are probably to understand their bishops and pastors. If so, then we have a striking thought, symbolised by the juxtaposition. Christ, as it were, holds in the one hand the empty vessels, and in the other the brimming cup, from which He will pour out the supply for their emptiness.

The lesson taught us is, that in a dead church the teachers mostly partake of the deadness, and are responsible for it. But, further, we learn that Christ's way of reviving a decaying and all but effete church is oftenest by filling single men full of His Spirit, and then sending them out to kindle a soul under the ribs of death. So Luther brought back life to the churches in his day. So the Wesleys brought about the great evangelical revival of last century. So let us pray that it may be again in our day when another century is drawing near its end, and the love of many has grown cold.

If we regard the 'angels' as being but ideal representatives of the churches themselves, then we may gather from the juxtaposition of the two clauses a lesson which is ever true. In Christ's one hand is the perfect supply for all our need, wisdom for our blindness, might to clothe our weakness, righteousness for our sin, life to flood our drooping souls. In Christ's

Q

other hand He holds us all, and surely He will not leave us empty while we are within His arm's length of such fulness. Let us look to Him alone for all we need, and rejoice to know that we, held in His grasp, are near His heart, the home of infinite love, and near His hand, the source of infinite supply of strength and grace.

III. Consider, now, the practical uses of these thoughts.

That vision should shame us into penitent consciousness of our own deadness. When we contrast the little life we possess with the abundance waiting to be given, like the poor scanty supply in some choked mill-stream compared with the full-flashing store in the brimming river, we may well be stricken with shame. So much offered and so little possessed; such fiery energy of love possible, and poor tepid feeling, actual! Such a mighty breath of God blowing all about us, and we lying as if enchanted and becalmed, with scarce wind enough to keep our idle sails from flapping. There in Jesus Christ is the measure of what we might possess, and the pattern of what we should possess— does it not bow us in penitence, because of what we do possess?

But while ashamed and penitent, we should be kept by that vision from despondent thoughts, as if the future could never be different from the past. It is not good to think too much of our failure and emptiness, lest penitence darken into despair, and shame cut the sinews of our souls and unfit them for all brave endeavour. Let us think of Christ's fulness and hope, as well as repent.

Let it stir us too to seek for the reason why we have not more of Christ's life. What is the film which prevents the light from reaching our eyes? I remember once seeing by a roadside a stone trough for cattle to drink from empty, because the pipe from which it was fed was stopped by a great plug of ice. That is the reason why many of our hearts are so empty of Christ's Spirit. We have plugged the channel with a mass of ice. Close communion with Jesus Christ is the only means of possessing His Spirit. With penitence let us go back to Him, and let us hold fast by His hand. If we listen to Him, trust Him, keep our minds and hearts attent on Him, He will breathe on us as of old, and as we hear Him say, 'Receive ye the Holy Ghost,' a diviner life will pass into our veins, and the law of the Spirit of life in Christ will make us free from the law of sin and death.

WALKING IN WHITE

'Thou hast a few names even in Sardis which have not defiled their garments; and they shall walk with Me in white: for they are worthy.'—REV. iii. 4.

THE fond fancy that the primitive Church was a better Church than to-day's is utterly blown to pieces by the facts that are obvious in Scripture. Here, in the Apostolic time, under the very eye of the fervent Apostle of Love, and so recently after the establishment of Christianity on the seaboard of Asia, was a church, a young church, with all the faults of a decrepit old one, and in which Jesus Christ Himself could find nothing to commend, and about which He could only say that it had a name to live and was dead. The church at Sardis suffered no persecution. It was much too like the world to be worth the trouble of persecuting. It had no heresy; it did not care enough about religion to breed heresies. It was simply utterly

apathetic and dead. And yet there was a salt in it, or
it would have been rotten as well as dead. There were
'a few names, even in Sardis,' which, in the midst of
all the filth, had kept their skirts white. They had
'not defiled their garments,' and so with beautiful
congruity the promise is given to them—'they shall
walk with Me in white, for they are worthy.' The
promise, I said. It would have been wiser to have said
the *promises*, for there are a great many wrapped up in
germ in these quiet, simple words. Nearly all that we
know, and all that we need to know, about that
mysterious future is contained in them. So my purpose now is, with perfectly inartificial simplicity, just
to take these words and weigh them as a jeweller
might weigh in his scales stones which are very small
but very precious.

I. We have here, then, the promise of continuous
and progressive activity—'they shall walk.'

In Scripture we continually find that metaphor of
the 'walk' as equivalent to an outward life of action.
To make that idea prominent in our conceptions of the
future is a great gain, for it teaches us at once how
imperfect and one-sided are the thoughts about it which
come with such fascination to most of us wearied men.
It is a wonderful, unconscious confession of the troubled,
toilsome, restless lives which most of us live, that the
sweetest and most frequently recurring thought about
the great future is, 'There remaineth a rest for the
people of God'; where the wearied muscles may be
relaxed, and the tortured hearts may be quiet. But
whilst we must not say one word to break or even to
diminish the depth and sweetness of that aspect of the
Christian hope, neither must we forget that it is only
one phase of the complete whole, and that this promise

of the text has to be taken with it. 'They shall walk,' in all the energies of a constant activity, far more intense than it was at its highest here, and yet never, by one hair's breadth, trenching upon the serenity and indisturbance of that perpetual repose. We have to put together the two ideas, which to all our experience are antagonistic, but which yet are not really so, but only complementary, as the two halves of a sphere may be, in order to get the complete round. We have to say, with this very book of the Apocalypse, which goes so deep into the secrets of heaven, 'His servants serve Him and see His face'—uniting together in one harmonious whole the apparent and, as far as earth's experience goes, the real opposites of continual contemplation and continual activity of service. It is so hard for us in this life to find out practically for ourselves how much to give to each of these, that it is blessed to know that there comes a time for all of us, if we will, when that difficulty will solve itself, and Mary and Martha shall be one person, continually serving and yet continually sitting, no more troubled about many things, in the quiet of the Master's presence. 'They shall walk,' harmonising work and rest, contemplation and service.

And then there is the other thought, too, involved in that pregnant word, of continuous advancement, growing every moment, through the dateless cycles, nearer and nearer to the true centre of our souls, and up into the loftiness of perfection. We do not know what ministries of love and service may wait for Christ's servants yonder, but of this we can be quite sure, that all the faculties for service which we see crippled and limited by the hindrances of earth will find in the future a worthier sphere. Do you think it likely that

God should so waste His wealth as to take men and
redeem them and sanctify them, and prepare them by
careful discipline and strengthen their powers by work,
and then, just when they are out of their apprenticeship and ready for larger service, should condemn them
to idleness? Is that like Him? Must it not rather be
that there is a wider field for the faculties that were
trained here; and that, whatsoever there may be in
eternity, there will be no idleness there?

II. Still further, here is the further promise of companionship with Christ. 'They shall walk *with Me*.'

'How can two walk together except they be agreed?'
If there be this promised union, it can only be because
of the completeness of sympathy and the likeness of
character between Christ and His companions. The
unity between Christ and His followers in the heavens
is but the carrying into perfectness of the imperfect
union that makes all the real blessedness of life here
upon earth.

'*With Me*.' Why! that union with Christ is all we
know about heaven. All the rest is imagery, that is
reality. All the rest is material symbol, that is what it
all means.

In the sweet, calm words of Richard Baxter's simple,
but deep song—

> 'My knowledge of that life is small,
>   The eye of faith is dim;
> But 'tis enough that Christ knows all,
>   And I shall be with Him.'

We ask ourselves and one another, and God's Word, a
great many questions about that unseen life; and
sometimes it seems to us as if it would have been so
much easier for us to bear the burdens that are laid
upon us if some of these questions could have been

answered. But we do not really need to know more than that we shall be ' ever with the Lord.' Two, who are ever with Him, cannot be far from one another. So we may thankfully feel that the union of all is guaranteed by the union of each with Him. And for the rest we can wait.

Only remember that to walk with Him implies that those who were but little children here have grown up to maturity. We try to tread in His footsteps here, but at the best we follow Him with tottering feet and short steps, as children trying to keep up with an elder brother. But there we shall keep step and walk in His company, side by side. For earth the law is, 'leaving us an example that we should follow His steps.' For heaven the law is 'they shall walk with Me '; or, as the other promise of this book has it, 'they shall follow the Lamb whithersoever He goeth.' No heights are so high to which He rises but He will make our feet like hind's feet to tread upon the high places; no glories so great but we shall share them. Nothing in His divine nature shall part Him from us, but we shall be ever with Him. Let us comfort one another with these words.

III. Further, my text speaks a promise of the perfection of purity. 'They shall walk with Me *in white.*'

The white garment, of course, is a plain metaphor for unsullied purity of moral character. And it is worth notice that the word employed by the Apocalyptic seer here for white, as indeed is the case throughout the manifold references to that heavenly colour which abound in this book, implies no dead ghastly white, but a flashing glistering whiteness, as of sunshine upon snow, which, I suppose, is the whitest thing that human eyes can look upon undazzled. So of the same radiant tint as the great White Throne on which He sits shall be the vestures of those that follow Him. The white robe is the conqueror's robe, the white robe is the priest's robe, the white robe is the copy of His who stood in that solitary spot on Mount Hermon, just below its snowy summit, with garments 'so as no fuller on earth could white them'; white as the driven and sunlit snow that sparkled above. Perhaps we are to think of a glorified body as being the white garment. Perhaps it may be rather that the image expresses simply the conception of entire moral purity, but in either case it means the loftiest manifestation of the most perfect Christlike beauty as granted to all His followers.

IV. And so, lastly, note the condition of all these promises.

'Thou hast a few names, even in Sardis, which have not defiled their garments; and they shall walk with Me in white: for they are worthy.' The only thing that makes it possible for any man to have that future life of active communion with Jesus Christ, in perfect beauty of inward character and of outward form, is that here he shall by faith keep himself 'unspotted from the world.' There is a congruity and proportion between the earthly life and the future life. Heaven is but the life of earth prolonged and perfected by the dropping away of all the evil, the strengthening and lifting to completeness of all the good. And the only thing that fits a man for the white robe of glory is purity of character down here on earth.

There is nothing said here directly about the means by which that purity can be attained or maintained. That is sufficiently taught us in other places, but what in this saying Christ insists upon is that, however it is

got, it *must* be got, and that there is no life of blessedness, of holiness and glory, beyond the grave, except
for those for whom there is the life of aspiration after,
and in some real measure possession of, moral purity
and righteousness and goodness here upon earth.

Do not be surprised at that word—'They are *worthy*.'
It is an evangelical word. It declares the perfect congruity between the life on earth and the issue and
reward of the life in heaven. And it holds up to us
the great principle that purity here is crowned with
glory hereafter. If the white garments could be put
upon a black soul they would be like the poisoned
shirt on the demigod in the Greek legend, they would
bite into the flesh, and burn and madden. But it is
impossible, and for ever and ever it remains true that
only those who have kept their garments undefiled
here shall 'walk in white.' It does not need absolute
cleanness from all spot, God be thanked! But it does
need, first, that we shall have 'washed our robes and
made them white' in the 'blood of the Lamb.' And
then that we shall keep them white, by continual
recourse to the blood that cleanses from all sin, and by
continual effort after purity like His own and received
from Him. They who come back as prodigals in rags,
and have their filthy tatters exchanged for the clean
garment of Christ's righteousness, with which by faith
they are invested, and who then take heed to follow
Him, with loins girt and robes kept undefiled, and ever
washed anew in His cleansing blood, shall be of the
heavenly companions of the glorified Christ, joined to
Him in all His dominion, and clothed in flashing whiteness like the body of His glory.

V.—THE VICTOR'S LIFE-ROBE

'He that overcometh, the same shall be clothed in white raiment; and I will not blot out his name out of the book of life, but I will confess his name before My Father, and before His angels.'—REV. iii. 5.

THE brightest examples of earnest Christianity are generally found amidst widespread indifference. If a man does not yield to the prevailing tone, it is likely to quicken him into strong opposition. So it was in this Church of Sardis. It was dead. That was the summing up of its condition. It had a name to live, and the name only made the real deadness more complete. But there were exceptions: souls ablaze with Divine love, who in the midst of corruption had kept their robes clean, and whom Christ's own voice declared to be worthy to walk with Him in white.

That great eulogium, which immediately precedes our text, is referred to in the first of its triple promises; as is even more distinctly seen if we read our text as the Revised Version does: 'He that overcometh, the same shall thus be clothed in white raiment'; the 'thus' pointing back to the preceding words, and widening the promise to the faithful few in Sardis so as to extend to all victors in all Churches throughout all time.

Now the remaining two clauses of our text also seem to be coloured by the preceding parts of this letter. We read in it, 'Thou hast a *name* that thou livest'; and again, 'Thou hast a few *names* even in Sardis which have not defiled their garments.' Our text catches up the word, and moulds its promises accordingly. One is more negative, the other more positive; both link on to a whole series of Scriptural representations.

Now all these declarations of the blessedness of the victors are, of course, intensely symbolical, and we can but partially translate them. I simply seek now to take them as they stand, and to try to grasp at least some part of the dim but certain hopes which they partly reveal and partly hide. There are, then, three things here.

I. The victor's robes.

'He that overcometh, the same shall (thus) be clothed in white raiment.' White, of course, is the festal colour. But it is more than that: it is the heavenly colour. In this book we read of white thrones, white horses, hairs 'white as snow,' white stones. But we are to notice that the word here employed does not merely mean a dead whiteness, which is the absence of colour, but a lustrous and glistering white, like that of snow smitten by sunshine, or like that which dazzled the eyes of the three on the Mount of Transfiguration, when they saw the robes of the glorified Christ 'whitened as no fuller on earth could white them.' So that we are to associate with this metaphor, not only the thoughts of purity, festal joy, victory, but likewise the thought of lustrous glory.

Then the question arises, can we translate that metaphor of the robe into anything that will come closer to the fact? Now I may remind you that this figure runs through the whole of Scripture. We find, for instance, in one of the old prophets, a vision in which the taking away of Israel's sin is represented by the high priest, the embodiment of the nation, standing in filthy garments, which were stripped off him and fair ones put on him. We find our Lord giving forth a parable of a man who came to the feast not having on a wedding garment. We find the Apostle

Paul speaking frequently, in a similar metaphor, of putting off an ancient nature and putting on a new one. We find in this book, not only the references in my text and the context, but the great saying concerning those that have 'washed their robes and made them white in the blood of the Lamb,' and the final benediction pronounced upon those who washed their robes, that they may 'have a right to enter through the gate into the city.'

Putting all these things together—and the catalogue might be extended—we have to observe that the signification of this symbol is not that of something wholly external to or apart from the man, but that it is rather that part of his nature, so to speak, which is visible to beholders, and we may translate it very simply—the robe is character. So the promise of my text, brought down so far as we can bring it to its primary element, is of a purity and lustrous glory of personal character, which shall be visible to any eye that may look upon the wearer. What more there may be found in it when we are 'clothed upon with our house which is from heaven,' if so be that 'being clothed we shall not be found naked,' I do not presume to say. I do not speculate, I simply translate the plain words of Scripture into the truth which they represent.

But now I would have you notice that this, like all the promises of the New Testament in regard to a future life, lays main stress on what a man is. Not where we are, not what we have, not what we do or know, make heaven, but *what we are*. The promises are clothed for us, as they must needs be, in sensuous images, which sensuous men have interpreted in far too low a sense; or sometimes have not been even at the trouble of interpreting. But in reality there are but two facts

that we *know* about that future, and they are smelted
together, as cause and effect, in the great saying of the
most spiritual of the Apostles: ' We shall be like Him'
—that is what we shall be—' for we shall see Him as
He is.' So, then, purity of character, when all the
stains on the garments, spotted by the flesh, shall have
melted away; purity of character, when temptations
shall have no more food in us and so conflict shall not
be needful; purity like Christ's own, and derived from
the vision of Him, according to the great law that
beholding is transformation, and the light we see is
the light which we reflect—this is the heart of this
great promise.

But notice that the main thing about it is that this
lustrous purity of a perfected character is declared to
be the direct outcome of the character, that was made
by effort and struggle carried on in faith here upon
earth. In this clause the familiar ' I will give' does
not appear; and the thought of the condition upon earth
working itself out into the glory of lustrous purity in
the heavens is made even more emphatic by the adoption
of the reading to which I have referred: 'Shall *thus* be
clothed,' which points us backwards to what preceded,
where our Lord's own voice declares that the men who
have not defiled their garments upon earth are they who
' shall walk with Him in white.' The great law of
continuity and of increase, so that the dispositions
cultivated here rise to sovereign power hereafter, and
that what was tendency, and struggle, and imperfect
realisation upon earth becomes fact and complete possession in the heavens, is declared in the words before
us.

What solemn importance that thought gives to the
smallest of our victories or defeats here on earth! They

are threads in the web out of which our garment is
to be cut. After all, yonder as here, we are dressed in
homespun, and we make our clothing and shape it for
our wear. That truth is perfectly consistent with the
other truth on which it reposes—that the Christian man
owes to Christ the reception of the new garment of
purity and holiness. The evangelical doctrine, 'not by
works of righteousness which we have done,' and its
complement in the words of my text, are perfectly
harmonious. We cannot weave the web except Christ
gives us yarn, nor can we work out our own salvation
except Christ bestows upon us the salvation which we
work out. The two things go together. Let us remember that, whilst in one aspect the souls that were
all clad in filthy garments are arrayed as a bridegroom
decketh his bride with a fair vesture, in another aspect
we ourselves, by our own efforts, by our own struggles,
by our own victories, have to weave and fashion and
cut and sew the dress which we shall wear for ever.

II. Notice here the victor's place in the Book of
Life.

'I will not blot out his name out of the Book of
Life.' I have pointed out that in the former clause
the characteristic ' I will give ' is omitted, in order that
emphatic expression might be secured for the thought
that in one aspect the reward of the future is automatic
or self-working. But that thought is by no means a
complete statement of the truth with regard to this
matter; and so, in both of the subsequent clauses, we
have our Lord representing Himself (for it is never to
be forgotten that these promises are Christ's own words
from heaven) as clothed with His judicial functions,
and as determining the fates of men. 'I will not blot
out his name out of the Book of Life.' That is a solemn

and tremendous claim, that Christ's finger can write, and Christ's finger can erase, a name from that register.

Now I have said that all these clauses link themselves on to a whole series of Scriptural representatives. I showed that briefly in regard to the former; I would do so in regard to the present one.

You will remember, perhaps, in the early history of Israel, that Moses, with lofty self-devotion, prayed God to blot his name out of His book, if only by that sacrifice Israel's sin might be forgiven. You may recall too, possibly, how one of the prophets speaks of ' those that are written amongst the living in Jerusalem,' and how Daniel, in his eschatological vision, refers to those whose names were or were not written in the book. I need not remind you of how our Lord commanded His disciples to rejoice not in that the spirits were subject to them, but rather to rejoice because their names were written in heaven. Nor need I do more than simply refer to the Apostle's tender and pathetic excuse for not remembering the names of some of his fellow-workers, that it mattered very little, because their names were written in the Book of Life. Throughout this Apocalypse, too, we find subsequent allusions of the same nature, just as in the Epistle to the Hebrews we read of the 'Church of the first-born whose names are written in heaven.' Now all these, thus put together, suggest two ideas: one which I do not deal with here—viz., that of a burgess-roll—and the other that of a register of those who truly live. And that is the thought that is suggested here. The promise of my text links on to the picture in the letter of the condition of the Church at Sardis, which was dead, and says that the victor will truly and securely and for

ever possess life, with all the clustered blessedness
which, like a nebula unresolved, gather themselves, dim
yet radiant, round that great word.

But what I especially note here is, not so much this
reiteration of the fundamental and all-embracing
promise which has met us in preceding letters, the promise of a secure, eternal life, as that plain and solemn
implication that a name *may* be struck out of that book.
Theological exigencies compelled our fathers to deny
that, but surely the words of our text are too plain
to be neglected or misunderstood. It is possible that
a name, like the name of a dishonest attorney, shall
be struck off the rolls.   Do not let any desire for
theological symmetry blind you, brother, to that fact.
Take it into account in your daily lives. It is possible
for a man to 'cast away his confidence.' It is possible
for him to make shipwreck of the faith. Some of you
will remember that pathetic story of Cromwell's death-
bed, when he asked one of his ghostly counsellors
whether it was true that ' once in the covenant, always
in the covenant?'   He got the answer, 'Yes'; and
then he said, 'I know I once was,' and so died.
Brethren, it is the victors whose names are kept upon
the roll. These people at Sardis had a name to live,
and they thought that their names were in the Book
of Life. And when it was opened, lo! a blot. Some
of us have seen upon the granite of Egyptian temples
the cartouches of a defeated dynasty chiselled out by
their successors. The granite on which this list is
written is not so hard but that a man, by his own sin,
falling away from the Master, may chisel out his name.
A student goes up for his examination. He thinks he
has succeeded. The pass-lists come out, and his name
is not there. Take care that you are not building upon

past faith, but remember that it is the *victor's* name
that is not blotted out of the Book of Life.

III. Lastly, the victor's recognition by the Commanding Officer.

'I will confess his name before My Father, and before
His angels.' There, too, we have a kind of mosaic,
made up of previous Scripture declarations. Our Lord,
twice in the Gospels—and on neither occasion in the
Gospel according to St. John—has similar sayings;
once about confessing the name of him who confesses
His name 'before the Father'; once about confessing
it 'before the holy angels.' Here these are smelted
together into the one great recognition by Jesus Christ
of the victor as being His.

Now I need not remind you of how emphatically,
to this clause also, the remark which I have made with
regard to the former one applies, and how tremendous
and inexplicable, except on one hypothesis, is this same
assumption by Christ of judicial functions which determine the fate and the standing of men.

But I would rather point to the thought that this
promise carries with it, not only Christ's judicial recognition of the victor, but also the thought of loving
relationship, of close friendship, of continual regard.
He 'confesses the name'—that means that He takes to
His heart, and loves and cares for the person.

Is it not the highest honour that can be given to
any soldier, to have honourable mention in the general's
despatches? It matters very little what becomes of
our names upon earth, though there they be dark,
and swift oblivion devours them almost as soon as we
are dead, except in so far as they may live for a little
while in the memory of two or three that loved us.
That is the fate of most of us. And surely 'the hollow

wraith of dying fame' may 'fade wholly,' and we
'exult,' if Jesus Christ confess our name.   It matters
little who forgets us if He remembers us.   It matters
even less what the judgments pronounced in our obitu-
aries may be, if He says, 'That man is Mine, and I own
him.' Ah! brethren, what a reversal of the world's
judgments there will be one day; and how names that
have been blown through a thousand trumpets, and
had hosannas sung to them, and been welcomed with
a tumult of acclaim through generations, will sink into
oblivion and never be heard of any more, and the unseen and obscure men who lived by, and for, and with
Jesus Christ, will come to the front!   Praise from Him
is praise indeed.

Now, brethren, the upshot of it all is that life here
derives its meaning and its consecration from life hereafter.   The question for us is, do we habitually realise
that we are weaving the garment we must wear, be it
a poisoned robe that shall eat into our flesh like fire,
or be it a vesture clean and white?   Do we brace ourselves for the obscure struggles of our little lives, feeling that they are not small because they carry eternal
consequences? Are we content to be unknown because
well known by Him, and to live so that He shall ac-
knowledge us in the day when to be acknowledged by
Him means glory and blessedness beyond all hopes and
all symbols; and to be disowned by Him means ruin
and despair? You know the conditions of victory. Lay
them to heart, and its issues, and the tragical results
of death; and then cleave, with mind and heart and
will, to Him who can make you more than conquerors,
who will change your frayed and dinted armour for
the fine linen, clean and white, and will point to you,
before His Father and the universe, and say, 'This

man was one of Thy faithful soldiers.' That will be honour indeed. Do you see to it that you make it yours.

KEEPING AND KEPT

'Because thou hast kept the word of My patience, I also will keep thee from the hour of temptation.'—REV. iii. 10.

THERE are only two of the seven churches which receive no censure or rebuke from Jesus Christ; and of these two—viz., the churches of Smyrna and Phila-delphia—the former receives but little praise though much sympathy. This church at Philadelphia stands alone in the abundance and unalloyed character of the eulogium which Christ passes upon it. He doles out His praise with a liberal hand, and nothing delights Him more than when He can commend even our imperfect work. He does not wait for our perform-ances to reach the point of absolute sinlessness before He approves them. Do you think that a father or a mother, when its child was trying to please him or her, would be at all likely to say, 'Your gift is worth very little. I could buy a far better one in a shop'? And do you think that Jesus Christ's love and delight in the service of His children are less generous than ours? Surely not.

So here we are not to suppose that these good souls in Philadelphia lived angelic lives of unbroken holi-ness because Jesus Christ has nothing but praise for them. Rather we are to learn the great thought that, in all our poor, stained service, He recognises the central motive and main drift, and, accepting these, is glad when He can commend. 'Thou hast kept the word of My patience,' and, with a beautiful reciprocity, 'I will keep those that keep My word from' and 'in the hour of temptation.'

I. Now notice, in the first place, the thing kept.

That is a remarkable phrase 'the word of My patience.' A verse or two before, our Lord had said to the same church, evidently speaking about the same thing in them, 'Thou hast a little strength, and hast kept My word.' This expression, 'the word of My patience,' seems to be best understood in the same general way as that other which precedes it, and upon which it is a commentary and an explanation. It refers, not to individual commandments to patience, but to the entire gospel message, the general whole of 'the Word of Jesus Christ' communicated therein to men. That is a profound and beautiful way of characterising the sum of the revelation of God in Christ as 'the word of His patience,' and is one which yields ample reward to meditative thought.

The whole gospel, then, is so named, inasmuch as it all records the patience which Christ exercised.

What does the New Testament mean by 'patience'? Not merely endurance, although, of course, that is included, but endurance of such a sort as will secure persistence in work, in spite of all the opposition and sufferings which may come in the way. The world's patience simply means, 'Pour on, I will endure.' The New Testament patience has in it the idea of perseverance as well as of endurance, and means, not only that we bow to the pain or the sorrow, but that nothing in sorrow, nothing in trial, nothing in temptation, nothing in antagonism, has the smallest power to divert us from doing what we know to be right. The man who will reach his hand through the smoke of hell to lay hold of plain duty is the patient man of the New Testament. 'Though there were as many devils in Worms as there are tiles on the housetops, I will go in.' That speech of Luther's, though uttered with a little too much energy, expressed the true idea of Christian patience. High above the stormy and somewhat rough determination of the servant towers, calm and gentle, and therefore stronger, the 'patience' of the Lord, and the whole story of His life on earth may well be regarded, from this point of view, as the record of His unfaltering and meek continuance in obedience to the Father's will, in the face of opposition and suffering. His life, to use a secular word, was the most 'heroic' ever lived. Before Him was the thing to be done, and between Him and it were massed such battalions of antagonism and evil as never were mustered in opposition to any other saintly soul upon earth. And through all He went persistently, with 'His face like a flint,' of set purpose to do the work for which He came into the world.

But there was no fierce antagonism about Jesus Christ's patience. His persistence, in spite of all obstacles and opposition, was the persistence of meekness, the heroism of gentleness. Patience in the lower sense of quiet endurance, as well as in the higher, of heroic scorn of all that opposition could do to hinder the realisation of the Father's will, is deeply stamped upon His life. We think of His gentleness, of His meekness, of His humility, of all the softer, and, as men insolently call them, the more feminine virtues in Christ's character. But I do not know that we often enough think of what men, with equal insolence and shortsightedness, call the masculine virtues of which,

too, He is the great Exemplar, that magnificent, un-
paralleled, and perfectly quiet and unostentatious in-
vincibility of will and heroism of settled resolve with
which He pressed towards the mark, though the mark
was a cross.

This is the theme of the gospel story, and this
Apocalypse of a gentle Christ, whose gentleness was
the gentleness of inflexible strength, this story, or
word 'of My patience,' is that which we are to lay upon
our hearts. For that name is fitly applied to the
gospel, inasmuch as it enjoins upon every one of us in
our degree, and in regard of the far easier tasks and
slighter antagonisms with which we have to do and
which we have to meet, to make Christ's persistence the
model for our lives. So the whole morality of Christianity may almost be gathered up into this one expression,
which sets forth at once the law and the supreme motive
for fulfilling it. Unwelcome and hard tasks are made
easy and delightsome when we hear Jesus say, 'The
record of My patience is thy pattern and thy power.
Be like Me, and thou shalt be perfect and entire, wanting nothing.'

II. Notice, next, the keepers of this word.

The metaphor represents to us the action of one who,
possessing some valuable thing, puts it into some safe
place, takes great care of it, carries it very near to the
heart, perhaps within the robe, and watches tenderly
and jealously over it. So 'thou hast kept the word of
My patience.'

There are two ways by which Christians are to do
that; the one is by inwardly cherishing the word, and
the other by outwardly obeying it. There should be
both the inward counting it dear and precious, and
treasuring it in mind and heart, as the Psalmist says,

'Thy word have I hid in my heart, that I should not offend against Thee,' and also the regulation of conduct which we more usually regard as keeping the commandment.

Let me say a word, and it shall only be a word, about each of these two things. I am afraid that the plain practical duty of reading their Bibles is getting to be a much neglected duty amongst professing Christian people. I do not know how you are to keep the words of Christ's patience in your hearts and minds if you do not read them. I am afraid that most Christian congregations nowadays do their systematic and prayerful study of the New Testament by proxy, and expect their ministers to read the Bible for them and to tell them what is there. A mother will sometimes take a morsel of her child's food into her mouth, and half masticate it first before she passes it to the little gums. I am afraid that newspapers, and circulating libraries, and magazines, and little religious books—very good in their way, but secondary and subordinate—have taken the place that our fathers used to have filled by honest reading of God's Word. And that is one of the reasons, and I believe it is a very large part of the reason, why so many professing Christians do not come up to this standard; and instead of '*running* with patience the race that is set before them,' *walk* in an extraordinarily leisurely fashion, by fits and starts, and sometimes with long intervals, in which they sit still on the road, and are not a mile farther at a year's end than they were when it began. There never was, and there never will be, vigorous Christian life unless there be an honest and habitual study of God's Word. There is no short-cut by which Christians can reach the end of the race. Foremost

among the methods by which their eyes are enlightened and their hearts rejoiced are application to the
eyes of their understanding of that eye-salve, and the
hiding in their hearts of that sweet solace and fountain
of gladness, the Word of Christ's patience, the revelation of God's will.   The trees whose roots are laved
and branches freshened by that river have leaves that
never wither, and all their blossoms set.

But the word is kept by continual obedience in
action as well as by inward treasuring.   Obviously the
inward must precede the outward.   Unless we can say
with the Psalmist, 'Thy word have I hid in my heart,'
we shall not be able to say with him, 'I have not hid
Thy righteousness within my heart.'   If the Word of
the Lord is to sound like a rousing trumpet-blast
from our lives, it must first be heard in secret by us,
and its music linger in our listening hearts.

We need this brave persistence in daily life if we are
not to fail wholly.   Very instructive in this aspect
are many of the Scripture allusions to 'patience' as
essential to the various virtues and blessednesses of
Christian life.

For example, 'In your patience ye shall win your
souls.'   Only he who presses right on, in spite of all
that externals can do to hinder him from realising his
conviction of duty, is the lord of his own spirit.   All
others are slaves to something or some one.   By persistence in the paths of Christian service, no matter
what around or within us may rise up to hinder us,
and by such persistence only, do we become masters of
ourselves.   Many a man has to walk, as in the old days
of ordeal by fire, over a road strewn with hot plough-
shares, to get to the place where God will have him to
be.   And if he does not flinch, though he may reach

the goal with scorched feet, he will reach it with a
quiet heart, and possess himself, whatever he may lose.

Again, the Lord Himself says to us, ʻThese are those
which bring forth fruit with patience.ʼ There is no
growth of Christian character, no flowering of Christian
conduct, no setting of incipient virtues into the mature
fruit of settled habit, without this persistent adher-
ence in the face of all antagonism, to the dictates of
conscience and the commandment of Christ. It is the
condition of bringing forth fruit, some thirty, some
sixty, and some a hundredfold.

Again the Scripture says, demanding this same persistence, gentle abstinence, and sanctified stiffnecked-
ness, ʻRun with perseverance the race that is set
before you.ʼ There is no progress in the Christian
course, no accomplishing the *stadia* through which we
have to pass, except there be this dogged keeping at
what we know to be duty, in spite of all the reluctance
of trembling limbs, and the cowardice of our poor
hearts.

III. We have here Christ keeping the keepers of
His word.

ʻBecause thou hast kept the word of My patience I
will keep thee from,ʼ and *in*, ʻthe hour of temptation.ʼ
There is a beautiful reciprocity, as I said. Christ will
do for us as we have done with His word. Christ still
does in heaven what He did upon earth. In the great
high priestʼs prayer recorded by the evangelist who
was also the amanuensis of these letters from heaven,
Jesus said, ʻI kept them in Thy name which Thou hast
given Me, and I guarded them, and not one of them
perished.ʼ And now, speaking from heaven, He con-
tinues His earthly guardianship, and bids us trust that,
just as when with His followers here, He sheltered

them as a parent bird does its young, fluttering round
them, bearing them up on its wings, and drew them
within the sacred circle of His sweet, warm, strong,
impregnable protection, so, if we keep the word of His
patience, cherishing the story of His life in our hearts,
and humbly seeking to mould our lives after its sweet
and strong beauty, He will keep us in the midst of,
and also from, the hour of temptation. The Christ in
heaven is as near each trembling heart and feeble
foot, to defend and to uphold, as was the Christ upon
earth.

He does not promise to keep us at a distance from
temptation, so as that we shall not have to face it, but
from means, as any that can look at the original will
see, that He will save us *out of it*, we having previously
been in it, so as that 'the hour of temptation' shall not
be the hour of falling. Yes! the man whose heart is
filled with the story of Christ's patience, and who is
seeking to keep that word, will walk in the midst of the
fire-damp of this mine that we live in, as with a safety
lamp in his hand, and there will be no explosion. If
we keep our hearts in the love of God, and in that great
word of Christ's patience, the gunpowder in our nature
will be wetted, and when a spark falls upon it there
will be no flash. Outward circumstances will not be
emptied of their power to tempt, but our susceptibility
will be deadened in proportion as we keep the word of
the patience of the patient Christ. The lustre of earthly
brightnesses will have no glory by reason of the glory
that excelleth, and when set by the side of heavenly
gifts will show black against their radiance, as would
electric light between the eye and the sun.

It is great to wrestle with temptation and fling it,
but it is greater to be so strong that it never grasps us.

It is great to be victor over passions and lusts, and to put our heel upon them and suppress them, but it is better to be so near the Master that they have crouched before Him, and 'the lion eats straw like the ox.'

To such blessed state we attain if, and only if, we draw near to Him and in daily communion with Him secure that the secret of His patient continuance in well-doing is repeated in us. So we shall be lifted above temptation. That great word of His patience, and the spirit which goes with the word, will be for us like the cotton wool that chemists put into the flask which they wish to seal hermetically from the approach of microscopic germs of corruption. It will let all the air through, but it will keep all the infinitesimal animated points of poison out. It will filter the most polluted atmosphere, and bring it to our lungs clean and clear. 'If thou keep the word of My patience I will keep thee from the hour of temptation.'

'THY CROWN'

'. . . Hold that fast which thou hast, that no man take thy crown.'—REV. iii. 11.

THE Philadelphian Church, to which these stirring words are addressed, is the only church of the seven in which there was nothing that Christ rebuked. It had no faults, or at least no recorded faults, either of morals or of doctrine. It had had no great storm of persecution beating upon it, although one was threatened. But yet, although thus free from blame and occasion for censure, it was not beyond the need of stimulating exhortation, not beyond the need of wholesome warning, not beyond the reach of danger and possible loss. 'That no man take thy crown'—as long as Christian

men are here, so long have they to watch against the
tendency of received truth to escape their hold because
of its very familiarity; of things that are taken for
granted to become impotent and to slip, and so for the
crown to fall from the head, which is all unconscious
of its discrowned shame.

We have here, then, three things: 'thy crown'; the
possibility of losing it; the way to secure it.

I. Now, as to the first. It contributes to the understanding of the meaning of the metaphor to remember
that the crown spoken of here is not the symbol of
royalty, not the golden or other circlet which kings and
emperors wore, but the floral wreath or garland which
in ancient social life played many parts: was laid on
the temples of the victors in the games, was wreathed
around the locks of the conquering general, was
placed upon the anointed heads of brides and of
feasters, was the emblem of victory, of festivity, of joy.
And it is this crown, not the symbol of dominion, but
the symbol of a race accomplished and a conquest won,
an outward and visible sign of a festal day, with all its
abundance and ease and abandonment to delight, which
the apocalyptic vision holds out before the Christian
man.

The crown is a common figure all through the New
Testament, and it may help us to grasp the fulness of
the meaning of the metaphor if we just recall in a
sentence or two the various instances of its occurrence.
It is spoken about under three designations, as a crown
of 'life,' of 'righteousness,' of 'glory'; the first and last
designating it in reference to that of which it may be
supposed to consist, namely, life and glory; the centre
one designating it rather in reference to that of which
it is the reward. The righteousness of earth is crowned

by the more abundant life and the more radiant glory
of the future. The roses that were wreathed round
the flushed temples of the revellers withered and faded,
and their petals drooped in the hot atmosphere of the
banqueting hall, laden with fumes of wine. The parsley
wreath, that was twined round the locks of the young
athlete who had been victorious in the games, was
withered to-morrow and cast into the dust heap. 'But,'
says one of the New Testament writers, 'the crown
of glory fadeth not away.' And the other wreaths, in-
trinsically worthless, were only symbols of victory
and honour, but this itself is full of preciousness and of
substance and of power.

So the crown is the reward of righteousness, and
consists of life so full that our present experience con-
trasted with it may almost be called an experience
of death; of glory so flashing and wonderful that, if
our natures were not strengthened, it would be an
'exceeding weight of glory' that would crush them
down, and upon all the life and all the glory is stamped
the solemn signature of eternity, and they are for ever.
Now, says my text to each Christian, all this, the
consequence and reward of sore toil, faithfully done,
and of effort that strains every muscle in the race—the
festal participation in life and glory for evermore—is
'thy crown'; not because thou hast it now, but because,
as sure as God is God and righteousness is righteousness, nothing can prevent the man who, holding by
Jesus Christ, has become possessor of the righteousness, which is of God by faith, from receiving that great
reward. It is his already in the Divine destination;
his by the immutable laws of proprietorship in God's
kingdom; his upon the simple condition of his con-
tinuing to be what he is. Like Peter's saying about

the inheritance 'reserved in heaven for you,' this representation treats the perfect future blessedness of us who are toiling and struggling here as already in existence and waiting for us, beyond the dust of the wrestling-ground, and the fury of the battlefield. Of course that is not meant to be taken in prosaic literality. The 'place' may indeed be 'prepared' in which that blessedness is to be realised, but the blessedness itself can have no existence apart from those who possess it. The purpose of the representations is to put in the strongest possible way the absolute certainty of the heads that now are pressed by the helmet being then encircled with the crown, and of the strangers scattered abroad reaching and resting for ever in the promised land to which they journey. The reward is as sure as if each man's crown, with his name engraved upon it, lay safely guarded in the treasure-house of God.

The light of that great certainty should ever draw our weary eyes, weary of false glitter and vulgar gauds. The assurance of that joy unspeakable makes the best joy here. Future blessedness, apprehended by the long arm of faith, brings present blessedness. The gladness and the power of the Christian life largely depend on the habitual beholding, with yearning and hope, of 'the King in His beauty and of the land that is very far off,' and yet so near, and of our own proper 'portion of the inheritance of the saints in light.' Christian men, it much concerns the vigour of your Christianity that you should take time and pains to cultivate the habit of looking forward through all the mists and darkness of this petty and unsubstantial present, and of thinking of that future as a certainty more certain than the contingencies of earth and as a present possession,

moro real by far than any of the fleeting shadows which
we proudly and falsely call our own. They pass from
hand to hand. They are mine to-day, another's to-
morrow. I have no real possession of them while
they were called mine. We truly possess but two
possessions—God and ourselves. We possess both by
the same way of giving ourselves to God in love and
obedience; and of such surrender and possession the
crown is the perfecting and the reward. 'Thy crown'
will fit no temples but thine. It is part of thy perfected
self, and certain to be thine, if thou hold fast the
beginning of thy confidence firm unto the end.

II. Note next the grim possibility of losing the crown.

'That no man take' it. Of course we are not to
misunderstand the contingency shadowed here, as if it
meant that some other person could filch away and put
on his own head the crown which once was destined
for us, which is a sheer impossibility and absurdity.
No man would think to win heaven by stealing
another's right of entrance there. No man could, if
he were to try. The results of character cannot be
transferred. Nor are we to suppose reference to the
machinations of tempters, either human or diabolic,
who deliberately and consciously try to rob Christians
of their religion here, and thereby of their reward
hereafter. But it is only too possible that men and
things round about us may upset this certainty that
we have been considering, and that though the crown
be 'thine,' it may never come to be thy actual possession in the future, nor ever be worn upon thine own
happy head in the festival of the skies.

That is the solemn side of the Christian life, that it is
to be conceived of as lived amidst a multitude of men
and things that are always trying to make us unfit to

receive that crown of righteousness. They cannot work directly upon *it*. It has no existence except as the efflorescence of our own character crowned by God's approbation. It is an ideal thing; but they can work upon *us*, and if they stain our heads with foul dust, then they make them unfit for our crown.   So here are we, Christian men and women! in a world all full of things that tend and may be regarded as desiring to rob us of our crowns. This is not the way in which we usually think of the temptations that assail us. For instance, there comes some sly and whispering one to us and suggests pleasant hours, bought at a very small sacrifice of principle; delights for sense or for ambition, or for one or other of the passions of our nature, and all looks very innocent, and the harm seems to be comparatively small. Ah! let us look a little bit deeper. That temptation that seems to threaten so little and to promise so much is really trying to rob us of the crown. If we would walk through life with this thought in our minds, how it would strip off the masks of all these temptations that buzz about us! If once we saw their purpose and understood the true aim of the flattering lies which they tell us, should we not see over the lies, and would not they lose their power to deceive us? Be sure—and oh! let us hold fast by the illuminating conviction when the temptations come— be sure that, with all their glozing words and false harlot kisses, their meaning is this, to rob us of the bright and precious thing that is most truly ours; and so let us put away the temptations, and say to them, 'Ah! you come as a friend, but I know your meaning; and forewarned is forearmed.'

III. Lastly, note the way to secure the crown which is ours.

'Hold fast that thou hast.' For if you do not hold it fast, it will slip. The metaphor is a plain one—if a man has got something very precious, he grips it with a very tight hand. The slack hand will very soon be an empty hand. Anybody walking through the midst of a crowd of thieves with a bag of gold in charge would not hold it dangling from a finger-tip, but he would put all five round it, and wrap the strings about his wrist.

The first shape which we may give to this exhortation is—hold fast by what God has given in His gospel; hold fast His Son, His truth, His grace. Use honestly and diligently your intellect to fathom and to keep firm hold of the great truths and principles of the gospel. Use your best efforts to keep your wandering hearts and mobile wills fixed and true to the revealed love of the great Lover of souls, which has been given to you in Christ, and to obey Him. You have got a Christ that is worth keeping, see to it that you keep Him, and do not let Him slip away out of your fingers. When the storms come a wise captain lashes all the light articles, and then they are safe. You and I have to struggle through many a storm, and all the loose stuff on deck will be washed off or blown away long before we get into calm water. Lash it by meditation, by faithful obedience, and by constant communion, and hold fast the Christian gospel, and, in the Christ whom the gospel reveals, the spiritual life that you possess.

But there is another aspect of the same commandment which applies not so much to that which is given us in the objective revelation and manifestation of God in Christ, as to our own subjective degrees of progress in the appropriation of Christ, and in likeness to Him. And possibly that is what my text more especially means, for just a little before, the Lord has said to that Church, 'Thou hast a little strength, and hast kept My word, and hast not denied My name.' 'Thou hast a little strength . . . hold fast that which thou hast.' See to it that thy present attainment in the Christian life, though it may be but rudimentary and incomplete, is at least kept. Cast not away your confidence, hold fast the beginning of your confidence firm, with a tightened hand, unto the end. For if we keep what we have, it will grow. Progress is certain, if there be persistence. If we do not let it go, it will increase and multiply in our possession. In all branches of study and intellectual pursuit, and in all branches of daily life, to hold fast what we have, and truly to possess what we possess, is the certain means to make our wealth greater. And so it is in the Christian life. Be true to the present knowledge, and use it, as it is meant to be used, and it will daily increase. 'Hold fast that thou hast.' Thou *hast* the 'strength'; thou hast not yet the crown. Keep what God has committed to you, and God will keep what He has reserved for you.

And so the sure way to get the crown is to keep the faith; and then the life and the glory, which are but the outcome and the fruit of the faithful, persistent life here, are as sure as the cycles of the heavens, or as the throne and the will of God. Men and things and devils may try to take your crown from you, but nobody can deprive you of it but yourself. Hold fast the present possession, and make it really your own, and the future crown which God has promised to all who love and thereby possess Him will, in due time, be twined around your head. He who has and holds fast Christ here cannot fail of the crown yonder.

VI.—THE VICTOR'S LIFE-NAMES

'**Him** that overcometh will I make a pillar in the temple of My God, and he shall go no more out: and I will write upon him the name of My God, and the name of the city of My God, which is new Jerusalem, which cometh down out of heaven from My God: and I will write upon him My new name.'—REV. iii. 12.

THE eyes which were as a flame of fire saw nothing to blame in the Philadelphian Church, and the lips out of which came the two-edged sword that cuts through all hypocrisy to the discerning of the thoughts and intents of the heart, spoke only eulogium—'Thou hast kept My word, and hast not denied My name.' But however mature and advanced may be Christian experience, it is never lifted above the possibility of temptation; so, with praise, there came warning of an approaching hour which would try the mettle of this unblamed Church. Christ's reward for faithfulness is not immunity from, but strength in, trial and conflict. As long as we are in the world there will be forces warring against us; and we shall have to fight our worst selves and the tendencies which tempt us to prefer the visible to the unseen, and the present to the future. So the Church which had no rebuke received the solemn injunction: 'Hold fast that thou hast; let no man take thy crown.' There is always need of struggle, even for the most mature, if we would keep what we have. The treasure will be filched from slack hands; the crown will be stricken from a slumbering head. So it is not inappropriate that the promise to this Church should be couched in the usual terms, 'to him that *overcometh*,' and the conclusion to be drawn is the solemn and simple one that the Christian life is always a conflict, even to the end.

The promise contained in my text presents practically but a twofold aspect of that future blessedness;

the one expressed in the clause, 'I will make him a pillar'; the other expressed in the clauses referring to the writing upon him of certain names. I need not do more than again call attention to the fact that here, as always, Jesus Christ represents Himself as not only allocating the position and determining the condition, but as shaping, and moulding, and enriching the characters of the redeemed, and ask you to ponder the question, What in Him does that assumption involve?

Passing on, then, to the consideration of these two promises more closely, let us deal with them singly. There is, first, the steadfast pillar; there is, second, the threefold inscription.

I. The steadfast pillar.

Now I take it that the two clauses which refer to this matter are closely connected. 'I will make him a pillar in the temple of My God, and he shall go no more out.' In the second clause the figure is dropped, and the point of the metaphor is brought out more clearly. The stately column in the temples, with which these Philadelphian Christians, dwelling in the midst of the glories of Greek architecture, were familiar, might be, and often has been, employed as a symbol of many things. Here it cannot mean the office of sustaining a building, or pre-eminence above others, as it naturally lends itself sometimes to mean. For instance, the Apostle Paul speaks of the three chief apostles in Jerusalem, and says that they 'seemed to be pillars'; by which pre-eminence and the office of maintaining the Church are implied. But that obviously cannot be the special application of the figure here, inasmuch as we cannot conceive of even redeemed men sustaining that temple in the heavens, and also inasmuch as the promise here is perfectly universal, and is given to

all that overcome—that is to say, to all the redeemed.
We must, therefore, look in some other direction.
Now, the second of the two clauses which are thus
linked together seems to me to point in the direction
in which we are to look. 'He shall go no more out.'
A pillar is a natural emblem of stability and permanence,
as poets in many tongues and in many lands have felt it
to be. I remember one of our own quaint English writers
who speaks of men who 'are bottomed on the basis of
a firm faith, mounting up with the clear shaft of a
shining life, and having their persevering tops gar-
landed about, according to God's promise, "I will give
thee a crown of life."' That idea of stability, of permanence, of fixedness, is the one that is prominent in
the metaphor here.

But whilst the general notion is that of stability and
permanence, do not let us forget that it is permanence
and stability in a certain direction, for the pillar is 'in
the temple of My God.' Now I would recall to you
the fact that in other parts of Scripture we find the
present relation of Christian men to God set forth under
a similar metaphor: 'Ye are the temple of the living
God'; or again, 'In whom ye are builded for a habitation of God through the Spirit'; or again, in that great
word which is the foundation of all such symbols, 'We
will come and make our abode with Him.' So that
the individual believer and the community of all such
are, even here and now, the dwelling-place of God.
And whilst there are ideas of dignity and grace attaching to the metaphor of the pillar, the underlying meaning of it is substantially that the individual souls of
redeemed men shall be themselves parts of, and collectively shall constitute, the temple of God in the heavens.

This book of the Apocalypse has several points of view

in regard to that great symbol. It speaks, for instance,
of there being 'no temple therein,' by which is meant
the cessation of all material and external worships
such as belong to earth. It speaks also of God and the
Lamb as themselves being 'the Temple thereof.' And
here we have the converse idea that not only may we
think of the redeemed community as dwelling in God
and Christ, but of God and Christ as dwelling in the redeemed community. The promise, then, is of a thrilling consciousness that God is in us, a deeper realisation
of His presence, a fuller communication of His grace,
a closer touch of Him, far beyond anything that we can
conceive of on earth, and yet being the continuation
and the completion of the earthly experiences of those
in whom God dwells by their faith, their love, and their
obedience. We have nothing to say about the new
capacities for consciousness of God which may come to
redeemed souls when the veils of flesh and sense, and
the absorption in the present drop away. We have
nothing to say, because we know nothing about the
new manifestations and more intimate touches which
may correspond to these new capacities. There are
vibrations of sounds too rapid or too slow for our ears
as at present organised to catch. But whether these
be too shrill or too deep to be heard, if the ear were
more sensitive there would be sound where there is
silence, and music in the waste places. So with new
organs, with new capacities, there will be a new and
a deeper sense of the presence of God ; and utterances
of His lips too profound to be caught by us now, or too
clear and high to be apprehended by our limited sense,
will then thunder into melody and with clear notes
sound His praises. There are rays of light in the
spectrum, at both ends of it, as yet not perceptible to

human eyes; but then 'we shall, in Thy light, see light' flaming higher and deeper than we can do now. We dwell in God here if we dwell in Christ, and we dwell in Christ if He dwell in us, by faith and love. But in the heavens the indwelling shall be more perfect, and transcend all that we know now.

The special point in regard to which that perfection is expressed here is to be kept prominent. 'He shall go no more out.' Permanence, and stability, and uninterruptedness in the communion and consciousness of an indwelling God, is a main element in the glory and blessedness of that future life. Stability in any fashion comes as a blessed hope to us, who know the curse of constant change, and are tossing on the unquiet waters of life. It is blessed to think of a region where the seal of permanence will be set on all delights, and our blessedness will be like the bush in the desert, burning and yet not consumed. But the highest form of that blessedness is the thought of stable, uninterrupted, permanent communion with God and consciousness of His dwelling in us. The contrast forces itself upon us between that equable and unvarying communion and the ups and downs of the most uniform Christian life here—to-day thrilling in every nerve with the sense of God, to-morrow dead and careless. Sometimes the bay is filled with flashing waters that leap in the sunshine; sometimes, when the tide is out, there is only a long stretch of grey and oozy mud. It shall not be always so. Like lands on the equator, where the difference between midsummer and midwinter is scarcely perceptible, either in length of day or in degree of temperature, that future will be a calm continuance, a uniformity which is not monotony, and a stability which does not exclude progress.

I cannot but bring into contrast with that great promise 'he shall go no more out' an incident in the gospels. Christ and the Twelve were in the upper room, and He poured out His heart to them, and their hearts burned within them. But 'they went out to the Mount of Olives'—He to Gethsemane and to Calvary; Judas to betray and Peter to deny; all to toil and suffer, and sometimes to waver in their faith. 'He shall go no more out.' Eternal glory and unbroken communion is the blessed promise to the victor who is made by Christ 'a pillar in the temple of My God.'

II. Now, secondly, notice the threefold inscription.

We have done with the metaphor of the pillar altogether. We are not to think of anything so incongruous as a pillar stamped with writing, a monstrosity in Grecian architecture. But it is the man himself on whom Christ is to write the threefold name. The writing of a name implies ownership and visibility.

So the first of the triple inscriptions declares that the victor shall be conspicuously God's. 'I will write upon him the name of My God.' There may possibly be an allusion to the golden plate which flamed in the front of the high priest's mitre, and on which was written the unspoken name of Jehovah. But whether that be so or no, the underlying ideas are these two which I have already referred to—complete ownership, and that manifested in the very front of the character.

How do we possess one another? How do we belong to God? How does God belong to us? There is but one way by which a spirit can possess a spirit—by love, which leads to self-surrender and to practical obedience. And if—as a man writes his name in his books, as a farmer brands on his sheep and oxen the marks that express his ownership—on the redeemed there is written the name of God, that means, whatever else it may mean, perfect love, perfect self-surrender, perfect obedience, that the whole nature shall be owned, and know itself owned, and be glad to be owned, by God. That is the perfecting of the Christian relationship which is begun here on earth. And if we here yield ourselves to God and depart from that foolish and always frustrated attempt to be our own masters and owners, so escaping the misery and burden of self-hood, and entering into the liberty of the children of God, we shall reach that blessed state in which there will be no murmuring and incipient rebellions, no disturbance of our inward submission, no breach in our active obedience, no holding back of anything that we have or are ; but we shall be wholly God's—that is, wholly possessors of ourselves, and blessed thereby. 'He that loveth his life shall lose it; and he that loseth his life, the same shall find it.' And that Name will be stamped on us, that every eye that looks, whoever they may be, shall know 'whose we are and whom we serve.'

The second inscription declares that the victor conspicuously belongs to the City. Our time will not allow of my entering at all upon the many questions that gather round that representation of 'the New Jerusalem which cometh down out of heaven.' I must content myself with simply pointing to the possible allusion here to the promise in the preceding letter to Sardis. There we were told that the victor's name should not 'be blotted out of the Book of Life'; and that Book of Life suggested the idea of the burgess-roll of the city, as well as the register of those that truly live. Here the same thought is suggested by a converse metaphor. The name of the victor is written on the rolls of the city, and the name of the city is stamped

on the forehead of the victor. That is to say, the affinity
which, even here and now, has knit men who believe
in Jesus Christ to an invisible order, where is their true
mother-city and metropolis, will then be uncontradicted
by any inconsistencies, unobscured by the necessary
absorption in daily duties and transient aims and
interests, which often veils to others, and renders less
conscious to ourselves, our true belonging to the city
beyond the sea. The name of the city shall be stamped
upon the victor. That, again, is the perfecting and the
continuation of the central heart of the Christian life
here, the consciousness that we are come to the city of
the living God, the heavenly Jerusalem, and belong to
another order of things than the visible and material
around us.

The last of the triple inscriptions declares that the
victor shall be conspicuously Christ's. 'I will write
upon him My new name.' All the three inscriptions
link themselves, not with earlier, but with later parts
of this most artistically constructed book of the Revelation; and in a subsequent portion of it we read of a
new name of Christ's, which no man knoweth save
Himself. What is that new name? It is an expression
for the sum of the new revelations of what He is, which
will flood the souls of the redeemed when they pass
from earth. That new name will not obliterate the
old one—God forbid! It will not do away with the
ancient, earth-begun relation of dependence and
faith and obedience. 'Jesus Christ is the same . . .
for ever': and His name in the heavens, as upon earth,
is Jesus the Saviour. But there are abysses in Him
which no man moving amidst the incipiencies and imperfections of this infantile life of earth can understand. Not until we possess can we know the depths

of wisdom and knowledge, and of all other blessed treasures which are stored in Him. Here we touch but the fringe of His great glory; yonder we shall penetrate to its central flame.

That new name no man fully knows, even when he has entered on its possession and carries it on his forehead; for the infinite Christ, who is the manifestation of the infinite God, can never be comprehended, much less exhausted, even by the united perceptions of a redeemed universe; but for ever and ever, more and more will well out from Him. His name shall last as long as the sun, and blaze when the sun himself is dead.

'I will write upon him My new name' was said to a church, and while the eulogium was, 'Thou hast not denied My name.' If we are to pierce the heart and the glory there, we must begin on its edges here. If the name is to be on our foreheads then, we must bear in our body the marks of the Lord Jesus—the brand of ownership impressed on the slave's palm. In the strength of the name we can overcome; and if we overcome, His name will hereafter blaze on our foreheads—the token that we are completely His for ever, and the pledge that we shall be growingly made like unto Him.

LAODICEA

'I know thy works, that thou art neither cold nor hot . . . be zealous therefore, and repent.'—Rev. iii. 15, 19.

WE learn from Paul's Epistle to the Colossians that there was a very close connection between that Church and this at Laodicea. It is a probable conjecture that a certain Archippus, who is spoken of in the former Epistle, was the bishop or pastor of the Laodicean

Church.   And if, as seems not unlikely, the 'angels'
of these Asiatic churches were the presiding officers of
the same, then it is at least within the limits of possibility that the 'angel of the Church at Laodicea,' who
received the letter, was Archippus.

The message that was sent to Archippus by Paul was
this: 'Take heed to the ministry which thou hast
received of the Lord, that thou fulfil it.'   And if thirty
years had passed, and then Archippus got this message:
'Thou art neither cold nor hot,' you have an example
of how a little negligence in manifest duty on the part
of a Christian man may gradually grow and spread,
like a malignant cancer, until it has eaten all the life
out of him, and left him a mere shell.   The lesson is
for us all.

But whether we see an individual application in
these words or no, certainly the 'angel of the church'
is spoken of in his character of a representative of the
whole Church.   So, then, this Laodicean community
had no works.   So far had declension gone that even
Christ's eye could see no sign of the operation of the
religious principle in it; and all that He could say
about it was, 'thou art neither cold nor hot.'

It is very remarkable that the first and the last
letters to the seven Churches deal with the same phase
of religious declension, only that the one is in the
germ and the other is fully developed.   The Church of
Ephesus had still works abundant, receiving and deserving the warm-hearted commendation of the Master,
but they had 'left their first love.'   The Church at
Laodicea had no works, and in it the disease had sadly,
and all but universally, spread.

Now then, dear friends, I intend, not in the way of
rebuke, God knows, but in the way of earnest remon-

strance and appeal to you professing Christians, to draw some lessons from these solemn words.

I. I pray you to look at that loving rebuke of the faithful Witness : 'Thou art neither cold nor hot.'

We are manifestly there in the region of emotion. The metaphor applies to feeling. We talk, for instance, about warmth of feeling, ardour of affection, fervour of love, and the like. And the opposite, cold, expresses obviously the absence of any glow of a true living emotion.

So, then, the persons thus described are Christian people (for their Christianity is presupposed), with very little, though a little, warmth of affection and glow of Christian love and consecration.

Further, this defectiveness of Christian feeling is accompanied with a large amount of self-complacency : —'Thou sayest I am rich, and increased with goods, and have need of nothing; and knowest not that thou art wretched, and miserable, and poor, and blind, and naked.' Of course it is so. A numbed limb feels no pain. As cold increases the sensation of cold, and of everything else, goes away. And a sure mark of defective religious emotion is absolute unconsciousness on the man's part that there is anything the matter with him. All of you that have no sense that the indictment applies to you, by the very fact show that it applies most especially and most tragically to you. Self-complacency diagnoses spiritual cold, and is an inevitable and a constantly accompanying symptom of a deficiency of religious emotion.

Then again, this deficiency of warmth is worse than absolute zero. 'I would thou wert cold or hot.' That is no spurt of impatience on the part of the 'true Witness.' It is for their sake that He would they were

cold or hot. And why? Because there is no man
more hopeless than a man on whom the power of
Christianity has been brought to bear, and has failed
in warming and quickening him. If you were cold, at
absolute zero, there would be at least a possibility that
when you were brought in contact with the warmth
you might kindle. But you have been brought in
contact with the warmth, and this is the effect. Then
what is to be done with you? There is nothing more
that can be brought to bear on your consciousness to
make you anything higher or better than you are,
than what you have already had in operation in your
spiritual life. And if it has failed, all God's armoury is
empty, and He has shot His last bolt, and there is
nothing more left. 'I would thou wert cold or hot.'

Now, dear friends, is that our condition? I am
obliged sadly to say that I believe it is to a fearful
extent the condition of professing Christendom to-day.
'Neither cold nor hot!' Look at the standard of
Christian life round about us. Let us look into our
own hearts. Let us mark how wavering the line is
between the Church and the world; how little upon
our side of the line there is of conspicuous consecration
and unworldliness; how entirely in regard of an
enormous mass of professing Christians, the maxims
that are common in the world are their maxims; and
the sort of life that the world lives is the sort of life
that they live. 'Oh! thou that art named the House of
Israel,' as one of the old prophets wailed out, 'is the
Spirit of the Lord straitened? Are these His doings?'
And so I would say, look at your churches and mark
their feebleness, the slow progress of the gospel among
them, the low lives that the bulk of us professing
Christians are living, and answer the question: Is that

the operation of a Divine Spirit that comes to transform and to quicken everything into His own vivid
and flaming life? or is it the operation of our own
selfishness and worldliness, crushing down and hem-
ming in the power that ought to sway us? Brethren!
it is not for me to cast condemnation, but it is for each
of us to ask ourselves the question: Do we not hear
the voice of the 'faithful and true Witness' saying to
us, 'I know thy works, that thou art neither cold
nor hot'?

II. And now will you let me say a word next as to
some of the plain causes of this lukewarmness of
spiritual life?

Of course the tendency to it is in us all. Take a bar
of iron out of the furnace on a winter day, and lay it
down in the air, and there is nothing more wanted.
Leave it there, and very soon the white heat will
change into livid dulness, and then there will come a
scale over it, and in a short time it will be as cold as
the frosty atmosphere around it. And so there is
always a refrigerating process acting upon us, which
needs to be counteracted by continual contact with the
fiery furnace of spiritual warmth, or else we are cooled
down to the degree of cold around us. But besides
this universally operating cause there are many others
which affect us.

Laodicea was a great commercial city, an emporium
of trade, which gives especial point and appropriateness
to the loving counsel of the context. 'I advise thee to
buy of Me gold tried in the fire.' And Manchester life,
with its anxieties, with its perplexities for many of
you, with its diminished profits, and apparently dimin-
ishing trade, is a fearful foe to the warmth and reality
of your Christian life. The cares of this world, and

the riches of this world are both amongst the thorns
which choke the Word and make it unfruitful. I find
fault with no man for the earnestness which he flings
into his business, but I ask you to contrast this entire
absorption of spirit, and the willing devotion of hours
and strength to *it*, with the grudging, and the partial,
and the transient devotion of ourselves to the religious
life; and say whether the relative importance of the
things seen and unseen is fairly represented by the
relative amount of earnestness with which you and I
pursue these respectively.

Then, again, the existence among us, or around us,
of a certain widely diffused doubt as to the truths of
Christianity is, illogically enough, a cause for diminished fervour on the part of the men that do not doubt
them. That is foolish, and it is strange, but it is true.
It is very hard for us, when so many people round
about us are denying, or at least are questioning, the
verities which we have been taught to believe, to keep
the freshness and the fervour of our devotion to these;
just as it is very difficult for a man to keep up the
warmth of his body in the midst of some creeping mist
that enwraps everything. So with us, the presence, in
the atmosphere of doubt, depresses the vitality and the
vigour of the Christian Church where it does not
intensify its faith, and make it cleave more desperately
to the things that are questioned. Beware, then, of
unreasonably yielding so far to the influence of prevailing unbelief as to make you grasp with a slacker
hand the thing which still you do not say that you
doubt.

And there is another case, which I name with some
hesitation, but which yet seems to me to be worthy of
notice; and that is, the increasing degree to which

Christian men are occupied with what we call, for
want of a better name, *secular* things. The leaders in
the political world, on both sides, in our great commercial cities, are usually professing Christians. I am
the last man to find fault with any Christian man for
casting himself, so far as his opportunities allow, into
the current of political life, if he will take his Christianity with him, and if he will take care that he does
not become a great deal more interested in elections,
and in pulling the strings of a party, and in working
for 'the cause,' than he is in working for his Master.
I grudge the political world nothing that it gets of
your strength, but I do grudge, for your sakes as well
as for the Church's sake, that so often the two forms
of activity are supposed by professing Christians to be
incompatible, and that therefore the more important is
neglected, and the less important done. Suffer the
word of exhortation.

And, in like manner, literature and art, and the
ordinary objects of interest on the part of men who
have no religion, are coming to absorb a great deal
of our earnestness and our energy. I would not with-
draw one iota of the culture that now prevails largely
in the Christian Church. All that I plead for, dear
brethren, is this, 'Ye are the salt of the earth.' Go
where you like, and fling yourselves into all manner of
interests and occupations, only carry your Master with
you. And remember that if you are not salting the
world, the world is putrefying you.

There I think you have some, though it be imperfect,
account of the causes which operate to lower the temperature of the Christian Church in general, and of
this Christian Church, and of you as individual members of it.

T

III. Now, further, note the loving call here to deep-ened earnestness.

'Be zealous, therefore.' The word translated, and rightly translated, *zealous* means literally *boiling with heat*. It is an exhortation to fervour. Now there is no worse thing in all this world than for a man to try to work up emotion, nothing which is so sure, sooner or later, to come to mischief, sure to breed hypocrisy and all manner of evil. If there be anything that is worse than trying to work up emotion, it is attempting to pretend it. So when our Master here says to us, 'Be zealous, therefore,' we must remember that zeal in a man ought to be a consequence of knowledge; and that, seeing that we are reasonable creatures, intended to be guided by our understandings, it is an upsetting of the whole constitution of a man's nature if his heart works independently of his head. And the only way in which we can safely and wholesomely increase our zeal is by increasing our grasp of the truths which feed it.

Thus the exhortation, 'Be zealous,' if we come to analyse it, and to look into its basis, is this—Lay hold upon, and meditate upon, the great truths that will make your heart glow. Notice that this exhortation is a consequence, 'Be zealous, therefore,' and repent. *Therefore*, and what precedes? A whole series of con-siderations—such as these: 'I counsel thee to buy of Me gold tried in the fire . . . and white raiment . . . and anoint thine eyes with eyesalve.' That is to say, lay hold of the truth that Christ possesses a full store of all that you can want. Meditate on that great truth and it will kindle a flame of desire and of fruition in your hearts. 'Be zealous, *therefore*.' And again, 'As many as I love I rebuke and chasten.' 'Be zealous, therefore.' That is to say, grasp the great thought of the loving Christ, all whose dealings, even when His voice assumes severity, and His hand comes armed with a rod, are the outcome and manifestation of His love; and sink into that love, and that will make your hearts glow. 'Behold, I stand at the door and knock.' 'Be zealous, therefore.' Think of the earnest, patient, long-suffering appeal which the Master makes, bearing with all our weaknesses and our shortcomings, and not suffering His gentle hand to be turned away, though the door has been so long barred and bolted in His face. And let these sweet thoughts of a Christ that gives everything, of a Christ all whose dealings are love, of a Christ who pleads with us through the barred door, and tries to get at us through the obstacles which ourselves have fastened against Him, let them draw us to Him, and kindle and keep alight a brighter flame of consecration and of devotion in our hearts to Him. '*Be zealous.*' Feed upon the great truths of the Gospel which kindles zeal.

Brethren, the utmost warmth is reasonable in religion. If Christianity be true, there is no measure of ardour or of consecration which is beyond the reasonable requirements of the case. We are told that 'a sober standard of feeling in matters of religion' is the great thing to aim at. So I say. But I would differ, perhaps, with the people that are fond of saying so, in my definition of sobriety. A sober standard is a standard of feeling in which the feeling does not outrun the facts on which it is built. Enthusiasm is disproportionate or ignorant feeling; warmth without light. A sober, reasonable feeling is the emotion which is correspondent to the truths that evoke it. And will any man tell me that any amount of earnestness, of

flaming consecration, of fiery zeal, is in advance of the
great truths that Christ loves me, and has given
Himself for me?

IV. And now, lastly, observe the merciful call to a
new beginning: 'Repent.'

There must be a lowly consciousness of sin, a clear
vision of my past shortcomings, an abhorrence of these,
and, joined with that, a resolute act of mind and heart
beginning a new course, a change of purpose and of
the current of my being.

Repentance is sorrow for the past, blended with a
resolve to paste down the old leaf and begin a new
writing on a new page. Christian men have need of
these fresh beginnings, and of new repentance, even as
the patriarch when he came up from Egypt went to
the place where 'he builded the altar *at the first*,'
and there offered sacrifice. Do not you be ashamed,
Christian men and women, if you have been living
low and inconsistent Christian lives in the past, to
make a new beginning and to break with that past.
There was never any great outburst of life in a Christian
Church which was not preceded by a lowly penitence.
And there is never any penitence worth naming which
is not preceded by a recognition, glad, rapturous, confident as self-consciousness, of Christ's great and infinite love to me.

Oh! if there is one thing that we want more than
another to-day, it is that the fiery Spirit shall come
and baptise all the churches, and us as individual members of them. What was it that finished the infidelity of
the last century? Was it Paley and Butler, with their
demonstrations and their books? No! it was John
Wesley and Whitefield. Here is a solution, full of
microscopic germs that will putrefy. Expose it to

heat, raise the temperature, and you will kill all the germs, so that you may keep it for a hundred years, and there will be no putrefaction in it. Get the temperature of the Church up, and all the evils that are eating out its life will shrivel and drop to the bottom dead. They cannot live in the heat; cold is their region.

So, dear brethren, let us get near to Christ's love until the light of it shines in our own faces. Let us get near to Christ's love until, like coal laid upon the fire, its fervours penetrate into our substance and change even our blackness into ruddy flame. Let us get nearer to the love, and then, though the world may laugh and say, 'He hath a devil and is mad,' they that see more clearly will say of us: 'The zeal of Thine house hath eaten him up,' and the Father will say even concerning us: 'This is My beloved son, in whom I am well pleased.'

CHRIST'S COUNSEL TO A LUKEWARM CHURCH

'I counsel thee to buy of Me gold tried in the fire, that thou mayest be rich ; and white raiment, that thou mayest be clothed, and that the shame of thy nakedness do not appear ; and anoint thine eyes with eyesalve, that thou mayest see.'— REV. iii. 18.

AFTER the scathing exposure of the religious condition of this Laodicean Church its members might have expected something sterner than 'counsel.' There is a world of love and pity, with a dash of irony, in the use of that softened expression. He does not willingly threaten, and He never scolds; but He rather speaks to men's hearts and their reason, and comes to them as a friend, than addresses Himself to their fears.

Whether there be any truth or not in the old idea that these letters to the seven churches are so arranged

as, when taken in sequence, to present a fore-glimpse
of the successive conditions of the Church till the
second coming of our Lord, it is at least a noteworthy
fact that the last of them in order is the lowest in
spiritual state.   That church was 'lukewarm'; 'neither
cold'—untouched by the warmth of the Spirit of
Christ at all—'nor hot'—adequately inflamed thereby.

That is the worst sort of people to get at, and it is
no want of charity to say that Laodicea is repeated in
a thousand congregations, and that Laodiceans are
prevalent in every congregation.   All our Christian
communities are hampered by a mass of loose adherents
with no warmth of consecration, no glow of affection,
no fervour of enthusiasm; and they bring down the
temperature, as snow-covered mountains over which
the wind blows make the thermometer drop on the
plains.   It is not for me to diagnose individual conditions, but it is for me to take note of widespread
characteristics and strongly running currents; and it
is for you to settle whether the characteristics are
yours or not.

So I deal with Christ's advice to a lukewarm church,
and I hope to do it in the spirit of the Master who
counselled, and neither scolded nor threatened.

I. Now I observe that the first need of the lukewarm
church is to open its eyes to see facts.

I take it that the order in which the points of this
counsel are given is not intended to be the order in
which they are obeyed.   I dare say there is no thought
of sequence in the succession of the clauses.   But if
there is, I think that a little consideration will show
us that that which comes last in mention is to be first
in fulfilment.

Observe that the text falls into two distinct parts,

and that the counsel to buy does not extend—and,and
it is ordinarily read as if it did—to the last item in one-
Lord's advice. These Laodiceans are bid to ' buy of '
Him ' gold ' and ' raiment,' but they are bid to use the
' eyesalve ' that they ' may see.' No doubt, whatever is
meant by that ' eyesalve ' comes from Him, as does
everything else. But my point is that these people are
supposed already to possess it, and that they are bid to
employ it. And, taking that point of view, I think we
can come to the understanding of what is meant.

No doubt the exhortation, 'anoint thine eyes with
eyesalve, that thou mayest see,' may be so extended as
to refer to the general condition of spiritual blindness
which attaches to humanity, apart from the illuminating and sight-giving work of Jesus Christ. That true
Light, which lighteneth every man that cometh into
the world, has a threefold office as the result of all the
parts of which there comes to our darkened eyes the
vision of the things that are. He reveals the objects
to see; He gives the light by which we see them; and
He gives us eyes to see with. He shows us God, immortality, duty, men's condition, men's hopes, and He
takes from us the cataract which obscures, the shortsightedness which prevents us from beholding things
that are far off, and the obliquity of vision which
forbids us to look steadily and straight at the things
which it is worth our while to behold. ' For judgment
am I come into the world,' said He, ' that they which
see not might see.' And it is possible that the general
illuminating influence of Christ's mission and work,
and especially the illuminating power of His Spirit
dwelling in men's spirits, may be included in the
thoughts of the eyesalve with which we are to anoint
our eyes.

as, where context seems to me rather to narrow the
of age of the meaning of this part of our Lord's counsel.
For these Laodiceans had the conceit of their own
sufficing wealth, of their own prosperous religious condition, and were blind as bats to the real facts that
they were 'miserable and poor and naked.' Therefore
our Lord says: 'Anoint thine eyes with eyesalve, that
thou mayest see—recognise your true state; do not
live in this dream that you are satisfactorily united to
Myself, when all the while the thread of connection is
so slender that it is all but snapped. Behold Me as I
am, and the things that I reveal to you as they are;
and then you will see yourselves as you are.'

So, then, there comes out of this exhortation this
thought, that a symptom constantly accompanying the
lukewarm condition is absolute unconsciousness of it.
In all regions the worse a man is the less he knows it.
It is the good people that know themselves to be bad;
the bad ones, when they think about themselves,
conceit themselves to be good. It is the men in the
van of the march that feel the prick of the impulse to
press farther: the laggards are quite content to stop
in the rear. The higher a man climbs, in any science,
or in the practice of any virtue, the more clearly he
sees the unscaled peaks above him. The frost-bitten
limb is quite comfortable. It is when life begins to
come back into it that it tingles and aches. And so
these Laodiceans were like the Jewish hero of old, who
prostituted his strength, and let them shear away his
locks while his lazy head lay in the harlot's lap: he
went out 'to shake himself' as of old times, and knew
not that the Spirit of God had departed from him. So,
brethren, the man in this audience who most needs
to be roused and startled into a sense of his tepid

religionism is the man that least suspects the need, and
would be most surprised if a more infallible and penetrating voice than mine were to come and say to him,
'Thou—*thou* art the man.'   'Anoint thine eyes with
eyesalve, that thou mayest see'; and let the light,
which Christ pours upon unseen things, pour itself
revealing into your hearts, that you may no longer
dream of yourselves as 'rich, and increased with goods,
and having need of nothing'; but may know that you
are poor and blind and naked.

Another thought suggested by this part of the counsel is that the blind man must himself rub in the
eyesalve. Nobody else can do it for him. True! it
comes, like every other good thing, from the Christ in
the heavens; and, as I have already said, if we will
attach specific meanings to every part of a metaphor,
that 'eyesalve' may be the influence of the Divine
Spirit who convicts men of sin. But whatever it is,
you have to apply it to your own eyes. Translate that
into plain English, and it is just this, by the light of
the knowledge of God and duty and human nature,
which comes rushing in a flood of illumination from
the central sun of Christ's mission and character, test
yourselves. Our forefathers made too much of self-
examination as a Christian duty, and pursued it often
for mistaken purposes. But this generation makes far
too *light* of it. Whilst I would not say to anybody,
'Poke into the dark places of your own hearts in order
to find out whether you are Christian people or not,'
for that will only come to diffidence and despair, I
would say, 'Do not be a stranger to yourselves, but
judge yourselves rigidly, by the standard of God's
Word, of Christ's example, and in all your search, ask
Him to give you that 'candle of the Lord,' which will

shine into the dustiest corners and the darkest of our
hearts, and reveal to us, if we truly wish it, all the
cobwebs and unconsidered litter and rubbish, if not
venomous creatures, that are gathered there. Apply
the eyesalve; it will be keen, it will bite; welcome the
smart, and be sure that anything is good for you which
takes away the veil that self-complacency casts over
your true condition, and lets the light of God into the
cellars and dark places of your souls.

II. The second need of the lukewarm church is the
true wealth which Christ gives.

'I counsel thee to buy of Me gold tried in the fire.'
Now there may be many different ways of putting the
thought that is conveyed here, but I think the deepest
truth of human nature is that the only wealth for a
man is the possession of God. And so instead of, as
many commentators do, suggesting interpretations
which seem to me to be inadequate, I think we go to
the root of the matter when we find the meaning of
the wealth which Christ counsels us to buy of Him in
the possession of God Himself, who is our true treasure
and durable riches.

That wealth alone makes us paupers truly rich. For
there is nothing else that satisfies a man's craving and
supplies a man's needs. 'He that loveth silver shall
not be satisfied with silver, nor he that loveth abundance, with increase'; but if we have the gold of God,
we are rich to all intents of bliss; and if we have Him
not, if we are 'for ever roaming with a hungry heart,'
and though we may have a large balance at our
bankers, and much wealth in our coffers, and 'houses
full of silver and gold,' we are poor indeed.

That wealth has immunity from all accidents. No
possession is truly mine of which any outward con-

tingency or circumstance can deprive me.   But this
wealth, the wealth of a heart enriched with the possession of God, whom it knows, loves, trusts, and obeys,
this wealth is incorporated with a man's very being,
and enters into the substance of his nature; and so
nothing can deprive him of it.   That which moth or
rust can corrupt; that which thieves can break through
and steal; that which is at the mercy of the accidents
of a commercial community or of the fluctuations of
trade; that is no wealth for a man.   Only something
which passes into me, and becomes so interwoven with
my being as is the dye with the wool, is truly wealth
for me.   And such wealth is God.

The only possession which we can take with us when
our nerveless hands drop all other goods, and our hearts
are untwined from all other loves, is this durable riches.
'Shrouds have no pockets,' as the grim proverb has it.
But the man that has God for his portion carries all
his riches with him into the darkness, whilst of the
man that made creatures his treasure it is written:
'His glory shall not descend after him.'   Therefore,
dear brethren, let us all listen to that counsel, and buy
of Jesus gold that is tried in the fire.

III. The third need of a lukewarm church is the
raiment that Christ gives.

The wealth which He bids us buy of Him belongs
mostly to our inward life; the raiment which He prof-
fers us to wear, as is natural to the figure, applies
mainly to our outward lives, and signifies the dress
of our spirits as these are presented to the world.

I need not remind you of how frequently this metaphor is employed throughout the Scriptures, both in the
Old and the New Testament—from the vision granted
to one of the prophets, in which he saw the high priest

standing before God, clothed in filthy garments, which
were taken off him by angel hands, and he draped in
pure and shining vestures—down to our Lord's parable
of the man that had not on the wedding garment; and
Paul's references to putting off and putting on the old
and the new man with his deeds. Nor need I dwell
upon the great frequency with which, in this book of
the Revelation, the same figure occurs. But the sum
and substance of the whole thing is just this, that we
can get from Jesus Christ characters that are pure and
radiant with the loveliness and the candour of His
own perfect righteousness. Mark that here we are
not bidden to put on the garment, but to take it from
His hands. True, having taken it, we are to put it on,
and that implies daily effort. So my text puts this
counsel in its place in the whole perspective of a combined Christian truth, and suggests the combination
of faith which receives, and of effort which puts on,
the garment that Christ gives. No thread of it is
woven in our own looms, nor have we the making of
the vesture, but we have the wearing of it.

There is nothing in the world vainer than effort after
righteousness which is not based on faith. There is
nothing more abnormal and divergent from the true
spirit of the New Testament than faith, so-called,
which is not accompanied with daily effort. On the
one hand we must be contented to receive; on the
other hand we must be earnest to appropriate. 'Buy
of Me gold,' and then we are rich. 'Buy of Me raiment,'
and then—listen to the voice that says, 'Put off the old
man with his deeds, and put on the new man of God
created in righteousness and holiness of truth.'

IV. Lastly, all supply of these needs is to be
bought.

'*Buy* of Me.' There is nothing in that counsel con-

tradictory to the great truth that 'the *gift* of God is
eternal life.' That buying is explained by the great
gospel invitation, long centuries before the gospel—
'Ho! every one that thirsteth, come ye to the waters,
... buy, and eat, ... without money and without
price.' It is explained by our Lord's twin parables of
the treasure hid in a field, which, when a man had
found, he went and sold all that he had and bought the
field; and of the pearl of great price which, when the
merchantman searching had discovered, he went and
sold all that he had that he might possess the one.

For what is 'all that we have'? Self! and we have
to give away self that we may buy the riches and the
robes. The only thing that is needed is to get rid, once
and for all, of that conceit that we have anything that
we can offer as the equivalent for what we desire. He
that has opened his eyes, and sees himself as he is, poor
and naked, and so comes to sue *in formâ pauperis*, and
abandons all trust in self, he is the man who buys of
Christ the gold and the vesture. If we will thus rightly
estimate ourselves, and estimating ourselves, have not
only the negative side of faith, which is self-distrust,
but the positive, which is absolute reliance on Him, we
shall not ask in vain. He counsels us to buy, and if we
take His advice and come, saying, 'Nothing in my hand
I bring,' He will not stultify Himself by refusing to
give us what He has bid us ask. 'What things were
given to me; those I counted loss for Christ. Yea!
doubtless, and I count all things but loss for the excel-
lency of the knowledge of Christ Jesus my Lord.' If
we, with opened eyes, go to Him thus, we shall come
away from Him enriched and clothed, and say, 'My
soul shall be joyful in my God, for He hath clothed me
with the garments of salvation; He hath covered me
with the robe of righteousness.'

CHRIST AT THE DOOR

'Behold, I stand at the door, and knock: if any man hear My voice, and open the door, I will come in to him, and will sup with him, and he with Me.'—REV. iii. 20.

MANY of us are familiar, I dare say, with the devoutly imaginative rendering of the first part of these wonderful words, which we owe to the genius of a living painter. In it we see the fast shut door, with rusted hinges, all overgrown with rank, poisonous weeds, which tell how long it has been closed. There stands, amid the night dews and the darkness, the patient Son of man, one hand laid on the door, the other bearing a light, which may perchance flash through some of its chinks. In His face are love repelled, and pity all but wasted; in the touch of His hand are gentleness and authority.

But the picture pauses, of course, at the beginning of my text, and its sequel is quite as wonderful as its first part. 'I will come in to him, and sup with him, and he with Me.' What can surpass such words as these? I venture to take this great text, and ask you to look with me at the three things that lie in it; the suppliant for admission; the door opened; the entrance, and the feast.

I. Think, then, first of all, of that suppliant for admission.

I suppose that the briefest explanation of my text is sufficient. Who knocks? The exalted Christ. What is the door? This closed heart of man. What does He desire? Entrance. What are His knockings and His voice? All providences; all monitions of His Spirit in man's spirit and conscience; the direct invitations of His written or spoken word; in brief, whatsoever sways our hearts to yield to Him and enthrone Him. This is the meaning, in the fewest possible words, of the great utterance of my text.

Here is a revelation of a universal truth, applying to every man and woman on the face of the earth; but more especially and manifestly to those of us who live within the sound of Christ's gospel and of the written revelations of His grace. True, my text was originally spoken in reference to the unworthy members of a little church of early believers in Asia Minor, but it passes far beyond the limits of the lukewarm Laodiceans to whom it was addressed. And the 'any man' which follows is wide enough to warrant us in stretching out the representation as far as the bounds of humanity extend, and in believing that wherever there is a closed heart there is a knocking Christ, and that all men are lightened by that Light which came into the world.

Upon that I do not need to dwell, but I desire to enforce the individual bearing of the general truth upon our own consciences, and to come to each with this message: The saying is true about thee, and at the door of thy heart Jesus Christ stands, and there His gentle, mighty hand is laid, and on it the flashes of His light shine, and through the chinks of the unopened door of thy heart comes the beseeching voice, 'Open! Open unto Me.' A strange reversal of the attitudes of the great and of the lowly, of the giver and of the receiver, of the Divine and of the human! Christ once said, 'Knock and it shall be opened unto you.' But He has taken the suppliant's place, and, standing by the side of each of us, He beseeches us that we let Him bless us, and enter in for our rest.

So, then, there is here a revelation, not only of a universal truth, but a most tender and pathetic disclosure of Christ's yearning love to each of us. What do you call that emotion which more than anything else desires that a heart should open and let it enter? We call it love when we find it in one another. Surely it bears the same name when it is sublimed into all but infinitude, and yet it is as individualising and specific as it is great and universal, as it is found in Jesus Christ. If it be true that He wants me, if it be true that in that great heart of His there are a thought and a wish about His relation to me, and mine to Him, then, then, each of us is grasped by a love that is like our human love, only perfected and purified from all its weaknesses.

Now we sometimes feel, I am afraid, as if all that talk about the love which Jesus Christ has to each of us was scarcely a prose fact. There is a woeful lack of belief among us in the things that we profess to believe most. You are all ready to admit, when I preach it, that it is true that Jesus Christ loves us. Have you ever tried to realise it, and lay it upon your hearts, that the sweetness and astoundingness of it may soak into you, and change your whole being? Oh! listen, not to my poor, rough notes, but to His infinitely sweet and tender melody of voice, when He says to you, as if your eyes needed to be opened to perceive it, ' Behold ! I stand at the door and knock.'

There is a revelation in the words, dear friends, of an infinite long-suffering and patience. The door has long been fastened; you and I have, like some lazy servant, thought that if we did not answer the knock, the Knocker would go away when He was weary. But we have miscalculated the elasticity and the

unfailingness of that patient Christ's love. Rejected,
He abides; spurned, He returns. There are men and
women who all their lives long have known that Jesus
Christ coveted their love, and yearned for a place in
their hearts, and have steeled themselves against the
knowledge, or frittered it away by worldliness, or
darkened it by sensuality and sin. And they are once
more brought into the presence of that rejected,
patient, wooing Lord, who courts them for their souls,
as if they were, which indeed they are, too precious to
be lost, as long as there is a ghost of a chance that
they may still listen to His voice. The patient Christ's
wonderfulness of long-suffering may well bow us all
in thankfulness and in penitence. How often has He
tapped or thundered at the door of your heart, dear
friends, and how often have you neglected to open?
Is it not of the Lord's mercies that the rejected or
neglected love is offered you once more? and the voice,
so long deadened and deafened to your ears by the
rush of passion, and the hurry of business, and the
whispers of self, yet again appeals to you, as it does
even through my poor translation of it.

And then, still further, in that thought of the
suppliant waiting for admission there is the explanation for us all of a great many misunderstood facts in
our experience. That sorrow that darkened your days
and made your heart bleed, what was it but Christ's
hand on the door? Those blessings which pour into
your life day by day ' beseech you, by the mercies of
God, that ye yield yourselves living sacrifices.' That
unrest which dogs the steps of every man who has not
found rest in Christ, what is it but the application of
His hand to the obstinately closed door? The stings
of conscience, the movements of the Spirit, the definite

U

proclamation of His Word, even by such lips as mine, what are they all except His appeals to us? And this is the deepest meaning of joys and sorrows, of gifts and losses, of fulfilled and disappointed hopes. This is the meaning of the yearning of Christless hearts, of the stings of conscience which come to us all. 'Behold! I stand at the door and knock.' If we understood better that all life was guided by Christ, and that Christ's guidance of life was guided by His desire that He should find a place in our hearts, we should less frequently wonder at sorrows, and should better understand our blessings.

The boy Samuel, lying sleeping before the light in the inner sanctuary, heard the voice of God, and thought it was only the grey-bearded priest that spoke. We often make the same mistake, and confound the utterances of Christ Himself with the speech of men. Recognise who it is that pleads with you; and do not fancy that when Christ speaks it is Eli that is calling; but say, 'Speak, Lord! for Thy servant heareth.' 'Lift up your heads, O ye gates, even lift them up, ye everlasting doors, and the King of Glory shall come in.'

II. And that leads me, secondly, to ask you to look at the door opened.

I need not enlarge upon what I have already suggested, the universality of the wide promise here— 'If *any* man open the door'; but what I want rather to notice is that, according to this representation, 'the door' has no handle outside, and is so hinged that it opens from within, outwards. Which, being taken out of metaphor and put into fact, means this, you are the only being that can open the door for Christ to come in. The whole responsibility, brother, of accepting or rejecting God's gracious Word, which comes to you all in good faith, lies with yourself.

I am not going to plunge into theological puzzles, but I appeal to consciousness. You know as well as I do—better a great deal, for it is *yourself* that is in question—that at each time when your heart and conscience have been brought in contact with the offer of salvation through faith in Jesus Christ, if you had liked you could have opened the door, and welcomed His entrance. And you know that nobody and nothing kept it fast except only yourselves. 'Ye *will* not come to Me,' said Christ, 'that ye might have life.' Men, indeed, do pile up such mountains of rubbish against the door that it cannot be opened, but it was they that put them there; and they are responsible if the hinges are so rusty that they will not move, or the doorway is so clogged that there is no room for it to open. Jesus Christ knocks, but Jesus Christ cannot break the door open. It lies in your hands to decide whether you will take or whether you will reject that which He brings.

The door is closed, and unless there be a definite act on your parts it will not be opened, and He will not enter. So we come to this, that to do nothing is to keep your Saviour outside; and that is the way in which most men that miss Him do miss Him.

I suppose there are very few of us who have ever been conscious of a definite act by which, if I might adhere to the metaphor, we have laid hold of the door on the inside, and held it tight lest it should be opened. But, I fear me, there are many who have sat in the inner chamber, and heard the gracious hand on the outer panel, and have kept their hands folded and their feet still, and done nothing. Ah! brethren, to do nothing is to do the most dreadful of things, for it is to keep the shut door shut in the face of Christ. No passionate antagonism is needed, no vehement rejection, no intellectual denial of His truth and His promises. If you want to ruin yourselves, you have simply to do nothing! All the dismal consequences will necessarily follow.

'Well,' you say, 'but you are talking metaphors; let us come to plain facts. What do you want me to do?' I want you to listen to the message of an infinitely loving Christ who died on the Cross to bear the sins of the whole world, including you and me; and who now lives, pleading with each of us from heaven that we will take by simple faith, and keep by holy obedience, the gift of eternal life which He offers, and He alone can give. The condition of His entrance is simple trust in Him, as the Saviour of my soul. That is opening the door, and if you will do that, then, just as when you open the shutters, in comes the sunshine; just as when you lift the sluice in flows the crystal stream into the slimy, empty lock, so—I was going to say by gravitation, rather by the diffusive impulse that belongs to light, which is Christ—He will enter in, wherever He is not shut out by unbelief and aversion of will.

III. And so that brings me to my last point, viz., the entrance and the feast.

My text is a metaphor, but the declaration that 'if any man open the door' Jesus Christ 'will come *in to him*,' is not a metaphor, but is the very heart and centre of the Gospel, 'I will come in to him,' dwell in him, be really incorporated in his being, or inspirited, if I may so say, in his spirit. Now you may think that that is far too recondite and lofty a thought to be easily grasped by ordinary people, but its very loftiness should recommend it to us. I, for my part, believe that there is no more prose fact in the whole world than the actual dwelling of Jesus Christ, the Son of God who is in heaven, in the spirits of the people that love Him and trust Him. And this is one great part of the Gospel that I have to preach to you, that into our emptiness He will come with His fulness; that into our sinfulness He will come with His righteousness; that into our death He will come with His triumphant and immortal life; and He being in us and we in Him, we shall be full and pure and live for ever, and be blessed with the blessedness of Jesus. So remember that embedded in the midst of the wonderful metaphor of my text lies the fact, which is the very centre of the Gospel hope, the dwelling of Jesus Christ in the hearts even of poor sinful creatures like you and me.

But it comes into view here only as the basis of the subsequent promises, and on these I can only touch very briefly, 'I will come in to him and sup with him, and he with Me.' Well, that speaks to us in lovely, sympathetic language of a close, familiar, happy communication between Christ and my poor self, which shall make all life as a feast in company with Him. We remember who is the mouthpiece of Jesus Christ here. It is the disciple who knew most of what quietness of blessedness and serenity of adoring communion there were in leaning on Christ's breast at supper, casting back his head on that loving bosom; looking into those deep sad eyes, and asking questions which were sure of answer. And John, as he wrote down the words 'I will sup with him, and he with Me,' perhaps remembered that upper room where, amidst all

the bitter herbs, there was such strange joy and tranquillity. But whether he did or no, may we not take
the picture as suggesting to us the possibilities of
loving fellowship, of quiet repose, of absolute satisfaction of all desires and needs, which will be ours if
we open the door of our hearts by faith and let Jesus
Christ come in?

But, note, when He does come He comes as guest.
'I will sup with him.' 'He shall have the honour of
providing that of which I partake.' Just as upon earth
He said to the Samaritan woman, 'Give Me to drink,'
or sat at the table, at the modest village feast in
Bethany, in honour of the miracle of a man raised
from the dead, and smiled approval of Martha serving,
as of Lazarus sitting at table, and of Mary anointing
Him, so the humble viands, the poor man's fare that
our resources enable us to lay upon His table, are never
too small or poor for Him to delight in. This King
feasts in the neatherd's cottage, and He will even con-
descend to turn the cakes. 'I will sup with Him.' We
cannot bring anything so coarse, so poor, so unworthy,
if a drop or two of love has been sprinkled over it, but
that it will be well-pleasing in His sight, and He Himself will partake thereof. 'He has gone to be a guest
with a man that is a sinner.'

But more than that, where He is welcomed as guest,
He assumes the place of host. 'I will sup with him,
and *he with Me.*' You remember how, after the Resurrection, when the two disciples, moved to hospitality,
implored the unknown Stranger to come in and
partake of their humble fare, He yielded to their
importunity, and when they were in the guest-
chamber, took His place at the head of the table, and
blessed the bread and gave it to them. You remember

how, in the beginning of His miracles, He manifested forth His glory in this, that, invited as a common guest to the rustic wedding, He provided the failing wine. And so, wherever a poor man opens his heart and says, 'Come in,' and I will give Thee my 'best,' Jesus Christ comes in, and gives the man *His* best, that the man may render it back to Him. He owes nothing to any man, He accepts the poorest from each, and He gives the richest to each. He is Guest and Host, and what He accepts from us is what He has first given to us.

The promise of my text is fulfilled immediately when the door of the heart is opened, but it shadows and prophesies a nobler fulfilment in the heavens. Here and now Christ and we may sit together, but the feast will be like the Passover, eaten with loins girt and staves in hand, and the Red Sea and wilderness waiting to be trodden. But there comes a more perfect form of the communion, which finds its parallel in that wonderful scene when the weary fishers, all of whose success had depended on their obedience to the Master's direction, discerned at last, through the grey of the morning, who it was that stood upon the shore, and, struggling to His side, saw there a fire of coals, and fish laid thereon, and bread, to which they were bidden to add their modest contribution in the fish that they had caught; and the meal being thus prepared partly by His hand and partly by theirs, ennobled and filled by Him, His voice says, 'Come and dine.' So, brethren, Christ at the last will bring His servants to His table in His kingdom, and there their works shall follow them; and He and they shall sit together for ever, and for ever 'rejoice in the fatness of Thy house, even of Thy holy temple.'

I beseech you, listen not to my poor voice, but to **His** that speaks through it, and when He knocks do you open, and Christ Himself shall come in. 'If any man love Me he will keep My commandments, and My Father will love him, and *We* will come and make Our abode with him.'

VII.—THE VICTOR'S SOVEREIGNTY

'To him that overcometh will I grant to sit with Me in My throne, even as I also overcame, and am set down with My Father in His throne.'—REV. iii. 21.

THE Church at Laodicea touched the lowest point of Christian character. It had no heresies, but that was not because it clung to the truth, but because it had not life enough to breed even them. It had no conspicuous vices, like some of the other communities. But it had what was more fatal than many vices—a low temperature of religious life and feeling, and a high notion of itself. Put these two things together—they generally go together—and you get the most fatal condition for a Church. It is the condition of a large part of the so-called 'Christian world' to-day, as that very name unconsciously confesses; for 'world' is the substantive, and 'Christian' only the adjective, and there is a great deal more 'world' than 'Christian' in many so-called 'Churches.'

Such a Church needed, and received, the sharpest rebuke. A severe disease requires drastic treatment. But the same necessity which drew forth the sharp rebuke drew forth also the loftiest of the promises. If the condition of Laodicea was so bad, the struggle to overcome became proportionately greater, and, consequently, the reward the larger. The least worthy may rise to the highest position. It was not to the victors over persecution at Smyrna, or over heresies at Thyatira, nor even to the blameless Church of Philadelphia, but it was to the faithful in Laodicea, who had kept the fire of their own devotion well alight amidst the tepid Christianity round them, that this climax of all the seven promises is given.

In all the others Jesus Christ stands as the bestower of the gift. Here He stands, not only as the bestower, but as Himself participating in that which He bestows. The words beggar all exposition, and I have shrunk from taking them as my text. We seem to see in them, as if looking into some sun with dazzled eyes, radiant forms moving amidst the brightness, and in the midst of them one like unto the Son of man. But if my words only dilute and weaken this great promise, they may still help to keep it before your own minds for a few moments. So I ask you to look with me at the two great things that are bracketed together in our text; only I venture to reverse the order of consideration, and think of—

I. The Commander-in-Chief's conquest and royal repose.

'I also overcame, and am set down with My Father in His throne.' It seems to me that, wonderful as are all the words of my text, perhaps the most wonderful of them all are those by which the two halves of the promise are held together—'Even as I also.' The Captain of the host takes His place in the ranks, and, if I may so say, shoulders His musket like the poorest private. Christ sets Himself before us as pattern of the struggle, and as pledge of the victory and reward. Now let me say a word about each of the two halves of this great thought of our Lord's identification of Himself with us in our fight, and identification of us with Him in His victory.

As to the former, I would desire to emphasise, with all the strength that I can, the point of view from which Jesus Christ Himself, in these final words from the heavens, directed to all the Churches, looks back upon His earthly career, and bids us think of it as a true conflict. You remember how, in the sanctities of the upper room, and ere yet the supreme moment of the crucifixion had come, our Lord said, when within a day of the Cross and an hour of Gethsemane, 'I have overcome the world.' This is an echo of that never-to-be-forgotten utterance that the aged Apostle had heard when leaning on his Master's bosom in the seclusion and silence of that sacred upper chamber. Only here our Lord, looking back upon the victory, gathers it all up into one as a past thing, and says, 'I overcame,' in those old days long ago.

Brethren, the orthodox Christian is tempted to think of Jesus Christ in such a fashion as to reduce His conflict on earth to a mere sham fight. Let no supposed theological necessities induce you to weaken down in your thoughts of Him what He Himself has told us—that He, too, struggled, and that He, too, overcame. That temptation in the wilderness, where the necessities of the flesh and the desires of the spirit were utilised by the Tempter as weapons with which His unmoved obedience and submission were assailed, was repeated over and over again all through His earthly life. We believe—at least I believe—that Jesus Christ was in nature sinless, and that temptation found nothing in Him on which it could lay hold, no fuel or combustible material to which it could set light. But, notwithstanding, inasmuch as He became partaker of flesh and

blood, and entered into the limitations of humanity,
His sinlessness did not involve His incapacity for being
tempted, nor did it involve that His righteousness was
not assailed, nor His submission often tried. We believe — or at least I believe — that He 'did no sin,
neither was guile found in His mouth.' But I also
reverently listen to Him unveiling, so far as may need
to be unveiled, the depths of His own nature and
experience, and I rejoice to think that He fought the
good fight, and Himself was a soldier in the army
of which He is the General. He is the Captain, the
Leader, of the long procession of heroes of the faith;
and He is the 'perfecter' of it, inasmuch as His own
faith was complete and unbroken.

But I may remind you, too, that from this great
word of condescending self-revelation and identification,
we may well learn what a victorious life really is. 'I
overcame'; but from the world's point of view He was
utterly beaten. He did not gather in many who would
listen to Him or care for His words. He was misunderstood, rejected; lived a life of poverty; died
when a young man, a violent death; was hunted by
all the Church dignitaries of His generation as a
blasphemer, spit upon by soldiers, and execrated after
His death. And that is victory, is it? Well, then,
we shall have to revise our estimates of what is a
conquering career. If He, the pauper-martyr, if He,
the misunderstood enthusiast, if He conquered, then
some of our notions of a victorious life are very far
astray.

Nor need I say a word, I suppose, about the com-
pleteness, as well as the reality, of that victory of His.
From heaven He claims in this great word just what
He claimed on earth, over and over again, when He

fronted His enemies with, 'Which of you convinceth
Me of sin?' and when He declared in the sanctities
of His confidence with His friends, 'I do always the
things that please Him.' The rest of us partially overcome, and partially are defeated. He alone bears His
shield out of the conflict undinted and unstained. To
do the will of God, to dwell in continual communion
with the Father, never to be hindered by anything that
the world can present or my sins can suggest, whether
of delightsome or dreadful, from doing the will of the
Father in heaven from the heart—that is victory, and
all else is defeat. And that is what the Captain of our·
salvation, and only He, did.

Turn for a moment now to the other side of our
Lord's gracious identification of Himself with us.
'Even as I also am set down with My Father in His
throne.' That points back, as the Greek original shows
even more distinctly, to the historical fact of the
Ascension. It recalls the great words by which, with
full consciousness of what He was doing, Jesus Christ
sealed His own death-warrant in the presence of the
Sanhedrim when He said: 'Henceforth ye shall see
the Son of man sitting on the right hand of power.' It
carries us still further back to the psalm which our
Lord Himself quoted, and thereby stopped the mouths
of Scribes and Pharisees: 'The Lord said unto My Lord,
sit Thou at My right hand till I make Thine enemies
Thy footstool.' He laid His hand upon that great
promise, and claimed that it was to be fulfilled in His
case. And here, stooping from amidst the blaze of the
central royalty of the Universe, He confirms all that
He had said before, and declares that He shares the
Throne of God.

Now, of course, the words are intensely figurative,

and have to be translated as best we can, even though
it may seem to weaken and dilute them, into less
concrete and sensible forms than the figurative representation. But I think we shall not be mistaken if we
assert that, whatever lies in this great statement far
beyond our conception in the present, there lie in it
three things—repose, royalty, communion of the most
intimate kind with the Father.

There is repose. You remember how the first martyr
saw the opened heavens and the ascended Christ, in
that very hall, probably, in which Christ had said,
'Henceforth ye shall see the Son of man sitting at the
right hand of power.' But Stephen, as he declared,
with rapt face smitten by the light into the likeness of
an angel's, saw Him standing at the right hand. We
have to combine these two images, incongruous as they
are in prose, literally, before we reach the conception
of the essential characteristic of that royal rest of
Christ's. For it is a repose that is full of activity.
'My Father worketh hitherto,' said He on earth, ' and
I work.' And that is true with regard to His unseen
and heavenly life. The verses which are appended to
the close of Mark's gospel draw a picture for us—'They
went everywhere preaching the Word': He sat at
'the right hand of God.' The two halves do not fuse
together. The Commander is in repose; the soldiers
are bearing the brunt of the fight. Yes! but then
there comes the word which links the two halves
together. 'They went everywhere preaching, the Lord
also working with them.'

Christ's repose indicates, not merely the cessation
from, but much rather the completion of, His work on
earth, which culminated on the Cross; which work on
earth is the basis of the still mightier work which He

is doing in the heavens. So the Apostle Paul sets up a great ladder, so to speak, which our faith climbs by successive stages, when he says, 'He that died—yea, rather that is risen again—who is even at the right hand of God—who also maketh intercession for us.' His repose is full of beneficent activity for all that love Him.

Again, there is set forth royalty, participation in Divine dominion. The highly metaphorical language of our text, and of parallel verses elsewhere, presents this truth in two forms. Sometimes we read of 'sitting at the right hand of God'; sometimes, as here, we read of 'sitting on the throne.' The 'right hand of God' is everywhere. It is not a local designation. 'The right hand of the Lord' is the instrument of His omnipotence, and to speak of Christ as sitting on the right hand of God is simply to cast into symbolical words the great thought that He wields the forces of Divinity. When we read of Him as enthroned on the Throne of God, we have, in like manner, to translate the figure into this overwhelming and yet most certain truth, that the Man Christ Jesus is exalted to supreme, universal dominion, and that all the forces of omnipotent Divinity rest in the hands that still bear, for faith, the prints of the nails.

But again that session of Christ with the Father suggests the thought, about which it becomes us not to speak, of a communion with the Father—deep, intimate, unbroken, beyond all that we can conceive or speak. We listen to Him when He says, 'Glorify Thou Me with the glory which I had with Thee before the world was.' We bow before the thought that what He asked in that prayer was the lifting of one of ourselves, the humanity of Jesus, into this inseparable

unity with the very glory of God. And then we catch
the wondrous words: 'Even as I also.'

II. That brings me to the second of the thoughts
here, which may be more briefly disposed of after the
preceding exposition, and that is, the private soldier's
share in the Captain's victory and rest. 'I will grant
to sit with Me in My throne, even as I also.'

Now with regard to the former of these, our share
in Christ's triumph and conquest, I only wish to say
one thing, and it is this—I thankfully recognise that
to many who do not share with me in what I believe
to be the teaching of Scripture, viz., the belief that
Christ was more than example, their partial belief, as
I think it, in Him as the realised ideal, the living
Pattern of how men ought to live, has given
strength for far nobler and purer life than could
otherwise have been reached. But, brethren, it seems
to me that we want a great deal more than a pattern,
a great deal closer and more intimate union with
the Conqueror than the mere setting forth of the
possibility of a perfect life as realised in Him, ere we
can share in His victory. What does it matter to me,
after all, except for stimulus and for rebuke, that
Jesus Christ should have lived the life? Nothing.
But when we can link the words in the upper room, 'I
have overcome,' and the words from heaven, 'Even as
I also overcame,' with the same Apostle's words in his
epistle, 'This is the victory that overcometh the world,
even our faith,' then we share in the Captain's victory
in an altogether different manner from that which
they do who can see in Him only a pattern that stimu-
lates and inspires. For if we put our trust in that
Saviour, then the very life which was in Christ Jesus,
and which conquered the world in Him, will pass into

us; and the law of the spirit of life in Christ will make us more than conquerors through Him that loved us.

And then the victory being secured, because Christ lives in us and makes us victorious, our participation in His throne is secure likewise.

There shall be repose, the cessation of effort, the end of toil. There shall be no more aching heads, strained muscles, exhausted brains, weary hearts, dragging feet. There will be no more need for resistance. The helmet will be antiquated, the laurel crown will take its place. The heavy armour, that rusted the garment over which it was braced, will be laid aside, and the trailing robes, that will contract no stain from the golden pavements, will be the attire of the redeemed. We have all had work enough, and weariness enough, and battles enough, and beatings enough, to make us thankful for the thought that we shall *sit* on the throne.

But if it is a rest like His, and if it is to be the rest of royalty, there will be plenty of work in it; work of the kind that fits us and is blessed. I know not what new elevation, or what sort of dominion will be granted to those who, instead of the faithfulness of the steward, are called upon to exercise the activity of the Lord over ten cities. I know not, and I care not; it is enough to know that we shall sit on His throne.

But do not let us forget the last of the thoughts: 'They shall sit *with Me*.' Ah! there you touch the centre—'To depart and to be with Christ, which is far better'; 'Absent from the body; present with the Lord.' We know not how. The lips are locked that might, perhaps, have spoken; only this we know, that, not as a drop of water is absorbed into the ocean and

loses its individuality, shall we be united to Christ.
There will always be the two, or there would be no
blessedness in the two being one; but as close as is
compatible with the sense of being myself, and of His
being Himself, will be our fellowship with Him. 'He
that is joined to the Lord is one spirit.'

Brethren, this generation would be a great deal the
better for thinking more often of the promises and
threatenings of Scripture with regard to the future.
I believe that no small portion of the lukewarmness
of the modern Laodicea is owing to the comparative
neglect into which, in these days, the Christian teachings on that subject have fallen. I have tried in these
sermons on these seven promises to bring them at
least before your thoughts and hearts. And I beseech
you that you would, more than you have done, 'have
respect unto the recompense of reward,' and let that
future blessedness enter as a subsidiary motive into
your Christian life.

We may gather all these promises together, and
even then we have to say, 'the half hath not been told
us.' 'It doth not yet appear what we shall be.'
Symbols and negations, and these alone, teach us the
little that we know about that future; and when we
try to expand and concatenate these, I suppose that
our conceptions correspond to the reality about as
closely as would the dreams of a chrysalis as to what
it would be when it was a butterfly. But certainty and
clearness are not necessarily united. 'It doth not
yet appear what we shall be, but we *know* that when
He shall appear we shall be like Him.' Take 'even as
I also' for the key that unlocks all the mysteries of
that glorious future. 'It is enough for the servant
that he be as his Master.'

x

THE SEVEN EYES OF THE SLAIN LAMB

'...A Lamb as it had been slain, having...seven eyes, which are the seven Spirits of God sent forth into all the earth.'—REV. v. 6.

JOHN received a double commission, to write the things which are and the things which shall be. The things which are signify, I suppose, the unseen realities which flashed upon the inward eye of the solitary seer for a moment in symbol when the door was opened in Heaven. All that is here is seeming and illusion; the only substantial existences lie within the veil. And of all those 'things which are,' in timeless, eternal being, this vision of the throned 'Lamb, as it had been slain,' is the centre.

Between the Great White Throne and the outer ring of worshippers, representing in the 'living creatures' the crown and glory of creatural life, and in the elders, the crown and glory of redeemed humanity, stands the Lamb slain, which is the symbolical way of declaring that for ever and ever, through Christ and for the sake of His sacrifice, there pass to the universe all Divine gifts, and there rise from the universe all thankfulness and praise. His manhood is perpetual, the influence of His sacrifice in the Divine administration and government never ceases.

The attributes with which this verse clothes that slain Lamb are incongruous; but, perhaps, by reason of their very incongruity all the more striking and significant. The 'seven horns' are the familiar emblem of perfect power; the 'seven eyes' are interpreted by the seer himself to express the fulness of the Divine Spirit.

The eye seems a singular symbol for the Spirit, but it may be used as suggesting the swiftest and subtlest

way in which the influences of a human spirit pass out
into the external universe. At all events, whatever may
have been the reason for the selection of the emblem,
the interpretation of it lies here, in the words of our
text itself. The teaching of this emblem, then, is: 'He,
being by the right hand of God exalted, and having
received the promise of the Father, sheds forth this.'
The whole fulness of spiritual Divine power is in the
hand of Christ to impart to the world.

I. The 'slain Lamb' is the Lord and Giver of the
Spirit. He 'hath the seven Spirits of God' in the
simplest sense of all, that the manhood of our Brother
who died on the Cross for us, lifted up to the right
hand of God, is there invested and glorified with every
fulness of the Divine Spirit, and with all the mysteries
of the life of God. Whatsoever there is, in Deity, of
spirit and power; whatsoever of swift flashing energy;
whatsoever of gentleness and grace; whatsoever of
holiness and splendour; all inheres in the Man Christ
Jesus; unto whom even in His earthly lowliness and
humiliation the Spirit was not given by measure, but
unto whom in the loftiness of His heavenly life that
Spirit is given in yet more wondrous fashion than in
His humiliation. For I suppose that the exaltation
with which Christ is exalted is not only a change of
position, but in some sense His manhood is progressive;
and now in the Heavens is yet fuller of the indwelling Spirit than it was here upon earth.

But it is not as the recipient, but as the bestower of
the Spirit, that He comes before us in the great words
of my text. All that He has of God, He has that He
may give. Whatsoever is His is ours; we share in His
fulness and we possess His grace. He gives *His own*
life, and that is the very central idea of Christianity.

There are very many imperfect views of Christ's
work afloat in the world. The lowest of them, the
most imperfect, so imperfect and fragmentary as
scarcely to be worth calling Christianity at all, is the
view which recognises Him as being merely Example,
Guide, Teacher. High above that there comes the
view which is common amongst orthodox people of the
more superficial type—the view which is, I am afraid,
still too common amongst us—which regards the whole
work of Jesus Christ as terminated upon the Cross. It
thinks of Him as being something infinitely more than
Teacher and Guide and Example, but it stops at the
thought of His great reconciling death as being the
completion of His work, and hears Him say from the
Cross, 'It is finished,' with a faith which, however
genuine, cannot but be considered as imperfect unless
it is completed with the remembrance that it was but
one volume of His work that was finished when He
died upon the Cross. His death was really a transition
to a form of work which if not loftier was at all events
other than the work which was completed upon Calvary. His earthly life finished His perfect obedience
as Pattern and as Son; His death on the Cross finished
His mighty work of self-surrender and sacrifice, which
is propitiation and atonement for the sins of the whole
world. His life on earth and His death on the Cross
taken together finished His great work of revealing
the Father in so far as that revelation depended upon
outward, objective facts. But His life on earth and
His death on the Cross did not even begin the work,
but only laid the foundation for it, of communicating
to men the life which was in Himself. He lived that
He might complete obedience and manifest the Father.
He died that He might 'put away sin' and reveal the

Father still more fully. And now, exalted at the right hand of God, He works on through the ages in that which is the fruit of His Cross and the crown of His sacrifice, the communication to men, moment by moment, of His own perfect life, that they too may live for ever and be like Him.

He died that we might not die; He lives that the life which we live in the flesh may be His life and not ours. We may not draw comparisons between the greatness of the various departments of our Master's work, but we can say that His earthly life and His death of shame are the foundation of the work which He does to-day. And so, dear brethren, whilst nineteen centuries ago His triumphant words, 'It is finished,' rang out the knell of sin's dominion, and the first hope for the world's emancipation, another voice, far ahead still in the centuries, waits to be spoken; and not until the world has been filled with the glory of His Cross and the power of His life shall it be proclaimed: 'It is done!'

The interspace between these two is filled with the activity of that slain Lamb who, by His death, has become the Lord of the Spirit; and through His blood is able to communicate to all men the life of His own soul. The Lord of the Spirit is the Lamb that was slain.

II. Then let me ask you to look, secondly, at the representation here given of the infinite variety of gifts which Christ bestows.

Throughout this Book of the Revelation we find this remarkable expression, in which the Spirit of God is not spoken of as in His personal unity, but as in sevenfold variety. So at the beginning of the letter we find the salutation, 'Grace and peace from Him which is,

and was, and which is to come; and from the seven
Spirits which are before His Throne.' And again we
read, in one of the letters to the churches: 'These
things saith He that hath the seven Spirits of God, and
the seven stars'; the correspondence being marked
between the number of each. And again we read in
the earlier part of this same vision, in the preceding
chapter, that before the throne there were seven
torches flaming, 'which are the seven Spirits of God.'
And so, again, in my text, we read, 'seven Spirits of
God sent forth into all the earth.'

Now it is obvious that there is not any question
here of the personality and unity of the Divine Spirit,
which is sufficiently recognised in other parts of the
Apocalypse, such as 'the Spirit and the Bride say:
"Come!" ' and the like; but that the thing before the
Evangelist's mind is the variety of the operations and
activities of that one Spirit.

And the number 'seven,' of course, at once suggests
the idea of perfection and completeness.

So that the thought emerges of the endless, boundless, manifoldness, and wonderful diversity of the
operations of this great life-spirit that streams from
Jesus Christ.

Think of the number of designations by which that
Spirit is described in the New Testament. In regard
to all that belongs to intellectual life, He is 'the
Spirit of wisdom' and of 'illumination in the knowledge of Christ,' He is 'the Spirit of Truth.' In regard
to all that belongs to the spiritual life, He is 'the Spirit
of holiness,' the 'Spirit of liberty'; the Spirit of self-
control, or as rendered in our Bible, 'of a sound mind';
the 'Spirit of love.' In regard to all that belongs to
the practical life, He is 'the Spirit of counsel and

of might,' the 'Spirit of power.' In regard to all that
belongs to the religious life, He is 'the Spirit of
Adoption, whereby we cry, Abba! Father!'; the 'Spirit
of grace and of supplication,' the 'Spirit of life.' So
over the whole round of man's capacity and nature, all
his intellectual, moral, practical, and religious being,
there are gifts which fit each side and each part
of it.

Think of the variety of the symbols under which He
is presented: 'the oil,' with its soft, gentle flow; 'the
fire,' with its swift transmuting, purifying energy; the
water, refreshing, fertilising, cleansing; the breath,
quickening, vitalising, purifying the blood; the wind,
gentle as the sigh of an infant, loud and mighty as a
hurricane, sometimes scarcely lifting the leaves upon
the tender spring herbage, sometimes laying the city
low in a low place. It is various in manifestation,
graduating through all degrees, applying to every side
of human nature, capable of all functions that our
weakness requires, helping our infirmities, making
intercession for us and in us, with unutterable groan-
ings, sealing and confirming our possession of His
grace; searching the deep things of God and revealing
them to us; guiding into all truth, freeing us from the
law of sin and death. There are diversities of operation, but the same Spirit. It is protean, and takes
every shape that our necessities require.

Think of all men's diverse weaknesses, miseries, sins,
cravings—every one of them an open door through
which God's grace may come; every one of them a
form provided into which the rich molten ore of this
golden Spirit may flow. Whatsoever a man needs,
that he will find in the infinite variety of the spiritual
help and strength which the Lamb slain is ready to

give. It is like the old fable of the manna, which the
Rabbis tell us tasted upon each lip precisely what each
man chose. So this nourishment from above becomes
to every man what each man requires. Water will take
the shape of any vessel into which you choose to pour
it; the Spirit of God assumes the form that is imposed
upon it by our weaknesses and needs. And if you
want to know the exhaustless variety of the seven
Spirits which the Lamb gives, find out the multiplicity
and measure, the manifoldness and the depth, of man's
necessities, of weakness, of sorrow, and sin, and you
will know how much the Spirit of God is able to bestow
and still remain full and unexhausted.

III. Still further, my text suggests the unbroken continuity of the gifts which the slain Lamb has to give.

The language of the original, for any of you that can
consult it, will show you that the word ' sent' might
be rendered 'being sent,' expressive of a continual
impartation.

Ah! God's Spirit is not given once in a way and then
stops. It is given, not by fits and starts. People talk
about ' revivals,' as if there were times when the Spirit
of God came down more abundantly than at other
times upon the world, or upon churches, or upon individuals. It is not so. There are variations in our
receptiveness; there are no variations in its steady
efflux. Does the sun shine at different rates, are its
beams cut off sometimes, or poured out with less energy,
or is it only the position of the earth that makes the
difference between the summer and the winter, the days
and the nights, whilst the great central orb is raying out
at the same rate all through the murky darkness, all
through the frosty days? And so the gifts of Jesus
Christ pour out from Him at a uniform continuous

rate, with no breaks in the golden beams, with no pauses in the continual flow. Pentecost is far back, but the fire that was kindled then has not died down into grey ashes. It is long since that stream began to flow, but it is not yet shrunken in its banks. For ever and for ever, with unbroken continuity, whether men receive or whether they forbear, He shines on, communicating Himself and pouring out the Spirit of grace, ay! even into a non-receiving world! How much sunshine seems to be lost, how much of that Spirit's influence seems lost, and yet it pours on for ever.

Men talk about Christianity as being effete. People to-day look back upon the earlier ages, and say: 'Where is the Lord God of Elijah?' The earlier ages had nothing that you and I have not, and Christianity will not die out, and God's Church will not die out, until the sun that endureth for ever is shorn of its beams and forgets to shine. The seven Spirits are streaming out as they were at the beginning, and as— blessed be God!—they shall do to the end.

IV. And, lastly, my text suggests a universal diffusion of these gifts. 'Seven Spirits of God sent forth into all the earth.' The words are a quotation from a remarkable prophecy in the book of Zechariah, which speaks about the 'seven eyes of God,' running—

'To and fro over all the earth.'

There are no limitations of these gifts to any one race or nation as there were in the old times, nor any limitations either to a democracy. 'On My servants and on My handmaidens will I pour out of My Spirit.' In olden days the mountain-tops were touched with the rays, and all the lowly valleys lay deep in the shadow and the darkness. Now the risen sunshine

pours down into the deepest clefts, and no heart so
poor, so illiterate, so ignorant but that it may receive
the full sunshine of that Spirit.

Of course, in the very widest of all senses the words
are true of the universal diffusion of spiritual gifts
from Christ; for all the light with which men see is
His light; and all the eyes with which they have ever
looked at truth, or beauty, or goodness, come from
Him who is ' the Master-light of all our seeing.' And
poet, and painter, and thinker, and teacher, and phil-
anthropist, and every man that has helped his fellows
or has had any glimpse of any angle or bit of the
Divine perfection, has seen because the eye of the class
or order.   Christianity as the true Lord has been in
some measure granted to him, and ' the inspiration of
the Almighty has given him understanding.'

But the universal diffusion of spiritual gifts of this
sort is not what is meant in my text. It means the gifts
of a higher religious character. And I need not remind
you of how over broad lands that were heathen when
John in his rocky Patmos got this vision, there has
now dawned the glory of Christ and the knowledge of
His name. Think of all the treasures of the literature
of the Christian Church in Latin and African and
Teutonic lands that have come since the day when
this chapter was written. Think of what Britain was
then and of what it is to-day. Remember the heroisms,
holinesses, illuminations that have shone over these
then barbarous lands since that time ; and understand
how it has all come because from the Lamb by the
Throne there has been sent out over all the earth the
Spirit that is wisdom and holiness and life.

And think how steadily down through layers of
society that were regarded as outcast and contempt-

ible in the time of the founding of the Church, there has trickled and filtered the knowledge of Himself and of His grace; and how amongst the poor and the humble and the outcast, amongst the profligate and the sinful, there have sprung up flowers of holiness and beauty all undreamed of before; and we shall understand how all classes in all lands may receive a portion of the sevenfold Spirit.

Every Christian man and woman is inspired, not to be a teacher of infallible truth, but inspired in the true and deep sense that in them dwells the Spirit of Jesus Christ. 'If any man have not the Spirit he is none of His.' All of us, weak, sinful as we are, ignorant and bewildered often, may possess that Divine life to live in our hearts.

Only, dear brethren, remember it is the *slain* Lamb that gives the Spirit. And unless we are looking to that Lamb slain as our hope and confidence, we shall not receive it. A maimed Christianity that has a Christ, but no slain Lamb, has little of His Spirit; but if you trust to His Sacrifice, and rest your whole hopes on His Cross, then there will come into your hearts His own mighty grace, and 'the law of the Spirit of life in Christ Jesus will make you free from the law of sin and death.'

THE PALM-BEARING MULTITUDE

'. . . Lo, a great multitude . . . stood before the throne, and before the Lamb, clothed with white robes, and palms in their hands.'—REV. vii. 9.

THE Seer is about to disclose the floods of misery which are to fall upon the earth at the sound of the seven trumpets, like avalanches set loose by a noise. But before the crash of their descent comes there is a lull.

He sees angels holding back the winds, like dogs in a leash, lest they should blow, and all destructive agencies are suspended. In the pause before the storm he sees two visions: one, that of the sealing of the servants of God, the pledge that, amidst the world-wide calamities, they shall be secure; and one, this vision of my text, the assurance that beyond the storms there waits a calm region of life and glory. The vision is meant to brace all generations for their trials, great or small, to draw faith and love upwards and forwards, to calm sorrow, to diminish the magnitude of death and the pain of parting, and to breed in us humble desires that, when our time comes, we too may go to join that great multitude.

It can never be inappropriate to look with the eyes of the Seer on that jubilant crowd. So I turn to these words and deal with them in the plainest possible fashion, just taking each clause as it lies, though, for reasons which will appear, modifying the order in which we look at them. I think that, taken together, they tell us all that we can or need know about that future.

I. Note the palm-bearing multitude.

Now the palm, among the Greeks and Romans, was a token of victory. That is usually taken to be the meaning of the emblem here, as it was taken in the well-known hymn—

'More than conquerors at last.'

But it has been well pointed out that there is no trace of such a use of the palm in Jewish practice, and that all the emblems of this Book of the Revelation move within the circle of Jewish ideas. Therefore, appropriate as the idea of victory may be, it is not, as I take it, the one that is primarily suggested here. Where, then, shall we look for the meaning of the symbol?

Now there was in Jewish practice a very significant use of the palm-branches, for it was the prescription of the ritual law that they should be employed in the Feast of Tabernacles, when the people were bidden to take palm-branches and 'rejoice before the Lord seven days.' It is that distinctly Jewish use of the palm-branch that is brought before our minds here, and not the heathen one of mere conquest.

So then, if we desire to get the whole significance and force of this emblem of the multitude with the palms in their hands, we have to ask what was the significance of that Jewish festival. Like all other Jewish feasts, it was originally a Nature-festival, applying to a season of the year, and it afterwards came to have associated with it the remembrance of something in the history of the nation which it commemorated. That double aspect, the natural and the historical, are both to be kept in view. Let us take the eldest one first. The palm-bearing multitude before the Throne suggests to us the thought of rejoicing reapers at the close of the harvest. The year's work is done, the sowing days are over, the reaping days have come. 'They that gather it shall eat it in the courts of the Lord.' And so the metaphor of my text opens out into that great thought that the present and the future are closely continuous, and that the latter is the time for realising, in one's own experience, the results of the life that we have lived here. To-day is the time of sowing; the multitude with the palms in their hands are the reapers. Brother! what are you sowing? Will it be for you a glad day of festival when you have to reap what you have sown? Are you scattering

poisoned seed? Are you sowing weeds, or are you
sowing good fruit that shall be found after many days
unto praise and honour and glory? Look at your life
here as being but setting in motion a whole series of
causes of which you are going to have the effects
punctually dealt out to you yonder in the time to
come. That great multitude reaped what they had
sown, and rejoiced in the reaping. Shall I? We are
like operators in a telegraph office, touching keys here
which make impressions upon ribbons in a land beyond
the sea, and when we get there we shall have to read
what we have written here. How will you like it,
when the ribbon is taken out of the machine and
spread before you, and you have to go over it syllable by
syllable and translate all the dots and dashes into what
they mean? It will be a feast or a day of sadness.
But, festival or no, there stands plain and irrefragable
the fact that 'whatsoever a man soweth, that shall he
also reap,' and he will not only have to reap it, but he
will have to eat it, and be filled with the fruit of his
own doings. That is the first thought.

Turn to the other one. That palm-bearing multitude
keeping their Feast of Tabernacles reminds us of the
other aspect of the festival in its original intention,
which was the commemoration of all that God had
done for the people as they passed through the wilderness, and the rejoicing, in their settled abode, over
'the way by which the Lord their God had led them,'
and over the rest to which He had led them. So the
other idea comes out that they who have passed into
that great Presence look back on the darkness and the
dreariness, on the struggles and the change, on the
drought and the desert, on the foes and the fears, and
out of them all find occasions for rejoicing and reasons

for thankfulness. There can be no personal identity
without memory, and the memory of sorrows changes
into joy when we come to see the whole meaning and
trend of the sorrow. The desert was dreary, solitary,
dry, and parched as they passed through it. But like
some grim mountain-range seen in the transfiguring
light of sunrise, and from the far distance, all grimness
is changed into beauty, and the long dreary stretch
looks, when beheld from afar, one unbroken manifestation of the Divine love and presence. What was grim
rock and cold ice when we were near it is clothed with
the violets and the purples that remoteness brings,
and there shines down upon it the illuminating and
interpreting light of the accomplished purpose of God.
So the festival is the feast of inheriting consequences,
and the feast of remembering the past.

There is one other aspect of this metaphor which I
may just mention in a sentence. Later days in Judaism
added other features to the original appointments of
the Feast of Tabernacles, and amongst them there was
one which our Lord Himself used as the occasion of
setting forth one aspect of His work. 'On the last day,
that great day of the feast,' the priests went down from
the Temple, and filled their golden vases at the fountain, brought back the water, and poured it forth in
the courts of the Temple, chanting the ancient song
from the prophet, 'With joy shall ye draw water out
of the wells of salvation.' And our Lord in His earthly
life used this last day of the feast and its ceremonial
as the point of attachment for His revelation of Himself,
as He who gave to men the true living water. In like
manner, the expansion of my text, which occurs in the
subsequent verses, refers, as it would seem, to the
festival, and to our Lord's own use of it, when we read

that the 'Lamb which is in the midst of the Throne shall be their Shepherd, and shall lead them to the fountains of living waters.'

So the emblem of the feast brings to our mind, not only the thought of retribution and of repose, but also the thought of the abundant communication of all supplies for all the desires and thirsts of the dependent and seeking soul. Whatsoever human nature can need there, it receives in its fulness from Jesus Christ. The Rabbis used to say that he who had not seen the joy of the Feast of Tabernacles did not know what joy meant; and I would say that until we, too, stand there, with the palms in our hands, we shall not know of how deep, fervent, calm, perpetual a gladness the human heart is capable.

II. Note their place and attitude.

They stand before the Throne, and before the Lamb. Now it would take me too far away from my present purpose to do more than point, in a sentence, to that remarkable and tremendous juxtaposition of the 'Throne' and the 'Lamb,' which Lamb is the crucified Christ. What did the man that ventured upon that form of speech, bracketing together the 'Throne' of the Divine Majesty and the slain 'Lamb' who is Christ, think about Christ that he should sever Him from all the multitude of men, and unite Him with the solitary God? I only ask. I leave you to answer.

But I turn to the two points—'before the Throne and the Lamb,' and 'standing'; and these two suggest, as it seems to me, the two thoughts which, though we cannot do much to fill them out, are yet all-sufficient for illumination, for courage, and for hope. These two are the thought of nearness and the thought of service. 'Before the Throne and the Lamb' is but a picturesque way of saying 'to depart and to be with Christ, which is far better.' I do not enter upon any attempt to expound the manner of such nearness. All that I say is that it is a poor affair if we are to let flesh and sense interpret for us what is meant by 'near' and 'far.' For even here, and whilst we are entangled with this corporeal existence and our dependence upon the conditions of time and space, we know that there is nearness mediated by sympathy and love which is independent of, which survives and disregards, external separation in space. Every loving heart knows that where the treasure is, there the heart is, and where the heart is, there the man is. And the very same thing that knits us together, though oceans wide between us roll, in its highest form will knit the souls that love Jesus Christ to Him, wherever in space they and He may be. Here we have five senses, five windows, five gates. If our ears were different we should hear sounds, shrill and deep, which now are silence to us. If our eyes were different we should see rays at both ends of the spectrum which now are invisible. The body hides as much as it reveals, and we may humbly believe that when the perfect spirit is clothed with its perfect organ, the spiritual body— that is to say, the body that answers to all the needs of the spirit, and is its fit instrument, then many of those melodies which now pass by us unheard will fill our senses with sweetness, and many of these flashing lustres which now we cannot gather into visual impressions will then blaze before us in the perfect light. We shall be near Him, and to be with Christ, however it is mediated (and we cannot tell how), is all that you need, for peace, for nobleness, for blessedness, for immortality. Brethren! to have Christ with me here

Y

is my strength; to be with Christ yonder is my blessedness.   They are 'before the Throne of God and the
Lamb.' I do not believe that we know much beyond
that, and I am sure that we need nothing beyond it, if
we rightly understand all that it means.

But I said there was another idea here, and that is
implied by the words, they '*stood* before the Throne,'
and is further drawn out in the expansion of my text
which follows it as interpretation: 'Therefore are
they before the Throne of God, and serve Him day and
night in His Temple.' What the nature of the service
may be it boots not to inquire, only let us remember
that the caricature of the Christian heaven which has
often been flung at Christian people as a taunt, viz.,
that it is an eternity of idleness and psalm-singing, has
no foundation in Scripture, because the New Testament
conception unites the two thoughts of being with
Christ and of service for Christ.   Remember, for
instance, the parable of the pounds and the talents, in
which the great law is laid down.   'Thou hast been
faithful over a few things; I will make thee ruler over
many things,' and mark how here 'these . . . that
came out of great tribulation' are not only in His
presence, but active in His service. We have the same
blending still more definitely set forth in the last
chapter of this book, where we read of 'those who
serve Him, and see His face'; where the two ideas of
the life of contemplation and rapt vision, and of the
life of active service and joyful employment are welded
together as being not only not incompatible, but absolutely necessary for each other's completeness.

But remember that if there is to be service yonder,
here is the exercising ground, where we are to cultivate
the capacities and acquire the habitudes which there

will find ampler scope and larger field. I do not know
what we are here in this world for at all, unless it is to
apprentice us for heaven. I do not know that there
is anything that a man has to do in this life which is
worth doing unless it be as a training for doing something yonder that shall more entirely correspond with
his capacities. So what kind of work are you doing,
friend? Is it the sort of work that you will be able to
carry on when you pass beyond all the trivialities of
this life? I beseech you, remember this, that life on
earth is a bewilderment and an enigma for which
there is no solution, a long piece of irony, unless
beyond the grave there lie fields for nobler work for
which we are being trained here. And I pray you see
to it that your life here on earth is such as to prepare
you for the service, day and night, of the heavens.
How can I drive that home to your hearts and consciences? I cannot; you must do it for yourselves.

III. Lastly, note their dress.

'Clothed with white robes'—the robe is, of course, in
all languages, the character in which, as the result of
his deeds, a man drapes himself, that of him which is
visible to the world, the 'habit' of his spirit, as we say
(and the word 'habit' means both custom and costume).
'White' is, of course, the heavenly colour; 'white
thrones,' 'white horses' are in this book, and the white
is not dead but lustrous, like our Lord's garments on
the Mount of Transfiguration, such white as sunshine
smiting a snowfield makes. So, then, the dress, the
habit of the spirits is of lustrous purity, or *glory*, to
put it all into one word. But more important than
that is this question: How came they by such robes?
The expansion of our text, to which I have already
referred more than once, and which immediately fol-

lows, answers the question. 'They washed their robes,
and made them white in the blood of the Lamb.' '*They
washed*'; then there is something for them to do.
'The blood of the Lamb' was the means of cleansing;
then cleansing was not the result of their own effort.
The cleansing is not the mere forgiveness, but includes
also the making of the character, pure, white, lustrous.
And the blood of the Lamb does that. For Christ by
His death has brought to us forgiveness, and Christ by
His imparted life brings to each of us, if we will, the
cleansing which shall purify us altogether. Only we
have something to do. We cannot indeed cleanse ourselves. There is no detergent in any soap factory in
the world that will take the stains out of your character, or that will take away the guilt of the past. But
Jesus Christ by His death brings forgiveness, and by
His life imparted to us, will change the set of a
character, and make us gradually pure. He has
'washed us from our sins in His own blood.' We have
to wash our garments, and make them 'white in the
blood of the Lamb.' He has brought the means; we
have to employ them. If we do, if we not only trust
Him for pardon, but accept Him for purifyng, and
day by day honestly endeavour to secure greater and
greater whiteness of garments, our labour will not be
in vain. If, and only if, we do that, and see stain after
stain gradually fade away from the garment, under
our hands, we may humbly hope that when we die
there will be one more added to the palm-bearing,
white-robed multitude who stand before the Throne
and before the Lamb. 'Blessed are they that wash
their robes that they may have right to the Tree of
Life,' and may enter in through the gate into the City.

THE SONG OF MOSES AND THE LAMB

'And I saw as it were a sea of glass mingled with fire: and them that had gotten the victory over the beast, and over his image, . . . and over the number of his name, stand on the sea of glass, having the harps of God. 3. And they sing the song of Moses the servant of God, and the song of the Lamb.'—REV. xv. 2, 3.

THE form of this vision is moulded partly by the circumstances of the Seer, and partly by reminiscences of Old Testament history. As to the former, it can scarcely be an accident that the Book of the Revelation abounds with allusions to the sea. We are never far from the music of its waves, which broke around the rocky Patmos where it was written. And the 'sea of glass mingled with fire' is but a photograph of what John must have seen on many a still morning, when the sunrise came blushing over the calm surface; or on many an evening when the wind dropped at sundown, and the sunset glow dyed the watery plain with a fading splendour.—Nor is the allusion to Old Testament history less obvious. We cannot but recognise the reproduction, with modifications, of that scene when Moses and his ransomed people looked upon the ocean beneath which their oppressors lay, and lifted up their glad thanksgivings. So here, by anticipation, in the solemn pause before the judgment goes forth, there are represented the spirits that have been made wise by conquest, as gathered on the bank of that steadfast ocean, lifting up as of old a hymn of triumphant thankfulness over destructive judgments, and blending the song of Moses and of the Lamb, in testimony of the unity of spirit which runs through all the manifestations of God's character from the beginning to the end. Ever His judgments are right; ever the purpose of

His most terrible things is that men may know Him, and may love Him; and ever they who see deepest into the mysteries, and understand most truly the realities of the universe will have praise springing to their lips for all that God hath done.

I. Notice the Triumphant Choir.

'I saw them that had gotten the victory over the beast and over his image, and over the number of his name.' Now I am not going to plunge into Apocalyptic discussions. It is no part of my business now either to ask or answer the question as to whether this Beast of the Revelation is a person or a tendency. I do not care, for my present purpose, whether, supposing it to be a person, an embodiment of certain tendencies, it is a person in the past or in the future; whether it was a veiled designation of the Emperor Nero, or whether it is a prophecy of some yet unborn human embodiment of transcendent wickedness. The question that I would ask is rather this,—Whoever the beast is, what makes him a beast? And if we will think about that, we may get some good out of it. What is the bestial element in him, whoever he be? And the answer is not far to find—Godless selfishness, that is 'the mark of the beast.' Wherever a human nature is self-centred, God-forgetting, and, therefore, God-opposing (for whoever forgets God defies Him), that nature has gone down below humanity, and has touched the lower level of the brutes. Men are so made as that they must either rise to the level of God or certainly go down to that of the animal. And wherever you see men living by their own fancies, for their own pleasure, in forgetfulness and neglect of the sweet and mystic bonds that should knit them to God, there you see 'the image of the beast and the number of his name.'

But besides that godless selfishness, we may point to simple animalism as literally the mark of the beast. He who lives not by conscience and by faith, but by fleshly inclination and sense, lowers himself to the level of the instinctive brute-life, and beneath it, because he refuses to obey faculties which they do not possess, and what is nature in them is degradation in us. Look at the unblushing sensuality which marks many 're-spectable people' nowadays. Look at the foul fleshliness of much of popular art and poetry. Look at the way in which pure animal passion, the lust of the flesh, and the lust of the eye, and the love of good things to eat, and plenty to drink, is swaying and destroying men and women by the thousand among us. Look at the temptations that lie along every street in our great cities, for every young man, after dusk. Look at the thin veneer of culture over the ugliest lust. Scratch the gentleman, and you find the satyr. Is it much of an exaggeration, in view of the facts of English life to-day, to say that all the world wonders after and worships this beast?

Further, notice that to escape from the power of the beast it is needful to fight one's way out. The language of my text is remarkably significant. This Apocalyptic writer does not mind about grammar or smoothness so long as he can express his ideas; and he uses a form of speech here that makes the hair of grammatical purists stand on end, because it vigorously expresses his thought. He calls these triumphant choristers 'con-querors *out of* the beast,' which implies that victory over him is an escape from a dominion in which the conquerors, before their victory, were held. They have fought their way, as it were, out of the land of bondage, and, like revolted slaves, have won their liberty, and marched forth triumphant. The allusion to Israel's exodus is probable. 'Egypt was glad when they departed.' So the bondsmen of this new Pharaoh recover freedom by conflict, and the fruit of their victory is entire escape from the tyrant.

That victory is possible. The Apocalypse shows us that there are two opposing Powers—this said 'beast' on the one side, and 'the Lamb' on the other. In the Seer's vision these two divide the world between them. That is to say, Jesus Christ has conquered the bestial tendencies of our nature, the selfish godlessness which is apt to cast its spells and weave its chains over us all. The Warrior-Lamb, singular and incongruous as the combination sounds, is the Victor. He conquers because He is the Lamb of sacrifice; He conquers because He is the Lamb of innocence; He conquers because He is the Lamb of meekness, the gentle and, therefore, the all-victorious. By Christ we conquer. Through faith, which lays hold on His power and victory, we too may conquer. 'This is the victory which overcometh the world, even our faith.'

Young men and women, may I make my appeal specially to you? Do not let yourselves be led away captives, like cattle to the shambles, by the fascinations and seductions of this poor, fleeting present. Keep your heel on the neck of the animal that is within you; take care of that selfish godlessness into which we all are tempted to fall. Listen to the trumpet-call that ought to stir your hearts, and summons you to freedom and to victory through the blood of the Lamb. And by humbly clasping Him as your Sacrifice, your Leader, and your Power, enrol yourselves amongst those who, in His own good time, shall come victorious out from the beast and from his image.

II. Still further, notice the position of this victorious chorus.

'I saw as it were a sea of glass mingled with fire; and they stand on the sea of glass.' Of course the propriety of the image, as well as the force of the original language, suggests at once that by '*on* the sea of glass' here, we must understand, on the firm bank by its side. As Moses and the ransomed hosts stood on the shore of the Red Sea, so these conquerors are represented as standing on the safe beach, and looking out upon this sea of glass mingled with fire, which, calm, crystal, clear, stable, and yet shot through and through with the red lines of retributive judgment, sleeps above the buried oppressors.

Observe that besides its picturesque appropriateness and its historical allusion, this sea of glass has a distinct symbolical meaning. We find it appearing also in the great vision in the fourth chapter, where the Seer beholds the normal and ideal order of the universe, which is—the central throne, the 'Lamb that was slain' in the interspace between the Throne and the creatures as mediator; and round about, the four living beings, who represent the fulness of creation, and the four-and-twenty elders, who represent the Church in the Old and the New Covenants as one whole. Then follows, 'before the Throne was a sea of glass,' which cannot be any part of the material creation, and seems to have but one explanation, and that is that it means the aggregate of the Divine dealings. 'Thy judgments are a mighty deep.' 'Oh! the depth of the riches, both of the wisdom and of the knowledge of God; how unsearchable are His judgments and His ways past finding out.' Such a signification fits precisely our present passage, for the sea here repre-

sents that beneath which the tyrant lies buried for
evermore.

That great ocean of the judgment of God is crystal-
line—clear though deep. Does it seem so to us? Ah!
we stand before the mystery of God's dealings, often
bewildered, and not seldom reluctant to submit. The
perplexity arising from their obscurity is often almost
torture, and sometimes leads men into Atheism, or
something like it. And yet here is the assurance that
that sea is crystal clear, and that if we cannot look to
its lowest depths, that is not because there is any mud
or foulness there, but partly because the light from
above fails before it reaches the abysses, and partly
because our eyes are uneducated to search its depths.
In itself it is transparent, and it rises and falls without
'mire or dirt,' like the blue Mediterranean on the marble
cliffs of the Italian coast. If it is clear as far as the eye
can see, let us trust that beyond the reach of the eye
the clearness is the same.

And it is a crystal ocean as being calm. They who
stand there have gotten the victory and bear the image
of the Master. By reason of their conquest, and by
reason of their sympathy with Him they see that what
to us, tossing upon its surface, appears such a troubled
and tempestuous ocean, as calm and still. As from
some height, looked down upon, the ocean seems a
watery plain, and all the agitation of the billows has
subsided into a gentle ripple on the surface, so to them
looking down upon the sea that brought them thither,
it is quiet—and their vision, not ours, is the true one.

It is a 'sea of glass mingled with fire.' Divine acts
of retribution as it were flash through it, if I may so
say, like those streaks of red that are seen in Venice
glass, or like some ocean smitten upon the one side of

every wave by a fiery sunlight, while the other side of
each is dark.   So through that great depth of God's
dealings there flashes the fire of retribution.   They
who have conquered the animal, the godless self, see
into the meaning and the mercifulness of God's dealings
with the world; and we here, in the measure in which
we have become victors over the rude animalism and
the more subtle selfishness that tend to rule us all, and
in the measure in which we bear the image of Jesus
Christ, and therefore have come into sympathy with
Him, may come to discern with some clearer understanding, and to trust with more unfaltering faith, the
righteousness and the mercy of all that God shall do.

III. Lastly, notice the occasion of the song, and the
song itself.

'They sing the song of Moses and of the Lamb.'   The
Song of Moses was a song of triumph over destructive
judgment; the Song of the Lamb, says the text, is set
on the same key.   The one broad, general lesson to be
drawn from this, is one on which I have no time to
touch, viz., the essential unity, in spite of all superficial
diversities, of the revelation of God in the Old Covenant
by law and miracle and retributive acts, and the revelation of God in the New Covenant by the Cross and
Passion of Jesus Christ.   Men pit the Old Testament
against the New; the God of the Old Testament against
the God of the New.   They sometimes tell us that
there is antagonism.   Modern teachers are wanting us
to deny that the Old is the foreshadowing of the New,
and the New the fulfilment of the Old.   My text asserts,
in opposition to all such errors, the fruitful principle
of the fundamental unity of the two; and bids us find
in the one the blossom and in the other the fruit, and
declares that the God who brought the waters of the

ocean over the oppressors is the God that has mercy
upon all, in Jesus Christ, His dying Son.

And there is another principle here, upon which I
need not do more than touch, for I have already antici-
pated much that might have been said about it, and
that is the perfect harmony of the retributive acts
of God's destructive dealings in this world, and the
highest conception of His love and mercy which the
gospel brings us. 'When the wicked perish,' says one
of the old proverbs, 'there is shouting.' And so there
ought to be. When some hoary oppression that has
been deceiving mankind for centuries, with its instruments and accomplices, is swept off the face of the
earth, the more men have entered into the meaning of
Jesus Christ's mission and work, and the more they
feel the pitying indignation which they ought to feel
at seeing men led away by evil, and made miserable by
oppression, the more they will rejoice. God's dealings
are meant to manifest His character, and that in order
that all men may know and love Him. We may, therefore, be sure, and keep firm hold of the confidence, that
whatever He doeth, however the methods may seem
to vary, comes from one unalterable and fixed motive,
and leads to one unalterable and certain end. The
motive is His own love; the end the glory of His Name,
in the love and knowledge of men whose life and
blessedness depend on their knowing and loving Him.

So, dear friends, do not let us be too swift in saying
that this, that, and the other thing are inconsistent
with the highest conceptions of the Divine character.
I believe, as heartily as any man can believe, that God
has put His witness in our consciences and minds, and
that all His dealings will comply with any test that
man's reason and man's conscience and man's heart

can subject them to. Only we have not got all the
materials; we look at half-finished work; our eyes are
not quite so educated as that we can pronounce infallibly, on seeing a small segment of a circle, what are its
diameter and its sweep.

I am always suspicious of that rough-and-ready way
of settling questions about God's revelation, when a
man says: 'I cannot accept this or that because it con-
tradicts my conception of the Divine nature.' Unless
you are quite sure that your conceptions are infallibly
accurate, unless you deny the possibility of their being
educated, you must admit that agreement with them
is but a leaden rule. And it seems to me a good deal
wiser, and more accordant with the modesty which
becomes us, to be cautious in pronouncing what does
or does not befit God to do, and, until we reach that
loftier point of vision, where being higher up we can
see deeper down, to say 'the Judge of all the earth
must do right. If He does this, then it is right.' At
any rate let us lay hold of the plain truth: 'O Lord!
Thou preservest man and beast,' and then we may
venture to say, 'Thy judgments are a mighty deep,' and
beneath that deepest depth, as the roots of the hills
beneath the ocean, is God's righteousness, which is like
the great mountains.

The last thought that I would suggest is that,
according to the teaching of my text, we may take that
old, old story of the ransomed slaves and the baffled
oppressor and the Divine intervention and the overwhelming ocean, as prophecy full of radiant hope for
the world. That is how it is used here. Pharaoh is
the beast, the Red Sea is this 'sea of glass mingled
with fire,' the ransomed Israelites are those who have
conquered their way out of the dominion of the beast,

and the song of Moses and of the Lamb is a song parallel to the cadences of the ancient triumphant chorus,
and celebrating the annihilation of that power which
drew the world away from God. So we may believe
that as Israel stood on the sands, and saw the Egyp-
tians dead on the seashore, humanity will one day,
delivered from all its bestiality and its selfishness, lift
up a song of thanksgiving to the conquering King who
has drowned its enemies in the depths of His own
righteous judgments.

And as for the world, so for individuals. If you take
the Beast for your Pharaoh and your task-master, you
will 'sink' with him 'like lead in the mighty waters.'
If you take the Lamb for your sacrifice and your King,
He will break the bonds from off your arms, and lift
the yoke from your neck, and lead you all your lives
long; and you will stand at last, when the eternal
morning breaks, and see its dawn touch with golden
light the calm ocean, beneath which your oppressors
lie buried for ever, and will lift up glad thanksgivings
to Him who has washed you from your sins in His own
blood, and made you victors over 'the beast, and his
image, and the number of his name.'

THE NEW JERUSALEM ON THE NEW EARTH

'And I saw a new heaven and a new earth : for the first heaven and the first
earth were passed away : and there was no more sea. 2. And I John saw the holy
city, new Jerusalem, coming down from God out of heaven, prepared as a bride
adorned for her husband. 3. And I heard a great voice out of heaven saying,
Behold, the tabernacle of God is with men, and He will dwell with them, and they
shall be His people, and God Himself shall be with them, and be their God. 4. And
God shall wipe away all tears from their eyes; and there shall be no more death,
neither sorrow, nor crying, neither shall there be any more pain : for the former
things are passed away. 5. And He that sat upon the throne said, Behold, I make
all things new. And He said unto me, Write: for these words are true and faithful. 6. And He said unto me, It is done. I am Alpha and Omega, the beginning
and the end. I will give unto him that is athirst of the fountain of the water of

life freely. 7. He that overcometh shall inherit all things ; and I will be his God, and He shall be My son. . . . 22. And I saw no temple therein : for the Lord God Almighty and the Lamb are the temple of it. 23. And the city had no need of the sun, neither of the moon, to shine in it : for the glory of God did lighten it, and the Lamb is the light thereof. 24. And the nations of them which are saved shall walk in the light of it : and the kings of the earth do bring their glory and honour into it. 25. And the gates of it shall not be shut at all by day : for there shall be no night there. 26. And they shall bring the glory and honour of the nations into it. 27. And there shall in no wise enter into it any thing that defileth, neither whatsoever worketh abomination, or maketh a lie : but they which are written in the Lamb's book of life.'—REV. xxi. 1-7 ; 22-27.

THE 'new Jerusalem' can be established only under a 'new heaven' and on a 'new earth.' The Seer naturally touches on these before he describes it. And the fact that they come into view here as supplying the field for it makes the literal interpretation of their meaning the more probable. If 'a new heaven and a new earth' means a renovated condition of humanity, what difference is there between it and the new Jerusalem planted in it? We have to remember the whole stream of Old and New Testament representation, according to which the whole material creation is 'subject to vanity,' and destined for a deliverance. Modern astronomy has seen worlds in flames in the sky, and passing by a fiery change into new forms; and the possibility of the heavens being dissolved, the elements melted with fervent heat, and a new heavens and new earth emerging, cannot be disputed. In what sense are they 'new'? 'New' here, as the application of it to Jerusalem may show, does not mean just brought into existence, but renovated, made fresh, and implies, rather than denies, the fact of previous existence. So, throughout Scripture, the re-constitution of the material world, by which it passes from the bondage of corruption into 'the liberty of the glory of the children of God' is taught, and the final seat of the city of God is set forth as being, not some far-off, misty heaven in space, but 'that new world which is the old.'

'And the sea is no more' probably is to be taken in a
symbolic sense, as shadowing forth the absence of
unruly power, of mysterious and hostile forces, of
estranging gulfs of separation.   Into this renovated
world the renovated city floats down from God.   It
has been present with Him, before its manifestation on
earth, as all things that are to be manifested in time
dwell eternally in the Divine mind, and as it had been
realised in the person of the ascended Christ.   When
He comes down from heaven again, the city comes with
Him.   It is the 'new Jerusalem,' inasmuch as the ideas
which were partially embodied in the old Jerusalem
find complete and ennobled expression in it.   The
perfect state of perfect humanity is represented by
that society of God's servants, of which the ancient
Zion was a symbol.   In it all the glowing stream of
prophecy dealing with the 'bridal of the earth and of
the sky,' the marriage of perfect manhood with the
perfect King, is fulfilled.

II. The vision is supplemented by words explanatory
to the Seer of what he beheld (vs. 3, 4), and all turns
on two great thoughts—the blessed closeness of union
now perfected and made eternal between God and
men, and the consequent dawning of a new, unsetting
day in which all human ills shall be swept away.   The
former promise is cast in Old Testament mould, as are
almost all the symbols and prophecies of this Book of
Revelation.   In outward form the tabernacle had stood
in the centre of the wilderness encampment, and in
the symbol of the Shekinah, God had dwelt with Israel,
and they had been, in name, and by outward separation
and consecration, His people.   In the militant state of
the Church on the old earth, God had dwelt with His
people in reality, but with, alas! many a break in the

intercourse caused by His people defiling the temple. But in that future all that was symbol shall be spiritual reality, and there will be no separation between the God who tabernacles among men and the men in whom He dwells. The mutual relation of possession of each other shall be perfect and perpetual. That is the brightest hope for us, and from it all other blessedness flows. His presence drives away all evils, as the risen moon clears the sky of clouds. How can sorrow, or crying, or pain, or death, live where He is, as He will be in the perfected city? The undescribable future is best described by the negation of all that is sad and a foe to life. Reverse the miseries of earth, and you know something of the joys of heaven. But begin with God's presence, or you will know nothing of their most joyful joy.

III. The great voice speaks again, proclaiming the guarantees of the vision, and the conditions of possessing its fruition (vs. 5-7). How can we be sure that these radiant hopes are better than delusions, lights thrown on the black curtain of the unknown future by the reflection of our own imaginations? Only because ' He that sitteth on the throne,' and is therefore sovereign over all things, has declared that He will ' make all things new.' His power and faithful word are the sole guarantees. Therefore seers may write, and we may read, and be sure that when heaven and earth pass away His word shall not only not pass away, but bring the new heavens and the new earth. So sure is the fulfilment, that already, to the divine mind, these things ' are come to pass.' Faith may share in the di ae prerogative of seeing things that are not as though they were, and make the future present. He who is Alpha, the beginning, from whom are all things,

z

is Omega, the end, to whom are all things. There lies
the security that the drift of the universe is towards
God, its source, and that at last man, who came from
God, will come back to God, and Eden be surpassed by
the new Jerusalem.

The conditions of entering the city are gathered up
in words which recall many strains of prophecy and
promise. Thirst is the condition of drinking of the
water of life—as John the Evangelist delights to tell
that Jesus said by the well at Samaria and in the
temple court. Conflict and victory make His children
heirs of these things, as the Christ had spoken by the
Spirit to the churches. The Christian victory perfects
the paternal and filial relation between God and us.
And all three promises are but variations of the
answer to the question: How can I become a citizen of
that city of God?

IV. A fuller description, highly symbolical in colouring, of the city, comes next (vs. 22-27), on which space
will only allow us to remark that we have, first, two
representations, in each of which the city's glory is
expressed by the absence from it of a great good,
occasioned by the presence of a greater, of which the
lesser was but a shadowy similitude. There is no
temple, no outward shrine, no place of special communion, no dependence on externals, because the
communion with God and the Lamb is perfect, continuous, spiritual. There is no sun, moon, nor artificial
light, for far brighter than their feeble beams is the
light in which the citizens see light. That light is
perpetual, and no night ever darkens the sky. That
light draws all men to it. Possibly the Seer thinks of
kings and nations as still subsisting, but more probably
he carries over the features of the old earth into the

new, in order to express the great hope that all shall
be drawn to the light, and royalties and nations be
merged in citizenship. One solemn word limits the
universality of the vision. Nothing excludes but
uncleanness, but that does exclude. The roll of citizens
is the Lamb's book of life, and we may all have our
names written there. Only we must be pure, thirsty
for the water of life, and fight and conquer through
Jesus.

NO MORE SEA

'And there was no more sea.'—REV. xxi. 1.

'I JOHN,' says the Apocalypse at its commencement,
' was in the isle that is called Patmos, for the testimony
of Jesus.' In this, the one prophetic book of the New
Testament, we find the same fact that meets us in the
old prophecies, that the circumstances of the prophet
colour, and become the medium for, the representation
of the spiritual truths that he has to speak. All
through the book we hear the dash of the waves.
There was ' a sea of fire mingled with glass before the
throne.' The star Wormwood fell 'upon the sea.'
Out of the sea the beast rises. When the great angel
would declare the destruction of Babylon, he casts a
mighty stone into the ocean, and says, ' Thus suddenly
shall Babylon be destroyed.' And when John hears
the voice of praise of the redeemed, it is 'like the voice
of many waters,' as well as like the voice of 'harpers
harping on their harps.' And then, when there dawns
at the close of the vision, the bright and the blessed
time which has yet to come, the 'new heavens and the
new earth' are revealed to him; and that sad and

solitary and estranging ocean that raged around his
little rock sanctuary has passed away for ever. I suppose I need not occupy your time in showing that this
is a symbol; that it does not mean literal fact at all;
that it is not telling us anything about the geography of
a future world, but that it is the material embodiment
of a great spiritual truth.

Now what is meant by this symbol is best ascertained
by remembering how the sea appears in the Old Testament. The Jew was not a sailor. All the references
in the Old Testament, and especially in the prophets,
to the great ocean are such as a man would make who
knew very little about it, except from having looked
at it from the hills of Judea, and having often won-
dered what might be lying away out yonder at the
point where sky and sea blended together. There are
three main things which it shadows forth in the Old
Testament. It is a symbol of mystery, of rebellious
power, of perpetual unrest. And it is the promise of
the cessation of these things which is set forth in that
saying, 'There was no more sea.' There shall be no
more mystery and terror. There shall be no more 'the
floods lifting up their voice,' and the waves dashing
with impotent foam against the throne of God.
There shall be no more the tossing and the tumult of
changing circumstances, and no more the unrest and
disquiet of a sinful heart. There shall be the 'new
heavens and the new earth.' The old humanity will be
left, and the relation to God will remain, deepened and
glorified and made pure. But all that is sorrowful and
all that is rebellious, all that is mysterious and all that
is unquiet, shall have passed away for ever.

I. Let us then, by way of illustrating this great and
blessed promise, consider it first as the revelation of a

future in which there shall be no more painful mystery.

'Thy way is in the sea, and Thy path in the great waters, and Thy footsteps are not known.' 'Thy judgments are a mighty deep.' 'O the depth of the riches both of the wisdom and of the knowledge of God! How unsearchable are His judgments, and His ways past finding out!' Such is the prevailing tone of expression when the figure appears either in the Old or in the New Testament.

Most natural is it. There are, too, sources of obscurity there. We look out upon the broad ocean, and far away it seems to blend with air and sky. Mists come up over its surface. Suddenly there rises on the verge of the horizon a white sail that was not there a moment ago ; and we wonder, as we look out from our hills, what may be beyond these mysterious waters. And to these ancient peoples there were mysteries which we do not feel. Whither should they come, if they were to venture on its untried tides? And then, what lies in its sunless caves that no eyes have seen? It swallows up life and beauty and treasure of every sort, and engulfs them all in its obstinate silence. They go down in the mighty waters and vanish as they descend. What would it be if these were drained off? What revelations—wild sea-valleys and mountain-gorges; the dead that are in it, the power that lies there, all powerless now, the wealth that has been lost in it! What should we see if depth and distance were annihilated, and we beheld what there is out yonder, and what there is down there?

And is not our life, brethren, ringed round in like manner with mystery? And, alas! wherever to a poor human heart there is mystery, *there* will be terror.

The unknown is ever the awful. Where there is not certain knowledge, imagination works to people the waste places with monsters. There is a double limitation of our knowledge. There are mysteries that come from the necessary limitation of our faculties; and there are mysteries that come from the incompleteness of the revelation which God has been pleased to make. The eye is weak and the light is dim. There is much that lies beyond the horizon which our eyes cannot reach. There is much that lies covered by the deeps, which our eyes *could* reach if the deeps were away. We live—the wisest of us live—having great questions wrestling with us like that angel that wrestled with the patriarch in the darkness till the morning broke. We learn so little but our own ignorance, and we know so little but that we know nothing. There are the hard and obstinate knots that will not be untied; we bend all our faculties to them, and think they are giving a little bit, and they never give; and we gnaw at them, like the viper at the file, and we make nothing of it, but blunt our teeth!

Oh! to some hearts here, surely this ought to come as not the least noble and precious of the thoughts of what that future life is—'there shall be no more sea'; and the mysteries that come from God's merciful limitation of our vision, and some of the mysteries that come from God's wise and providential interposition of obstacles to our sight, shall have passed away. It is no dream, my brethren! Why, think how the fact of dying will solve many a riddle! how much more we shall know by shifting our position! 'There must be wisdom with great Death,' and he 'keeps the keys of all the creeds.' Try to conceive how some dear one that was beside us but a moment ago, perhaps but little conscious of his own ignorance, and knowing but little of God's ways, thinking as we did, and speaking as we did, and snared with errors as we were, has grown at a bound into full stature, and how a flood of new knowledge and Divine truth rushes into the heart the moment it passes the grave! If they were to speak to us, perhaps we should not understand their new speech, so wise have *they* become who have died.

What mysteries have passed into light for them? I know not. Who can tell what strange enlargement of faculty this soul of ours is capable of? Who can tell how much of our blindness comes from the flesh that clogs us, from the working of the animal nature that is so strong in us? Who can tell what unknown resources and what possibilities of new powers there lie all dormant and unsuspected in the beggar on the dunghill, and in the idiot in the asylum? This, at least, we are sure of: we shall 'know, even as also we are known.' God will not be fathomed, but God will be known. God will be incomprehensible, but there will be no mystery in God, except that most blessed mystery of feeling that the fulness of His nature still surpasses our comprehension. Questions that now fill the whole horizon of our minds will have shrunk away into a mere point, or been answered by the very change of position. How much of the knowledges of earth will have ceased to be applicable, when the first light-beam of heaven falls upon them! Those problems which we think so mysterious—why God is doing this or that with us and the world; what is the meaning of this and the other sorrow—what will have become of these? We shall look back and see that the bending line was leading straight as an arrow-flight, home to the centre, and that the end crowns and vindicates every step of

the road. Something of the mystery of God will have
been resolved, for man hath powers undreamed of yet,
and ' we shall see Him as He is.' Much of the mystery
of man, and of man's relation to God, will have ceased ;
for then we shall understand all the way, when we
have entered into the true sanctuary of God.

Men that love to know, let me ask you, where do you
get the fulfilment, often dreamed of, of your desires,
except here ? Set this before you, as the highest truth
for us : Christ is the beginning of all wisdom on earth.
Starting thence I can hope to solve the remaining
mysteries when I stand at last, redeemed by the blood
of the Lamb, in the presence of the great light of
God.

Not that we shall know everything, for that were to
cease to be finite. And if ever the blasphemous boast
come true that tempted man once, ' Ye shall be as gods,
knowing good and evil,' there were nothing left for the
soul that was filled with all knowledge but to lie down
and pant its last. It needs, by our very nature, and for
our blessedness, that there should be much unknown.
It needs that we should ever be pressing forward. Only,
the mysteries that are left will have no terror nor pain
in them. 'There shall be no more sea,' but we shall
climb ever higher and higher up the mountain of God,
and as we climb see farther and farther into the blessed
valleys beyond, and 'shall know, even as we are
known.'

II. Secondly, the text tells us of a state that is to
come, when there shall be no more rebellious power.
In the Old Testament the floods are often compared
with the rage of the peoples, and the rebellion of man
against the Will of God. 'The floods have lifted up,
O Lord, the floods have lifted up their voice. The Lord

on high is mightier than the noise of many waters ;
yea, than the mighty waves of the sea.' 'Thou stillest
the noise of the waves, and the tumult of the people.'
In like manner that symbolic reference surely supplies
one chief meaning of Christ's miracle of stilling the
tempest; the Peace-bringer bringing to peace the
tumults of men. Here, then, the sea stands as the
emblem of untamed power. It is lashed into yeasty
foam, and drives before it great ships and huge stones
like bulrushes, and seems to have a savage pleasure in
eating into the slow-corroding land, and covering the
beach with its devastation.

'There shall be no more sea.' God lets people work
against His kingdom in this world. It is not to be
always so, says my text. The kingdom of God *is* in the
earth, and the kingdom of God admits of opposition.
Strange! But the opposition, even here on earth, all
comes to nothing. 'Thou art mightier than the noise
of many waters '; the floods ' have lifted up their voice';
but Thou ' sittest upon the floods, yea, Thou sittest king
for ever.' Yes, it is an experience repeated over and
over again, in the history of individuals and in the
history of the world. Men, fancying themselves free,
resolved to be rebellious, get together and say, mutter-
ingly at first, and then boldly and loudly, ' Let us break
His bands asunder, and cast away His cords from us.'
And God sits in seeming silence in His heavens, and
they work on, and the thing seems to be prospering,
and some men's hearts begin to fail them for fear. The
great Armada comes in its pride across the waters—
and the motto that our England struck upon its medal,
when that proud fleet was baffled, serves for the
epitaph over all antagonism to God's kingdom, ' The
Lord blew upon them, and they were scattered.' The

tossing sea, that rages against the will and purpose of
the Lord, what becomes of all its foaming fury? Why,
this becomes of it—the ark of God 'moves on the face
of the waters,' and though wild tempests howl to beat
it from its course, yet beneath all the surface confusion
and commotion there is, as in the great mid-ocean, a
silent current that runs steady and strong, and it
carries the keel that goes deep enough down to rest in
it, safely to its port. Men may work against God's
kingdom, the waves may rave and rage; but beneath
them there is a mighty tidal sweep, and God's purposes
are wrought out, and God's ark comes to 'its desired
haven,' and all opposition is nugatory at the last.

But there comes a time, too, when there shall be no
more violence of rebellious wills lifting themselves
against God. Our text is a blessed promise that, in
that holy state to which the Apocalyptic vision carries
our longing hopes, there shall be the cessation of all
strife against our best Friend, of all reluctance to wear
His yoke whose yoke brings rest to the soul. The
opposition that lies in all our hearts shall one day be
subdued. The whole consent of our whole being shall
yield itself to the obedience of sons, to the service of
love. The wild rebellious power shall be softened into
peace, and won to joyful acceptance of His law. In all
the regions of that heavenly state, there shall be no
jarring will, no reluctant submission. Its 'solemn
troops and sweet societies' shall move in harmonious
consent of according hearts, and circle His throne in
continuousness of willing fealty. There shall be One
will in heaven. 'There shall be no more sea'; for
'His servants serve Him,' and the noise of the waves
has died away for ever.

Before I pass on, let me appeal to you, my friend, on

this matter. Here is the revelation for us of the utter
hopelessness and vanity of all opposition to God. Oh!
what a thought that is, that every life that sets itself
against the Lord is a futile life, that it comes to nothing
at last, that none hardens himself against God and
prospers! It is true on the widest scale. It is true on
the narrowest. It is true about all those tempests that
have risen up against God's Church and Christ's Gospel,
like 'waves of the sea foaming out their own shame,'
and never shaking the great rock that they break
against. And it is true about all godless lives; about
every man who carries on his work, except in loving
obedience to his Father in heaven. There is one
power in the world, and none else. When all is played
out, and accounts are set right at the end, you will find
that the power that seemed to be strong, if it stood
against God, was weak as water and has done nothing,
and is nothing! Do not waste your lives in a work
that is self-condemned to be hopeless! Rather ally
yourselves with the tendencies of God's universe, and
do the thing which will last for ever, and live the life
that has hope of fruit that shall remain. Submit
yourselves to God! Love Christ! Do His will! Put
your faith in the Saviour to deliver you from your
sins; and when the wild tossing of that great ocean of
ungodly power and rebellious opposition is all hushed
down into dead silence, you and your work will last
and live hard by the stable throne of God.

III. Lastly, the text foretells a state of things in which
there is no more disquiet and unrest. The old, old
figure which all the world, generation after generation
in its turn, has spoken, is a Scriptural one as well, and
enters into the fulness of the meaning of this passage
before us. Life is a voyage over a turbulent sea;

changing circumstances come rolling after each other,
like the undistinguishable billows of the great ocean.
Tempests and storms rise.   There is wearisome sailing,
no peace, but 'ever climbing up the climbing wave.'
That is life! But for all that, friends, there is an end
to it some day; and it is worth while for us to think
about our 'island home, far, far beyond the sea.'
Surely some of us have learned the weariness of this
changeful state, the weariness of the work and voyage
of this world. Surely some of us are longing to find
anchorage whilst the storm lasts, and a haven at the
end.   There *is* one, if only you will believe it, and set
yourselves towards it.   There is an end to all 'the
weary oar, the weary wandering fields of barren foam.'
On the shore stands the Christ; and there is rest *there*.
There is no more sea, but unbroken rest, unchanging
blessedness, perpetual stability of joy, and love in the
Father's house. Are *we* going there? Are *we* living
for Christ?   Are *we* putting our confidence in the
Lord Jesus?   Then, 'He brings us to the desired
haven.'

One thing more : not only does unrest come from the
chaos of changing circumstances, but besides that, there
is another source of disquiet, which this same symbol
sets forth for us. 'The wicked is like the troubled sea
which cannot rest, whose waters cast up mire and dirt.'
That restless, profitless working of the great homeless,
hungry, moaning ocean—what a picture it is of the heart
of a man that has no Christ, that has no God, that has
no peace by pardon! A soul all tossed with its own
boiling passion, a soul across which there howl great
gusts of temptation, a soul which works and brings
forth nothing but foam and mire! Unrest, perpetual
unrest is the lot of every man that is not God's child.

Some of you know that. Well, then, think of one
picture. A little barque pitching in the night, and one
figure rises quietly up in the stern, and puts out a re-
buking hand, and speaks one mighty word, ' Peace ! be
still.' And the word was heard amid all the hurly-
burly of the tempest, and the waves crouched at His
feet like dogs to their master. It is no fancy, brethren,
it is a truth. Let Christ speak to your hearts, and there
is peace and quietness. And if He do that, then your
experience will be like that described in the grand old
Psalm, ' Though the waters roar and be troubled, and
though the mountains shake with the swelling thereof,
yet will we not fear,' for the city stands fast, in spite
of the waves that curl round its lowest foundations.
Death, death itself, will be but the last burst of the ex-
piring storm, the last blast of the blown-out tempest.
And then, the quiet of the green inland valleys of our
Father's land, where no tempest comes any more, nor
the loud winds are ever heard, nor the salt sea is ever
seen ; but perpetual calm and blessedness ; all mystery
gone, and all rebellion hushed and silenced, and all unrest at an end for ever ! ' No more sea,' but, instead of
that wild and yeasty chaos of turbulent waters, there
shall be 'the river that makes glad the city of God,'
the river of water of life, that 'proceeds out of the
throne of God and of the Lamb.'

THE CITY, THE CITIZENS, AND THE KING

'And he shewed me a pure river of water of life, clear as crystal, proceeding out of the throne of God and of the Lamb. 2. In the midst of the street of it, and on either side of the river, was there the tree of life, which bare twelve manner of fruits, and yielded her fruit every month: and the leaves of the tree were for the healing of the nations. 3. And there shall be no more curse: but the throne of God and of the Lamb shall be in it; and His servants shall serve Him: 4. And they shall see His face; and His name shall be in their foreheads. 5. And there shall be no night there; and they need no candle, neither light of the sun; for the Lord God giveth them light: and they shall reign for ever and ever. 6. And He said unto me, These sayings are faithful and true: and the Lord God of the holy prophets sent His angel to shew unto His servants the things which must shortly be done. 7. Behold, I come quickly: blessed is he that keepeth the sayings of the prophecy of this book. 8. And I John saw these things, and heard them. And when I had heard and seen, I fell down to worship before the feet of the angel which shewed me these things. 9. Then saith he unto me, See thou do it not: for I am thy fellow-servant, and of thy brethren the prophets, and of them which keep the sayings of this book: worship God. 10. And he saith unto me, Seal not the sayings of the prophecy of this book: for the time is at hand. 11. He that is unjust, let him be unjust still: and he which is filthy, let him be filthy still: and he that is righteous, let him be righteous still: and he that is holy, let him be holy still.'— REV. xxii. 1-11.

Is the vision of the new Jerusalem to be realised in the present or in the future? Such features as the existence of 'nations' and 'kings of the earth' outside of it (vs. 21, 24), and leaves of the tree of life being 'for the healing of the nations,' favour the former reference, while its place in the book, after the first and second resurrections and the judgment and at the very end of the whole, seems to oblige us to hold by the latter. But the question must be answered in the light of the fact that the Christian life is one in essence in both worlds, and that the difference between the conditions of the society of the redeemed here and there is only one of degree. The 'city' has already come down from heaven; its perfect form waits to be manifested.

The passage is partly the close of that vision (vs. 1-5), and partly the beginning of the epilogue of the whole book (vs. 6-11). The closing description of the city is saturated with allusions to Old Testament prophecy.

It is like the finale of some great concerto, in which the themes that have sounded throughout it are all gathered up in the last majestic, melodious crash. Here at the farthest point to which mortal eyes are allowed to pierce, the 'tree of life' that the first of mortal eyes had looked on waves its branches again. The end has circled round to the beginning. But now there is no more prohibition to pluck and eat, and now it grows, not in a garden, but in a city where the perfection of human society is entered into.

Here, on the last page of Scripture, the river, the music of whose ripple had been heard by Ezekiel and Zechariah bringing life to everything that it laved, and by the Psalmist making 'glad the city of God,' flows with a broader, fuller stream, and is fouled by no stains, but is 'clear as crystal.' River and tree have the same epithet, and bring the same gift to the citizens. All the blessings which Jesus gives are summed up, both in John's Gospel and in the Apocalypse, as 'life.' The only true life is to live as God's redeemed servants, and that life is ours here and now if we are His. It is but a 'stream' of the river that gladdens us here, the fruit has not yet its full flavour nor abundance. 'It is life, more life, for which we pant,' and the desire will be satisfied there when the river runs always full, and every month the fruit hangs ripe and ready to be dropped into happy hands from among the healing leaves.

In verses 3 and 4 we pass from the city to the citizens. Perfect purity clothes them all. 'There shall be no more anything accursed'; that is, any unclean thing drawing down necessarily the divine 'curse,' and therefore there shall be no separation, no film of distance between the King and the people, but 'the throne

of God and the Lamb shall be therein.' The seer has
already beheld the Lamb close by the throne of God,
but now he sees Him sharing it in indissoluble union.
Perfect purity leads to perfect union with God and (or
rather in) Christ, and unbroken, glad submission to His
regal rule. And that perfect submission is the occupation and delight of all the citizens. They are His
'bond-servants,' and their fetters are golden chains of
honour and ornament. They 'do Him service,' ministering as priests, and all their acts are 'begun, continued, and ended in Him.' Having been faithful over
a few things, they are made rulers over many things,
and are yet bond-servants, though rulers.

In that higher service the weary schism between the
active and the contemplative life is closed up. Mary
and Martha end their long variance, and gazing on His
face does not hinder active obedience, nor does doing
Him service distract from beholding His beauty. 'His
name shall be in their foreheads,' conspicuous and un-
mistakable, no longer faintly traced or often concealed,
but flaming on their brows. They are known to be
His, because their characters are conformed to His.
They bear 'the marks of Jesus' in complete and visible
assimilation to Him.

The vision closes with an echo of Old Testament prophecy (Isaiah lx. 19). 'No night'—perhaps the most
blessed of all John's negative descriptions of the future
state, indicating the removal for ever of all the evil and
woe symbolised by darkness, and pointing to a state in
which no artifices of ours are needed to brighten our
gloom with poor, man-made candles, nor any created
light, though mighty and resplendent as the sun, whose
beams fade into invisibility before the immortal radiance that pours out for ever from the throne, brighten-

ing every glorified face that is turned to its lustre. Thus seeing, serving, and being like 'God and the Lamb,' they, as a consequence, 'shall reign for ever and ever,' for they are as He is, and while He lives and reigns they also live and reign.

With verse 6 begins the epilogue. An angel speaks, the same as in chapter i. 1—is represented as 'signifying' the 'revelation' to John. He now, as it were, sets his seal on his completed roll of prophecy. To discriminate between the words of the angel and of Jesus is impossible. Jesus speaks through him. 'Behold, I come quickly' cannot be merely the angel's voice. As in verse 12, a deeper voice speaks through his lips. The purpose of that solemn announcement is to impress on the Asiatic churches, and through them on the whole Church through all time, the importance of keeping 'the words of the prophecy of this book.' 'Quickly'— and yet nineteen hundred years have gone since then? Yes; and during them all Jesus has been coming, and the words of this book have progressively been in process of fulfilment.

Again, the speedy coming is enforced as a reason for not sealing up the prophecy, as had been commanded in chapter x. 4, and elsewhere in the Old Testament. And a very solemn thought closes our lesson—that there is a moment, the eve of any great 'day of the Lord,' when there is no more time or opportunity for change of moral or spiritual disposition. 'Too late, too late, ye cannot enter now.' Let us 'redeem the time,' buy back the opportunity while yet it is within our grasp.

THE TRIPLE RAYS WHICH MAKE THE WHITE LIGHT OF HEAVEN

'. . . His servants shall serve Him : 4. And they shall see His face ; and His name shall be in their foreheads.'—REV. xxii. 3, 4.

ONE may well shrink from taking words like these for a text. Their lofty music will necessarily make all words of ours seem thin and poor. The great things about which they are concerned are so high above us, and known to us by so few channels, that usually he who says least speaks most wisely about them. And yet it cannot be but wholesome if in a reverent spirit of no vain curiosity, we do try to lay upon our hearts the impressions of the great, though they be dim, truths which gleam from these words. I know that to talk about a future life is often a most sentimental, vague, unpractical form of religious contemplation, but there is no reason at all why it should be so. I wish to try now very simply to bring out the large force and wonderful meaning of the words which I have ventured to read. They give us three elements of the perfect state of man—Service, Contemplation, Likeness. These three are perfect and unbroken.

I. The first element, then, in the perfect state of man is perfect activity in the service of God. Now the words of our text are remarkable in that the two expressions for 'servant' and 'serve' are not related to one another in the Greek, as they are in the English, but are two quite independent words ; the former meaning literally 'a slave,' and the latter being exclusively confined in Scripture to one kind of service. It would never be employed for any service that a man did for a man ; it is exclusively a religious word, and

means only the service that men do for God, whether
in specific acts of so-called worship or in the wider
worship of daily life. So that if we have not here the
notion of priesthood, we have one very closely approximating towards it; and the representation is that the
activity of the redeemed and perfected man, in the
highest ideal condition of humanity, is an activity
which is all worship, and is directed to the revealed
God in Christ.

That, then, is the first thought that we have to look
at. Now it seems to me to be a very touching confession of the weariness and unsatisfactoriness of life in
general that the dream of the future which has
unquestionably the most fascination for most men, is
that which speaks of it as Rest. The religion which
has the largest number of adherents in the world—the
religion of the Buddhists—formally declares existence
to be evil, and preaches as the highest attainable good,
something which is scarcely distinguishable from
annihilation. And even though we do not go so far as
that, what a testimony it is of burdened hearts and
mournful lives, and work too great for the feeble
limits of our powers, that the most natural thought of
a blessed future is as rest! It is easy to laugh at
people for singing hymns about sitting upon green and
flowery mounts, and counting up the labours of their
feet: but oh! it is a tragical thought that whatsoever
shape a life has taken, howsoever full of joy and sunshine and brightness it may be, deep down in the man
there is such an experience as that the one thing he
wants is repose and to get rid of all the trouble and
toil.

Now this representation of my text is by no means
contradictory, but it is complementary, of that other

one. The deepest rest and the highest activity coincide.
They do so in God who 'worketh hitherto' in undis-
turbed tranquillity; they may do so in us. The wheel
that goes round in swiftest rotation seems to be standing still. Work at its intensest, which is pleasurable
work, and level to the capacity of the doer, is the
truest form of rest. In vacuity there are stings and
torment; it is only in joyous activity which is not
pushed to the extent of strain and unwelcome effort
that the true rest of man is to be found. And the two
verses in this Book of Revelation about this matter,
which look at first sight to be opposed to each other,
are like the two sides of a sphere, which unite and
make the perfect whole. 'They rest from their labours.'
'They rest *not*, day nor night.'

From their labours—yes; from toil disproportioned
to faculty—yes! from unwelcome work—yes! from
distraction and sorrow—yes! But from glad praise
and vigorous service—never! day nor night. And so
with the full apprehension of the sweetness and
blessedness of the tranquil Heaven, we say: It is found
only there, where His servants serve Him. Thus the
first thought that is presented here is that of an
activity delivered from all that makes toil on earth
burdensome and unwelcome; and which, therefore, is
coincident with the deepest and most perfect repose.

It may seem strange to think of a blessed life which
has no effort in it, for effort is the very salt and spice
of life here below, and one can scarcely fancy the
perfect happiness of a spirit which never has the glow
of warmth that comes from exercise in overcoming
difficulties. But perhaps effort and antagonism and
strain and trial have done their work on us when they
have moulded our characters, and when 'school is over

we burn the rod'; and the discipline of joy may evolve
nobler graces of character than ever the discipline of
sorrow did. At all events, we have to think of work
which also is repose, and of service in which is
unbroken tranquillity.

Then there is further involved in this first idea, the
notion of an outer world, on which and in which to
work; and also the notion of the resurrection of the
body, in which the active spirit may abide, and through
which it may work.

Perhaps it may be that they who sleep in Jesus, in
the period between the shuffling off of this mortal coil
and the breaking of that day when they are raised
again from the dead, are incapable of exertion in an
outer sphere. Perhaps, it may be, that by reason of
the absence of that glorified body of the Resurrection,
they sleep in Jesus in the sense that they couch at the
Shepherd's feet within the fold until the morning
comes, when He leads them out to new pastures. It
may be. At all events, this we may be sure of, that if
it be so they have no desires in advance of their
capacities; and of this also I think we may be sure,
that whether they themselves can come into contact
with an external universe or not, Christ is for them in
some measure what the body is to us here now, and
the glorified body will be hereafter; that being absent
from the body they are present with the Lord, and
that He is as it were the Sensorium by which they are
brought into contact with and have a knowledge of
external things, so that they may rest and wait and
have no work to do, and have no effort to put forth,
and yet be conscious of all that befalls the loved ones
here below, may know them in their affliction, and not
be untouched by their tears.

But all that is a dim region into which we have not any need to look. What I emphasise is, the service of Heaven means rest, and the service of Heaven means an outer universe on which, and a true bodily frame with which, to do the work which is delight.

The next point is this: such service must be in a far higher sphere and a far nobler fashion than the service of earth. That is in accordance with the analogy of the Divine dealings. God rewards work with more work. The powers that are trained and exercised and proved in a narrower region are lifted to the higher. As some poor peasant-girl, for instance, whose rich voice has risen up in the harvest-field only for her own delight and that of a handful of listeners, heard by some one who detects its sweetness, may be carried away to some great city, and charm kings with her tones, so the service done in some little corner of this remote, rural province of God's universe, apprehended by Him, shall be rewarded with a wider platform, and a nobler area for work. 'Thou hast been faithful in a few things, I will make thee ruler over many things.' God sends forth His children to work as apprentices here, and when they are 'out of their time,' and have 'got a trade,' He calls them home, not to let their faculties rest unused, but to practise on a larger theatre what they have learned on earth.

One more point must be noticed, viz., that the highest type of Heaven's service must be service for other people. The law for Heaven can surely not be more selfish than the law for earth, and that is, 'He that is chiefest amongst you let him be your servant.' The law for the perfect man can surely not be different from the law for the Master, and the law for Him is, 'Even Christ pleased not Himself.' The perfection of the child can surely not be different from the perfection of the Father, and the perfection of the Father is: 'He maketh His sun to "shine," and His blessings–to come —on the unthankful and on the good.'

So then the highest service for man is the service for others ;—how, where, or whom, we cannot tell. We too may be 'ministering spirits, sent forth to minister' (Heb. i. 14), but at all events not on ourselves can our activities centre ; and not in self-culture can be the highest form of our service to God.

The last point about this first matter is simply this— that this highest form of human activity is all to be worship; all to be done in reference to Him ; all to be done in submission to Him. The will of the man in His work is to be so conformed to the will of God as that, whatsoever the hand on the great dial points to, that the hand on the little dial shall point to also. Obedience is joy and rest. To know and to do His will is Heaven. It is Heaven on earth in so far as we partially attain to it, and when with enlarged powers and all imperfec- tions removed, and in a higher sphere, and without interruptions we do His commandments, hearkening to the voice of His word, then the perfect state will have come. Then shall we enter into the liberty of the glory of the children of God, when, as His slaves, we serve Him in the unwearied activities done for Him, which make the worship of Heaven.

II. Next, look at the second of the elements here :— 'They shall see His face.' Now that expression 'seeing the face of God' in Scripture seems to me to be employed in two somewhat different ways, according to one of which the possibility of seeing the face is affirmed, and according to the other of which it is denied.

The one may be illustrated by the Divine word to Moses: 'Thou canst not see My face. There shall no man see Me and live.' The other may be illustrated by the aspiration and the confidence of one of the psalms: 'As for me, I shall behold Thy face in righteousness.'

A similar antithesis, which is apparently a contradiction, may be found in setting side by side the words of our Saviour: 'Blessed are the pure in heart, for they shall see God,' with the words of the Evangelist: 'No man hath seen God at any time.' I do not think that the explanation is to be found altogether in pointing to the difference between present and possible future vision, but rather, I think, the Bible teaches what reason would also teach: that no corporeal vision of God is ever possible; still further, that no complete comprehension and knowledge of Him is ever possible, and, as I think further, that no direct knowledge of, or contact with, God in Himself is possible for finite man, either here or yonder. And the other side lies in such words as these, which I have already quoted: 'Blessed are the pure in heart, for they shall see God.' 'As through a glass darkly, but then face to face.' Where is the key to the apparent contradiction? Here, I think. Jesus Christ is the manifest God, in Him only do men draw near to the hidden Deity, the King Invisible, who dwelleth in the light that is inaccessible.

Here on earth we see by faith, and yonder there will be a vision, different in kind, most real, most immediate and direct, not of the hidden Godhood in itself, but of the revealed Godhood manifest in Jesus Christ, whom in His glorified corporeal Manhood we shall perceive, with the organs of our glorified body; whom in His Divine beauty we shall know and love with heart and mind, in knowledge direct, immediate, far surpassing in degree, and different in kind from, the knowledge of faith which we have of Him here below. But the infinite Godhood that lies behind all revelations of Deity shall remain as it hath been through them all—the King invisible, whom no man hath seen or can see. They shall see His face in so far as they shall hold communion with, and through their glorified body have the direct knowledge of Christ, the revealed Deity.

Whether there be anything more, I know not; I think there is not; but this I am sure of, that the law for Heaven and the law for earth alike are, 'He that hath seen Me hath seen the Father.'

But there is another point I would touch upon in reference to this second thought of our text, viz., its connection with the previous representation, 'They shall serve Him'—that is work in an outer sphere; 'they shall see His face'—that is contemplation. These two, the life of work and the life of devout communion —the Martha and the Mary of the Christian experience —are antagonistic here below, and it is hard to reconcile their conflicting, fluctuating claims and to know how much to give to the inward life of gazing upon Christ, and how much to the outward life of serving Him. But, says my text, the two shall be blended together. 'His servants shall serve Him,' nor in all their activity shall they lose the vision of His face. His servants 'shall see His face'; nor in all the still blessedness of their gaze upon Him shall they slack the diligence of the unwearied hands, or the speed of the willing feet. The Rabbis taught that there were angels who serve, and angels who praise, but the two classes meet in the perfected man, whose services shall be praise, whose praise shall be service. They go forth to do His will, yet are ever in the House of the

Lord. They work and gaze; they gaze and work. Resting they serve, and serving they rest; perpetual activity and perpetual vision are theirs. 'They serve Him, and see His face.'

III. The last element is, 'His name shall be in their foreheads.' That is, as I take it—a manifest likeness to the Lord whom they serve is the highest element in the perfect state of redeemed men. We hear a good deal in this Book of the Revelation about writing the names and numbers of persons and of powers upon men's faces and foreheads; as for instance, you remember we read about the 'number of the beast' written upon his worshippers, and about 'the name of the new Jerusalem, and the name of my God' being written as a special reward, 'upon him that overcomes.' The metaphor, as I suppose, is taken from the old, cruel practice of branding a slave with the name of his master. And so the primary idea of this expression: 'His slaves shall bear His name upon their foreheads,' is that their ownership shall be conspicuously visible to all that look.

But there is more than that in it. How is the ownership to be made visible? By His name being in their foreheads. What is 'His name'? Universally in Scripture 'His name' is His revealed character, and so we come to this: the perfect men shall be known to belong to God in Christ, because they are like Him. The ownership shall be proved by the likeness, and that likeness shall no longer be hidden in their *hearts*, no longer be difficult to make out, so blurred and obliterated the letters of the name by the imperfections of their lives and their selfishness and sin; but it shall flame in their foreheads, plain as the inscription on the high priest's mitre that declared him to be consecrated to the Lord.

And so that lovely and blessed thought is here of a perfect likeness in moral character, at all events, and a wonderful approximation and resemblance in other elements of human nature to the glorified humanity of Jesus Christ our Lord, which shall be the token that we are His.

Oh! what a contrast to the partial ownership, proved to be partial by our partial resemblance here on earth! We say, as Christian men and women, that we bear His name. Is it written so that men can read it, or is it like the name of some person traced in letters of gas jets over a shop-front—half blown out by every gust of wind that comes? Is that the way in which His name is written on your heart and character? My brother, a possibility great and blessed opens before us of a nobler union with Him, a closer approximation, a clearer vision, a perfecter resemblance. 'We shall be like Him, for we shall see Him as He is'!

One last word. These three elements, service, contemplation, likeness; these three are not different in kind from the elements of a Christian man's life here. You can enjoy them all sitting in these pews; in the bustle and the hurry of your daily life, you can have every one of them. If you do not enjoy them here you will never have them yonder. If you have never served anybody but yourself how shall death make you His servant? If all the days of your life you have turned away your ear when He has been saying to you 'Seek ye My face,' what reason is there to expect that when death's hammer smashes the glass through which you have seen darkly, 'the steady whole of that awful face' will be a pleasant sight to you? If all your life you have been trying, as some of you men and women, old and young, have been trying, and are trying now, to engrave the name of the beast upon your foreheads, what reason have you to expect that when you pass out of this life the foul signs shall disappear in a moment, and you will bear in your brow 'the marks of the Lord Jesus' in their stead? No! No! These things do not happen; you have got to begin here as you mean to end yonder. Trust Him here and you will see Him there. Serve Him here and you will serve Him yonder. Write His new Name upon your hearts, and when you pass from the imperfections of life you will bear His name in your foreheads.

And if you do not—I lay this upon the consciences of you all—if you do not you will see Christ;—and you will not like it! And you will bear, not the Image of the Heavenly, which is life, but the image of the earthy, which is death and hell!

THE LAST BEATITUDE OF THE ASCENDED
CHRIST

'Blessed are they that do His commandments, that they may have right to the Tree of Life, and may enter in through the gates into the city.'—REV. xxii. 14.

THE Revised Version reads: 'Blessed are they that wash their robes, that they may have the right to come to the Tree of Life.'

That may seem a very large change to make, from 'keep His commandments,' to 'wash their robes,' but in the Greek it is only a change of three letters in one word, one in the next, and two in the third. And the two phrases, written, look so like each other, that a scribe, hasty, or for the moment careless, might very easily mistake the one for the other. There can be no

doubt whatever that the reading in the Revised Version
is the correct one. Not only is it sustained by a great
weight of authority, but also it is far more in accordance with the whole teaching of the New Testament
than that which stands in our Authorised Version.

'Blessed are they that do His commandments, that
they may have right to the Tree of Life,' carries us
back to the old law, and has no more hopeful a sound
in it than the thunders of Sinai. If it were, indeed,
amongst Christ's last words to us, it would be a most
sad instance of His 'building again the things He had
destroyed.' It is relegating us to the dreary old round
of trying to earn Heaven by doing good deeds; and I
might almost say it is 'making the Cross of Christ of
none effect.' The fact that that corrupt reading came
so soon into the Church and has held its ground so
long, is to me a very singular proof of the difficulty
which men have always had in keeping themselves up
to the level of the grand central Gospel truth: 'Not by
works of righteousness which we have done, but by
His mercy, He saved us.'

'Blessed are they that wash their robes, that they may
have right to the Tree of Life,' has the clear ring of
the New Testament music about it, and is in full accord
with the whole type of doctrine that runs through this
book; and is not unworthy to be almost the last word
that the lips of the Incarnate Wisdom spoke to men
from Heaven. So then, taking that point of view, I
wish to look with you at three things that come plainly
out of these words:—First, that principle that if men
are clean it is because they are cleansed; 'Blessed are
they that wash their robes.' Secondly, It is the cleansed
who have unrestrained access to the source of life.
And lastly, It is the cleansed who pass into the society

of the city.   Now, let me deal with these three
things :—

First, If we are clean it is because we have been
made so.   The first beatitude that Jesus Christ spoke
from the mountain was, 'Blessed are the poor in spirit.'
The last beatitude that He speaks from Heaven is,
'Blessed are they that wash their robes.'   And the act
commended in the last is but the outcome of the spirit
extolled in the first.   For they who are poor in spirit
are such as know themselves to be sinful men; and
those who know themselves to be sinful men are they
who will cleanse their robes in the blood of Jesus
Christ.

I need not remind you, I suppose, how continually
this symbol of the robe is used in Scripture as an expression for moral character.   This Book of the
Apocalypse is saturated through and through with
Jewish implications and allusions, and there can be no
doubt whatever that in this metaphor of the cleansing
of the robes there is an allusion to that vision that the
Apocalyptic seer of the Old Covenant, the prophet
Zechariah, had when he saw the high priest standing
before the altar clad in foul raiment, and the word
came forth, 'Take away the filthy garments from him.'
Nor need I do more than remind you how the same
metaphor is often on the lips of our Lord Himself,
notably in the story of the man that had not on the
wedding garment, and in the touching and beautiful
incident in the parable of the Prodigal Son, where
the exuberance of the father's love bids them cast
the best robe round the rags and the leanness of
his long-lost boy.   Nor need I remind you how Paul
catches up the metaphor, and is continually referring
to an investing and a divesting—the putting on and the

putting off of the new and the old man. In this same Book of the Apocalypse we see, gleaming all through it, the white robes of the purified soul: 'They shall walk with Me in white, for they are worthy.' 'I beheld a great multitude, whom no man could number, who had washed their robes and made them white in the blood of the Lamb.'

And so there are gathered up into these last words, all these allusions and memories, thick and clustering, when Christ speaks from Heaven and says, 'Blessed are they that wash their robes.'

Well then, I suppose we may say roughly, in our more modern phraseology, that the robe thus so frequently spoken of in Scripture answers substantially to what we call character. It is not exactly the man—and yet it is the man. It is the self—and yet it is a kind of projection and making visible of the self, the vesture which is cast round 'the hidden man of the heart.'

This mysterious robe, which answers nearly to what we mean by character, is made by the wearer.

That is a solemn thought. Every one of us carries about with him a mystical loom, and we are always weaving—weave, weave, weaving—this robe which we wear, every thought a thread of the warp, every action a thread of the weft. We weave it as the spider does its web, out of its own entrails, if I might so say. We weave it, and we dye it, and we cut it, and we stitch it, and then we put it on and wear it, and it sticks to us. Like a snail that crawls about your garden patches, and makes its shell by a process of secretion from out of its own substance, so you and I are making that mysterious, solemn thing that we call character, moment by moment. It is our own self, modified by

our actions.   Character is the precipitate from the
stream of conduct which, like the Nile Delta, gradually
rises solid and firm above the parent river and confines
its flow.

The next step that I ask you to take is one that I
know some of you do not like to take, and it is this:
All the robes are foul. I do not say all are equally
splashed, I do not say all are equally thickly spotted
with the flesh. I do not wish to talk dogmas, I wish
to talk experience; and I appeal to your own consciences, with this plain question, that every man and
woman amongst us can answer if they like—Is it true
or is it not, that the robe is all dashed with mud
caught on the foul ways, with stains in some of us of
rioting and banqueting and revelry and drunkenness;
sins of the flesh that have left their mark upon the
flesh; but with all of us grey and foul as compared
with the whiteness of His robe who sits above us
there?

Ah! would that I could bring to all hearts that are
listening to me now, whether the hearts of professing
Christians or no, that consciousness more deeply than
we have ever had it, of how full of impurity and
corruption our characters are. I do not charge you
with crimes; I do not charge you with guilt in the
world's eyes, but, if we seriously ponder over our past,
have we not lived, some of us habitually, all of us far
too often, as if there were no God at all, or as if we
had nothing to do with Him? and is not that godlessness practical Atheism, the fountain of all foulness
from which black brooks flow into our lives, and stain
our robes?

The next step is, The foul robe can be cleansed. My
text does not go any further in a statement of the

method, but it rests upon the great words of this Book
of the Revelation, which I have already quoted for
another purpose, in which we read 'they washed their
robes, and made them white in the blood of the Lamb.'
And the same writer, in his Epistle, has the same paradox, which seems to have been, to him, a favourite
way of putting the central Gospel truth: 'The blood
of Jesus Christ cleanses from all sin.' John saw the
paradox, and saw that the paradox helped to illustrate
the great truth that he was trying to proclaim, that
the red blood whitened the black robe, and that in its
full tide there was a limpid river of water of life,
clear as crystal, proceeding out of the Cross of
Christ.

Guilt can be pardoned, character can be sanctified.
Guilt can be pardoned! Men say: 'No! We live in a
universe of inexorable laws; "What a man soweth
that he must also reap." If he has done wrong he
must inherit the consequences.'

But the question whether guilt can be pardoned or
not has only to do very remotely with consequences.
The question is not whether we live in a universe of
inexorable laws, but whether there is anything in the
universe but the laws; for forgiveness is a personal
act, and has only to do secondarily and remotely with
the consequences of a man's doings. So that, if we
believe in a personal God, and believe that He has got
any kind of living relation to men at all, we can
believe—blessed be His name!—in the doctrine of
forgiveness; and leave the inexorable laws full scope
to work, according as His wisdom and His mercy may
provide. For the heart of the Christian doctrine of
pardon does not touch those laws, but the heart of it is
this: 'O Lord! Thou wast angry with me, but Thine

anger is turned away, Thou hast comforted me!' So guilt may be pardoned.

Character may be sanctified and elevated. Why not, if you can bring a sufficiently strong new force to bear upon it? And you can bring such a force, in the blessed thought of Christ's death for me, and in the gift of His love. There is such a force in the thought that He has given Himself for our sin. There is such a force in the Spirit of Christ given to us through His death to cleanse us by His presence in our hearts. And so I say, the blood of Jesus Christ, the power of His sacrifice and Cross, cleanses from all sin, both in the sense of taking away all my guilt, and in the sense of changing my character into something loftier and nobler and purer.

Men and women! Do you believe that? If you do not, why do you not? If you do, are you trusting to what you believe, and living the life that befits the confidence?

One word more. The washing of your robes has to be done by you. 'Blessed are they that wash their robes.' On one hand is all the fulness of cleansing, on the other is the heap of dirty rags that will not be cleansed by you sitting there and looking at them. You must bring the two into contact. How? By the magic band that unites strength and weakness, purity and foulness, the Saviour and the penitent; the magic band of simple affiance, and trust and submission of myself to the cleansing power of His death and of His life.

Only remember, 'Blessed are they that *are washing*,' as the Greek might read. Not once and for all, but a continuous process, a blessed process running on all through a man's life.

These are the conditions as they come from Christ's own lips, in almost the last words that human ears, either in fact or in vision, heard Him utter. These are the conditions under which noble life, and at last Heaven, are possible for men, namely, that their foul characters shall be cleansed, and that continuously, by daily recurrence and recourse to the Fountain opened in His sacrifice and death.

Friends, you may know much of the beauty and nobleness of Christianity, you may know much of the tenderness and purity of Christ, but if you have not apprehended Him in this character, there is an inner sanctuary yet to be trod, of which your feet know nothing, and the sweetest sweetness of all you have not yet tasted, for it is His forgiving love and cleansing power that most deeply manifest His Divine affection and bind us to Himself.

II. The second thought that I would suggest is that these cleansed ones, and by implication these only, have unrestrained access to the source of life: 'Blessed are they that wash their robes, that they may have right "to the Tree of Life."' That, of course, carries us back to the old mysterious narrative at the beginning of the Book of Genesis.

Although it does not bear very closely upon my present subject, I cannot help pausing to point out one thing, how remarkable and how beautiful it is that the last page of the Revelation should come bending round to touch the first page of Genesis. The history of man began with angels with frowning faces and flaming swords barring the way to the Tree of Life. It ends here with the guard of Cherubim withdrawn; or rather, perhaps, sheathing their swords and becoming guides to the no longer forbidden fruit, instead of being its guards. That is the Bible's grand symbolical way of saying that all between—the sin, the misery, the death—is a parenthesis. God's purpose is not going to be thwarted, and the end of His majestic march through human history is to be men's access to the Tree of Life from which, for the dreary ages—that are but as a moment in the great eternities—they were barred out by their sin.

However, that is not the point that I meant to say a word about. The Tree of Life stands as the symbol here of an external source of life. I take 'life' to be used here in what I believe to be its predominant New Testament meaning, not bare continuance in existence, but a full, blessed perfection and activity of all the faculties and possibilities of the man, which this very Apostle himself identifies with the knowledge of God and of Jesus Christ. And that life, says John, has an external source in Heaven as on earth.

There is an old Christian legend, absurd as a legend, beautiful as a parable, that the Cross on which Christ was crucified was made out of the wood of the Tree of Life. It is true in idea, for He and His work will be the source of all life, for earth and for Heaven, whether of body, soul, or spirit. They that wash their robes have the right of unrestrained access to Him in whose presence, in that loftier state, no impurity can live.

I need not dwell upon the thought that is involved here, of how, whilst on earth and in the beginnings of the Christian career, life is the basis of righteousness: in that higher world, in a very profound sense, righteousness is the condition of fuller life.

The Tree of Life, according to some of the old Rabbinical legends, lifted its branches, by an indwelling

motion, high above impure hands that were stretched
to touch them, and until our hands are cleansed through
faith in Jesus Christ, its richest fruit hangs unreach-
able, golden, above our heads. Oh! brother, the fulness of the life of Heaven is only granted to them who,
drawing near Jesus Christ by faith on earth, have
thereby cleansed themselves from all filthiness of the
flesh and spirit.

III. Finally, those who are cleansed, and they only,
have entrance into the society of the city.

There again we have a whole series of Old and New
Testament metaphors gathered together. In the old
world the whole power and splendour of great kingdoms
were gathered in their capitals, Babylon and Nineveh
in the past, Rome in the present. To John the forces
of evil were all concentrated in that city on the Seven
Hills. To him the antagonistic forces which were the
hope of the world were all concentrated in the real
ideal city which he expected to come down from Heaven
—the new Jerusalem. And he and his brother who
wrote the Epistle to the Hebrews, whoever *he* was—
trained substantially in the same school—have taught
us the same lesson that our picture of the future is not
to be of a solitary or self-regarding Heaven, but of 'a
city which hath foundations.'

Genesis began with a garden, man's sin sent him out
of the garden. God, out of evil, evolves good, and for
the lost garden comes the better thing, the found city.
'Then comes the statelier Eden back to man.' For
surely it is better that men should live in the activities
of the city than in the sweetness and indolence of the
garden; and manifold and miserable as are the sins
and the sorrows of great cities, the opprobria of our
modern so-called civilisation, yet still the aggregation

of great masses of men for worthy objects generates a form of character, and sets loose energies and activities which no other kind of life could have produced.

And so I believe a great step in progress is set forth when we read of the final condition of mankind as being their assembling in the city of God. And surely there, amidst the solemn troops and sweet societies, the long-loved, long-lost will be found again. I cannot believe that, like the Virgin and Joseph, we shall have to go wandering up and down the streets of Jerusalem when we get there, looking for our dear ones. 'Wist ye not that I should be in the Father's house?' We shall know where to find them.

'We shall clasp them again,
And with God be the rest.'

The city is the emblem of security and of permanence. No more shall life be as a desert march, with changes which only bring sorrow, and yet a dreary monotony amidst them all. We shall dwell amid abiding realities, ourselves fixed in unchanging but ever-growing completeness and peace. The tents shall be done with, we shall inhabit the solid mansions of the city which hath foundations, and shall wonderingly exclaim, as our unaccustomed eyes gaze on their indestructible strength, 'What manner of stones and what buildings are here!'—and not one stone of these shall ever be thrown down.

Dear friends! the sum of all my poor words now is the earnest beseeching of every one of you to bring all your foulness to Christ, who alone can make you clean. 'Though thou wash thee with nitre, and take thee much soap, yet thine iniquity is marked before

Me, saith the Lord.' 'The blood of Jesus Christ cleanseth from all sin.' Submit yourselves, I pray you, to its purifying power, by humble faith. Then you will have the true possession of the true life to-day, and will be citizens of the city of God, even while in this far-off dependency of that great metropolis. And when the moment comes for you to leave this prison-house, an angel 'mighty and beauteous, though his face be hid,' shall come to you, as once of old to the sleeping Apostle. His touch shall wake you, and lead you, scarce knowing where you are or what is happening, from the sleep of life, past the first and second ward, and through the iron gate that leadeth unto the city. Smoothly it will turn on its hinges, opening to you of its own accord, and then you will come to yourself and know of a surety that the Lord hath sent His angel, and that he has led you into the home of your heart, the city of God, which they enter as its fitting inhabitants who wash their robes in the blood of the Lamb.

CHRIST'S LAST INVITATION FROM THE THRONE

'Let him that is athirst come. And whosoever will, let him take the water of life freely.'—Rev. xxii. 17.

THE last verses of this last book of Scripture are like the final movement of some great concerto, in which we hear all the instruments of the orchestra swelling the flood of triumph. In them many voices are audible alternately. Sometimes it is the Seer who speaks, sometimes an angel, sometimes a deeper voice from the Throne, that of Christ Himself. It is often difficult, therefore, amidst these swift transitions, to tell who is the speaker; but one thing is clear that, just before the verse from which my text is taken, our Lord has been proclaiming from the Throne His royalty and His swift coming 'to render to every man according' to his work, and to gather His own into the city.

After that solemn utterance He is silent for the moment, and there is a great hush. Then a voice is heard saying, 'Come!' It is the voice of the Bride in whom the Spirit speaks. What should she say, in answer to His promise, but pour out her wish for its fulfilment? How should the Bride not long for the bridegroom? Then apparently the Seer breaks in, summoning all who have heard Christ's promise, and the Church's prayer, to swell her cry of longing. For, indeed, His coming is the Divine 'event to which the whole Creation moves'; and in it all the world's dreams of a golden age are fulfilled, and all the world's wounds are healed. 'Let him that heareth say, Come!'

But who speaks my text? Apparently Christ Himself, though its force would not be materially modified if it were the voice of John, the Seer. It is His answer to the cry of the Church. He delays His coming; for this among other reasons that all the world may hear His gracious invitation. Then there are two comings in this verse—the final coming of Christ to the world; the invited coming of the world to Christ.

Now, it is obvious, I think, that such a way of understanding our text, with its vivid interchange of speakers and subjects, gives a far richer meaning to it than the interpretation which is so common amongst us, which recognises in all these 'Comes' only a reference to one and the same subject, the approach of men to Jesus Christ through faith in Him.

Let us, then, listen to this Voice from the Throne,

almost the last recorded words of the ascended Jesus, in which are gathered all His love for men and His longing to bless them.

I. Now, first let me suggest the question—To whom Christ from the Throne thus calls?

The persons addressed are designated by two descriptions: they that are 'athirst,' and those that 'will.' In one aspect of the former designation it is universal; in another aspect it is by no means so. The latter designation is, alas! anything but universal, because there are many men that thirst; and, strange as it seems, will not to be satisfied. But we take these two apart, and look at them separately.

The first qualification is need, and the sense of need. These two things, alas! do not go together. One is universal, the other by no means so. When a man is thirsty he knows that he is. But it is quite possible that your soul's lips may be cracking and black with thirst, and you may be all unconscious of it. There is a universal need stamped upon men, by the very make of their spirits, which declares that they must have something or some one external to themselves, on whom they can rest, and from whom they can be satisfied. The heart yearns for another's love; the mind is restless till it grasps reality and truth. The will longs to be mastered, even though it rebels against the Master, and the whole nature of man proclaims, 'My soul thirsteth for God; for the living God.' No man is at rest unless he is living in conscious amity with, and in possession of, the Father's heart and the Father's strength.

But, brethren, half of you do not know what ails you. You recognise the gnawing discontent, the urging restlessness, the continual feeling after something more than you have, and it often impels you on the wrong road. There is such a thing as misinterpreting the cry of the Spirit, and that misinterpretation is the crime and the misery of millions of men and of many in this building this evening. That they shall stifle their true need under a pile of worldly things, that they shall direct their longings to what can never satisfy them, that they shall put away all thoughts of the one sufficient anchorage, and hold, and nourishment, and refreshment, and gladness of the spirit, is indeed the state and the misery of many of us.

Perverted tastes are by no means confined to certain forms of disease of the body. There is the same perversion of taste in regard of higher things. You and I are made to feed upon God, and we feed upon ourselves, and one another, and the world, and all the trash, in comparison to our immortal desires and capacities, which we find around us. It seems to me sometimes, looking upon the busy life in the midst of which we live, and the way in which, from Monday morning to Saturday night, each man is hurrying after his chosen pursuits, as if we were all stricken with insanity, and chasing after dreams ; or as if, if I might take such an illustration, we were like the actors upon a stage, at some banquet in a play, pretending with great gusto to be drinking nothing, out of cups tinselled to look like gold, but which are only wood. Do you interpret aright the immortal thirst of your soul? Having the need, brother, are you conscious of the need ; and, if conscious, do you know where the fountain bubbles up that will supply it ? I fear—I fear that there are many who, if they would interrogate their own hearts honestly, and look this question in the face, would have to answer, No! It is 'as when a

thirsty man dreameth, and behold! he drinketh ; but
he awaketh ; and, behold! he is faint, and his soul
within him hath appetite.'

Now, I dare say there are many who are not aware of
this thirst of the soul. No! you have crushed it out,
and for a time you are quite satisfied with worldly
success, or with the various objects on which you have
set your hearts. It will not last! It will not last!
It is not likely to last even the length of your life. It
will not last any longer. Some of us may be like the
cactus that grows in hot, light soil in eastern lands,
having a considerable store of moisture in the fleshy
spike that will help it through a long time of drought,
but the store gets used up. Be sure of this, that, until
you go to Jesus Christ, you dwell in 'a dry and thirsty
land where no water is.' So far as the sense of need
goes this text may not appeal to you. So far as the
reality of the need goes it certainly does.

Then, look at the other designation of the persons to
whom Christ's merciful summons comes : 'Whosoever
will let him take.' Now, I said that the former designation, in one view of it, covered the whole ground of
humanity. We cannot say that of this other one, for
we are brought face to face with that strange and most
inexplicable and yet most certain and tragic of all facts
in regard to men, that they do turn away their wills
from the merciful call of God, and that some of them,
gnawing their very tongues with thirst, yet put away
with impatient hand the sparkling cup that He offers
to them freely. There is nothing sadder, there is
nothing more certain, than that we poor little creatures
can assert our will in the presence of the Divine loving-
kindness, and can thwart, so far as we are concerned,
the council of God against ourselves. 'How often

would I have gathered,' said the foiled, long-suffering
Christ—' how often would I have gathered . . . and ye
would not !' Oh ! brethren, it is an awful thing to think
that with this universal need there is such a partial
yielding of the will to Him.

I do not enter here and now upon the various reasons
or excuses which men offer to themselves and one
another for this disinclination to accept the Divine
mercy, but I do venture to say that the solid core of
unwillingness to be saved upon Christ's conditions
underlies a vast deal—not all, but a vast deal—of the
supposed intellectual difficulties of men in regard to the
Gospel. The will bribes the understanding, in a great
many regions. It is a very common thing all round
the horizon of thought and knowledge that a man
shall believe or disbelieve largely under the influence
of prejudice or inclination. So let no man be offended
if I say that what we have to guard against, in all
regions of thought, we have also to guard against in
our relation to the truths of the Gospel, and make very
sure that, when we think we are being borne along by
pure, impartial reason, the will has not put a bridle in
the nose of the steed, and is guiding it astray.

But for the most of you who stand apart from Jesus
Christ this is the truth, that your attitude is a merely
negative one. It is not that you will not to have Him
but that you do not will to have Him. But that negative attitude, that passive indifference which largely
comes from a heart that does not like to submit to
the conditions that Christ imposes, makes a positive
hindrance to your getting between your lips the water
of life. You know the old proverb: One man can
take a horse to the water, ten cannot make him drink.
We can bring you to the water, or the water to you,

but neither Christ nor His servants can put the refreshing, life-giving liquid into your mouth if you lock
your lips so tight that a bristle could not go in between
them.　You can thwart Christ, and when He says,
'Take, drink!' you can shake your head and mumble,
'I will not.'　So, dear friends, I beseech you to take
this solemnly into consideration, that the operative
cause why most of us who are not Christians are not,
is simply disinclination.　Wishing is one thing; willing
is quite another.　Wishing to be delivered from the
gnawing restlessness of a hungry heart, and to be satisfied, is one thing; willing to accept the satisfaction
which Christ gives on the terms which Christ lays
down is, alas! quite another.

Seeing that to know our need and to be willing to
let Him supply it in His own fashion are the only quali-
fications, then how magnificently from this last word
of the Christ from the Throne comes out the universality of His Gospel.　'Whosoever will,' that is all.　If
you choose you may.　No other conditions are laid
down.　If there had been any which were beyond the
power of every soul of man upon earth, then Christianity would have dwindled to a narrow, provincial,
sectional thing.　But, since it only demands the need,
which is universal; the sense of need, which every man
may feel; and willingness, which every man ought to,
and can, exercise, it is the Gospel for the world, and it
is the Gospel for me, and it is the Gospel for each of
you.　See that ye refuse not the offered draught.

II. That brings me, secondly, to say a word about
what Christ from heaven thus offers to us all.

This book of Revelation, as I have already remarked,
in another connection, is the close of the great Revelation of God; and it is full of the echoes of His earlier

words. The river of the water of life has been rippling and tinkling from the first chapter of Genesis to the last of Revelation. It is the river that flowed through Eden; the river which makes glad with its streams the City of God, the river of the Divine pleasures, of which God makes His children drink; the river which the prophet saw stealing out from under the Temple doors, and carrying life whithersoever it came; the river which Christ proclaimed should flow from because it had flowed into, all that should believe upon Him, 'the river of the water of life, clear as crystal,' which the Seer had just seen proceeding from the Throne of God and of the Lamb. Our Lord's words to the Samaritan woman, and His words on that last great day of the feast, when He stood and cried, 'If any man thirst let him come to Me and drink,' and many another gracious utterance, are all gathered up, as it were, in this last Voice from the Throne.

The water of life is not merely living water, in the sense that it flashes and sparkles and flows; but it is water which communicates life. 'Life' here is to be taken in that deep, pregnant, comprehensive sense in which the Apostle John uses it in all his writings. It is his shorthand symbol for the whole aggregate of the blessings which come to men through Jesus Christ, and which, received by men, make them blessed indeed.

The first thought that emerges from this 'water of life,' considered as being the sum of all that Christ communicates to humanity is—then, where it does not run or is not received, there is death. Ah, brother, the true death is separation from God, and the true separation from God is not brought about because He is in heaven, and we are upon earth; or because He is infinite and incomprehensible, and we are poor creatures

of an hour, but because we depart from Him in heart
and mind, and, as another Apostle says, are dead in
trespasses and sins. Death in life, a living death, is far
more dreadful than when the poor body is laid quiet
upon the bed, and the spirit has left the pale cheeks.
And that death is upon us, unless it has been banished
from us by a draught of the water of life.   Dear
brethren, that is not pulpit rhetoric; it is the deepest
fact about human nature. It is not a mere metaphor.
I take it that the death of the body is metaphor, so to
speak, the embodiment in material form, as a parable
of the far grimmer thing which goes on in the region
of the spirit. And I beseech you to remember that
according to the whole teaching of Scripture, which I
think is countersigned by the verdict of an awakened
conscience, death is the separation from God by sin;
and the only quickening potion is the water which
Christ gives; or rather, as He Himself said, 'He that
drinketh of My blood hath life indeed.'

But, then, besides all these thoughts, there come
others, on which I need not dwell, that in that great
emblem of the water that gives life is included the satisfaction of all desires, meeting and over-answering all
expectations, filling up every empty place in the heart,
in the hopes, in the whole inward nature of man, and
lavishing upon him all the blessings which go to make
up true gladness, true nobleness, and dignity.   Nor
does the eternal life cease when physical death comes.
The river—if I might modify the figure with which I
am dealing, and regard the man himself in his Christian
experience as the river—flows through a narrow, dark
gorge, like one of the cañons on American streams,
and down to its profoundest depths no sunlight can
travel. But the waters are not diminished though

they are confined, nor are they arrested by the black
rocks, but at the other end of the defile they come out
into flashing sunset and sparkle and flow. And away
somewhere in the dark gorge mighty tributaries have
poured in, so that the stream is broader and deeper,
and pours a more majestic volume towards the great
ocean from which it originally came.

Brother, here is the offer—life eternal, deliverance
from the death of sin both as guilt and power; the
pouring out upon us of all the blessing that our thirsty
spirits can desire, and the perpetuity of that blessed
existence and endless satisfaction through the infinite
ages of timeless being. These are the offers that Christ
makes to each of us.

III. Lastly, what Christ from heaven calls us to do.

'He that is athirst let him come; and whosoever will
let him take!' The two things, coming and taking, as
it seems to me, cover substantially the same ground.
You often hear earnest, evangelical preachers reiterate
that call—'Come to Jesus! come to Jesus!' with more
fervour than clearness of explanation of what they
mean. So, I would say, in one sentence emphatically,
and as plainly as I can put it, that Jesus Christ Himself
has told us what He means. Because when He was
here upon earth He stood and cried, 'If any man thirst
let him come to Me and drink.' And He explained
Himself when He said, 'He that cometh unto Me shall
never hunger, and he that believeth on Me shall never
thirst.' So let us put away the metaphors of 'coming'
and 'taking' and lay hold of the Christ-given interpretation of them, and say the one thing that Christ asks
me to do is to trust my poor, sinful self wholly and
confidently and constantly and obediently to Him.
That is all.

Ah! All! And that is just where the pinch comes. 'My father! my father!' remonstrated **Naaman's servants**, when he was in a towering passion **because he was** told to go wash in the Jordan; 'if the prophet had bidden thee do some great thing, wouldst thou not have done it? How much rather then when he saith to thee, Wash and be clean?' Naaman's strange reluctance to do a little thing in order to produce a great effect whilst he was willing to take a mint of trouble in order to produce it, is repeated over and over again amongst us. You will see men buy damnation dear who will not have salvation because it is a gift and they have nothing to do. I do believe that great multitudes of people would rather, like the Hindoos, stick hooks in the muscles of their backs, and swing at the end of a rope if that would get heaven for them, than simply be content to come *in formâ pauperis*, and owe everything to Christ's grace, and nothing to their own works.

Why! what is the meaning of all this new vitality of sacerdotal notions amongst us to-day, and of the efficacy of sacraments, and all the rest of it, except the purblindness to the flashing glory of the central truth of the Gospel that not by anything that we do, but simply by His Cross and passion received by faith into our hearts, are we saved? Brethren, it is not theology about Christ's sacrifice, but it is the Christ whom the theology about His sacrifice explains that you must get hold of. And if you trust **Him you** have come to Him in a very real sense, and have **His** presence with you, and you are present with Him far more really than were the men who companied with Him all the time that He went in and out amongst them here on this earth. So much for the 'come.'

'Let him take.' Well, that being translated, too, is

2 c

but the exercise of lowly trust in Him. Faith is the hand that, being put out, grasps this great gift. You must make the universal blessing your own. The river flows past your door, broader and deeper and more majestic than the 'father of waters' itself. But all that is naught to you unless you take your own little pitcher to the brink and fill it, and take it home. 'He loved *me*, and gave Himself for *me*.' Do you say that?

Dear brother! are you athirst? I know you are. Do you know it? Are you willing to take Christ's salvation on Christ's terms, and to live by faith in Him, communion with, and obedience to Him? If you are, then earth may yield or deny you its waters, but you will not be dependent on them. When all the land is parched and baked, and every surface well run dry, you will have a spring that fails not, and the water that Christ 'will give you will be in you a fountain of water leaping up into everlasting life.' Nor will your supplies fail when death cuts off all that flow from earthly cisterns, for they who here drink of the river will hereafter go up to the Source, and 'they shall hunger no more, neither thirst any more, for the Lamb that is in the midst of the Throne shall feed them, and shall lead them to living fountains of water, and God the Lord shall wipe away all tears from their eyes.'

Midnite
Treadmill
Sorrow
Lonely
Sickness,

CPSIA information can be obtained
at www.ICGtesting.com
Printed in the USA
LVHW082300031220
673139LV00009BA/308

9 781340 178079